LEAP OF
FAITH

LEAP OF FAITH

CONFRONTING
THE ORIGINS OF THE
BOOK OF MORMON

BOB BENNETT

DESERET
BOOK

SALT LAKE CITY, UTAH

Library of Congress Cataloging-in-Publication Data

Bennett, Robert F. (Robert Foster), 1933-
   Leap of faith : confronting the origins of the Book of Mormon / Bob Bennett.
     p. cm.
   Includes bibliographical references and index.
   ISBN 978-1-60641-053-0 (hardbound : alk. paper)
  1. Book of Mormon—Evidences, authority, etc.   2. Church of Jesus
Christ of Latter-day Saints—Apologetic works.   3. Mormon
Church—Apologetic works.   I. Title.
   BX8627.B36 2009
   289.3'22—dc22
                                        2009022806

Printed in the United States of America
Worzalla Publishing Co., Stevens Point, WI

10 9 8 7 6 5 4 3 2 1

To the memory of my cousin and friend

Truman Madsen

whose ability to combine serious scholarship
with steadfast faith set the standard
for us all

CONTENTS

CONTENTS

THE DOCTRINE

THE FINAL QUESTION

PREFACE

A book about the Book of Mormon by Bob Bennett? He's not an expert on the subject. What can he possibly say that will be either new or helpful?

If that is your first—and understandable—reaction to this book, give me a moment to explain what it is.

It directly probes the question of whether or not the Book of Mormon is a forgery. It describes that book's complexities and discusses the issues that arise from them. It is addressed to an audience who knows little or nothing about either the Book of Mormon or the church that is commonly called by its name. It is a sincere effort to be fair to all sides of the controversies.

Why did I write it? I take you back to 2001, when Utah was preparing to host the 2002 Winter Olympics and there was a good deal of press coverage about Mormons and what they believed. Most of it was evenhanded, but publications that discussed the Book of Mormon in any degree of detail almost universally treated it as an obvious fabrication, one whose claims and history were so bizarre that no one with any common sense could believe it to be authentic. That shallow treatment of a serious subject upset me, so I sat down at my computer and started writing answers to those articles.

As I wrote, visualizing an audience made up of people who might have read those articles, I was simply venting my frustration with what I considered sloppy journalism. I had no idea what might be done with my effort once—or even if—I ever finished it. Soon, however, the project took hold of me.

As I looked at the Book of Mormon from the vantage point of a neutral audience, I discovered aspects of it that I had never noticed before. As I probed the presentations of its critics, I discovered arguments that I had never understood before. As I recalled my own life experiences with forgeries, I saw applications that I had never thought of before. And, as I spread my net wider, taking advantage of my access to the Library of Congress to review other publications, I made connections with the book in areas I had never considered before.

I kept at it because the project provided a welcome break from the pressures of my political life as a Senator. Working on the manuscript became something for me to do on the long plane rides between Washington and Salt Lake, or during the late nights in the Capitol when we were waiting to vote but the speeches were still droning on, or while sitting in hotel rooms in distant cities where, after the political rallies were over, there was nothing left to do but play golf or drink, neither of which I do. The manuscript grew, even though my Senate schedule made me leave it alone for months at a time.

When I decided that I was finally finished and ready to run the risk of outside opinion, I turned to Greg Prince, a successful author with experience in writing for a wide audience. His response was encouraging, and he gave me a long list of helpful suggestions. I then contacted Jack Welch, a prolific scholar who has written a good deal about the subject. He and members of his family went through the manuscript and made additional valuable suggestions. I also got an encouraging response from Richard Bushman, the historian who has written the definitive biography of Joseph Smith. These positive comments, along with feedback from family and close friends, convinced me that, after seven years of writing in fits and starts, maybe I had something worthwhile after all. I was delighted when Sheri Dew, president of Deseret Book Company, called to say that she agreed.

Suzanne Brady, a senior editor at Deseret Book, was assigned to help with the final polishing, and I owe her and all the others who have been kind enough to read the manuscript and make suggestions—very much including members of my family—a great deal of gratitude. However, the final responsibility for the book you have in your hands, and any flaws that may be in it, is mine.

I offer it in the hope it will convince all who have an interest in the Book of Mormon, be they believers or skeptics, that any decision with respect to its origins requires a leap of faith.

PROLOGUE

GLASGOW, SCOTLAND, 1955

I WAS IN SCOTLAND AS A MISSIONARY for The Church of Jesus Christ of Latter-day Saints, going door to door with my companion, in apartment buildings in a new housing area, looking for people to teach.

Our method was simple. When a woman answered our knock on the door—very few women worked outside the home in those days—we would tell her that we were missionaries from America and ask if we could step inside for a moment. If she let us in, we gave her a copy of the Book of Mormon and asked if we could make an appointment to come back to discuss it in the evening when her husband would be home. Our goal was to set up as many such appointments as possible.

Marion Proctor was one woman who let us in and took the book. She was skeptical about how interested her husband would be, but she agreed to a time. We wrote it down in our appointment book and went on through the building, trying to set up similar appointments with her neighbors.

When we called at the Proctors' flat several days later, in the evening, Marion's husband, Bill, was sitting in a chair by the

1

fire reading the Book of Mormon. I took that as a good sign. Often when we returned to keep our appointment, the book was sitting on the doorstep with a note asking that we please go away.

Bill rose and greeted us warmly, but he didn't ask us to sit down. Instead, he said something like this, as best I can reconstruct the conversation:

"Look, lads, I know why you are here, and you are wasting your time. I have no intention of joining your church, and nothing you can say can change my mind.

"However, this is a very interesting book you have. I get in religious arguments with my mates down at work, and there is a lot in this book that I can use. So here's what we'll do. I'll buy the book from you, you can go on your way, and we'll both save time. Agreed?"

He was smiling as he said it, like a man sure of his ground and pleased with the logic of his argument. My response was something like this:

"Agreed. However, as long as we're here, would it be all right if we just sat down for a minute and explained some of the things that are in the book, to help you understand what it is?"

He seemed relieved that we had given in without a protest. "Sure," he said, "that would be fine."

We sat down and started through our prepared discussion.

He "really got into it," as the phrase goes. He picked up on the things we said; he pushed the discussion forward; he was clearly interested. When it was time for us to go and I asked the standard question—"When would be a good evening for us to come back?"—he didn't hesitate for a moment. A new appointment was set for the following week, and there was no more mention of our going on our way to save time.

When we came back, another couple was there. Bill and Marion had told their friends across the hall about us and the interesting new book in their lives. For the next several weeks we taught both couples, and soon both families were baptized.

Bill was the most enthusiastic new convert the local church had had in a long time, and Marion was the most surprised.

She told us, "Bill *never* went to church. He wouldn't have anything to do with church. When our youngest child was born, and I took the baby to be christened, Bill wouldn't go. I was embarrassed and made an excuse to the minister, telling him that Bill had had to work that day. My daughter pulled my skirt and said, 'No, he's not, Mummy. He's at home, making dinner for us so it will be ready when we get back.' Then I was really embarrassed."

So, a deep skeptic who wouldn't enter a church even on the occasion of his child's christening had become, almost overnight, a zealous follower of Jesus Christ, one who stayed on that path for the rest of his life. Before I left Scotland I asked him when it had happened. When had he known that what we were telling him was the truth?

"Oh," he said, "it was that first night. As we talked about the Book of Mormon, I just knew it was true. The Spirit was there right from the beginning."

The Book of Mormon has been around for close to two centuries. When it was first published, it appeared to be ludicrous on its face. It was full of very strange things. Its first printing didn't sell well, and it was ridiculed by every prominent scholar and commentator who reviewed it. Its prospects didn't look at all bright.

But it is still here because the Bill and Marion Proctor story has been duplicated, in different places and with different particulars, over millions of times. All sorts of people, in various parts of the world, have read it, prayed about it, and then embraced it, insisting that "the Spirit was there" telling them that it was true.

It's worth taking a look at.

THE BACKGROUND

INTRODUCTION

ALTHOUGH THERE HAVE BEEN A number of Christian denominations whose origins lie in American soil, the most successful one has been The Church of Jesus Christ of Latter-day Saints—the Mormons. In America, there are currently more of its members than there are Presbyterians, Episcopalians, or Jews, a statistic that would have been unthinkable at the time of the Church's formation in 1830.

Further, its success has not been limited to America. The Church's population is now larger outside of the United States than in it, with no signs that its exponential expansion will taper off anytime soon.

This continuing growth has given rise to a flow of books and articles on the Church, with new offerings appearing with increasing frequency. In all this flurry of commentary and analysis, however, comparatively little is said about the Church's premier publication, the Book of Mormon. It is usually mentioned only in passing, primarily as an explanation of why Church members are called Mormons. The book is seldom, if ever, carefully examined on its own merits.

Such shallow treatment of the book is found among believers as well as unbelievers. Inside the Church, too many members treat the book as something of a theological version of *Bartlett's Favorite Quotations*—a source for inspirational snippets that can be used to make various points in speeches and sermons but not a book to be read and pondered at length. Those Latter-day Saints who go no farther than that in their study of the book do not really understand it, and some make claims for it that go well beyond what the book itself maintains.

Outside the Church, commentators do the same thing in reverse. Instead of attempting to analyze it as a whole, they pick out passages that seem to them to be kind of silly or point to apparent anachronisms and then dismiss the rest of it as a rather clumsy fraud. They also often devote time to refuting what it does not say, or simply quote each other, giving full credence to sources that are quite outdated or hopelessly biased.

Some contemporary commentators who find much in the current Church that they approve of go so far as to suggest that the nineteenth-century Book of Mormon is an embarrassment to the twenty-first-century Mormon Church. They say that the book has been outgrown, that it has outlived its usefulness. In a somewhat patronizing tone, they suggest that perhaps it should be quietly abandoned so that the "good things" the Church accomplishes will cease to be tainted by the "weird things" that the book talks about.

The Church cannot do that, of course. Its founding prophet, Joseph Smith, called the book "the keystone of our religion."[1] It was the Church's first formal statement to the public, published prior to the Church's legal incorporation in April 1830. Every leader of the Church from Joseph Smith to the present has insisted that the book came to light through the intervention of an angel and contains the word of God, which puts it squarely at the heart of any discussion of the Church and its doctrine and history. The Church could not abandon it even if it wanted to.

The matter is as simple and stark as this: If the claims regarding the Book of Mormon are accurate, then the book is genuine scripture. If, however, the Book of Mormon is an invention of human origin—in short, a forgery—then the Church itself is a fraud.

Thus, for anyone truly interested in the Church and its claims, a thorough examination of the Book of Mormon as a possible forgery is a requirement. Instead of being just a footnote in an overall review of current Church activities, discussion of the book should be a primary focal point of the investigation. It should be held to the most rigorous tests for forgery.

What are those tests? They fall into the following categories:

INTERNAL ISSUES

Is the work consistent within itself? Is it consistent with its purported origin? Are there any loose ends—items or stories that start off in one direction but end up somewhere else—indicating that the forger, in his invention, lost track of where he was? What does the work tell us about the person who wrote it?

Any forgery is subject to internal structural errors if it is a long one, as the Book of Mormon is, and any work, forgery or not, contains valuable internal clues to the background and skill level of its author. Internal analysis can be quite revealing.

EXTERNAL ISSUES

Is there evidence external to its claims that either corroborates or contradicts those claims? Do the things that it says fit with facts that have come to light since its publication? Are there any anachronisms that its original readers may have missed but that are now obvious?

During the nearly two centuries since the appearance of the book, a great deal of scholarship has been developed around the history it claims to report. The area of external tests will be a fertile field.

Of course, in this effort, we must be careful to separate what the Book of Mormon says from what it does *not* say. Many of the external tests that its critics say it doesn't pass are tests of things that the book itself doesn't claim, but that some of its supporters do. The work cannot be held accountable for some of the errors of its more enthusiastic backers.

MOTIVE

Is there a reason why someone would want to fake this? What would he gain?

The usual motive for forgery is money, but there are always others that can come into play—fame, the thrill of pulling a fast one, whatever. Looking for possible motives for deception while questioning a possible forgery adds perspective to the effort.

To these three standard tests, which apply to any examination for forgery, we must add one more that is uniquely applicable to the Book of Mormon, as follows.

RELEVANCE

Is there a need, in contemporary times, for its message? Is there unique enlightenment here, for a modern person, that could not have come from some other source? Does this message truly qualify as something that God would want our age to understand?

The reason relevance is an issue is that the final authors of the Book of Mormon insist that it was written for our day, that is, for readers in the nineteenth, twentieth, and twenty-first centuries. Thus, if the answers to the relevance questions are no, the work is suspect, even if it passes the other three tests.

I am intrigued that no one, either in or out of the Church, has ever tried the Book of Mormon against these tests, as far as I know. Instead, authors who have written about the book have started out with a firm conclusion regarding it, for or against, and then assembled evidence to support that conclusion. It has not been examined solely as a possible forgery, drawing equally on the analytic efforts of both critics and believers.

Doing so is a fairly daunting task because it is very unlike any modern book with which we are familiar. It is a history of sorts, but its primary focus is on the divinity and mission of Jesus Christ as Savior of the world, and its purported authors regularly stop their historical narrative to insert long Christ-centered sermons, prophecies, or visions. There are also hard-to-follow flashbacks, obscure allegories, and extended biblical quotations that require considerable analysis if their relevance is to be properly understood—or challenged.

All of this makes it quite long—it filled 584 pages in its first edition—so it cannot be adequately devoured in one, or even several, sittings. Getting one's arms around it all can be very difficult.

To make it easier for those who are not fully familiar with the Book of Mormon to understand it, I approach it as if it were an American musical play, in which the actors constantly interrupt the plot by bursting into song and dance. Book of Mormon characters constantly interrupt the narrative by bursting into vision and sermon, many of which run on for so many pages that when they end, it is difficult to remember where you were in the story before they started. In order to make sense of it all, I first look at the Story and skip over the Doctrine— I separate the plot from the music, if you will—saving analysis of the book's religious message for later.

Looking at the Story first is exactly the reverse of the way most critical examinations of the book have been done. Alexander Campbell, the book's first serious critic, dismissed it as simply a "romance" and concentrated his fire on the book's theological and political opinions. Fawn Brodie did the same roughly a century later in *No Man Knows My History,* her biography of Joseph Smith. It is simply taken for granted by the critics that the Story is so ludicrous on its face that it is of no real consequence.

But the Story makes up most of the book. It is very intricate and densely packed with connecting narrative, explanatory flashbacks, and detailed descriptions of warfare. If it is forged, the forger must have worked extremely hard to produce it. As we look for signs of such forgery, we must not pass over the Story as lightly as Campbell and others have done.

Here is a brief summary of it, offered in chronological order and taking the book at face value, for now.

SUMMARY OF THE STORY

The Book of Mormon describes three migrations, all from the Eastern Hemisphere to the Western.

The first takes place at the time of the destruction of the Tower of Babel, when languages are confounded and peoples are scattered, as reported in the Bible.

A group of families living through that event manages to stay together. Led by a man named Jared, they cross vast distances in Asia until they come to the shore of a great sea, presumably the Pacific Ocean. They build barges in which they successfully navigate a year-long voyage across that ocean to the Western Hemisphere, where their descendants become a large society. They are called Jaredites, after the name of their first leader, and they keep records of their activities, which are eventually summarized by a man named Ether.

The second migration occurs thousands of years later, when two other families are prodded by divine revelation to leave their homes near Jerusalem in 600 B.C.E. to avoid the coming Babylonian invasion. Led by a man named Lehi, they wander in the Arabian desert for eight years and then build a ship and sail to the Western Hemisphere. They settle somewhere to the south of the Jaredites and, after Lehi's death, split into two groups, known as Lamanites and Nephites after the names of the two sons of Lehi who compete for leadership. It is the Nephites who keep records.

The third migration comes when the Babylonians descend on Jerusalem in 587 B.C.E. A group led by a man named Mulek escapes and travels to the Americas to settle on land that is somewhere between Jaredite and Nephite/Lamanite territory.

They build a large city known as Zarahemla but keep no records.

For centuries, these three different societies—Jaredite, Lamanite/Nephite, and Mulekite—live on the same continent without any knowledge of one another.

Then migrations take place within the lands the three groups occupy. Lamanite armies move toward Nephite lands in force, and the Nephites move out in an effort to escape the attacks. After a long journey in the wilderness (presumably north) the Nephites come across Zarahemla and the Mulekites who are living there. The two groups combine under the leadership of the Nephite leader, named Mosiah.

Around the same time, the Jaredites engage in a war of extinction. The last known Jaredite survivor wanders (presumably south) into Mulekite territory and is found by members of that society; he lives among them for nine months. When the Mulekites and Nephites combine, Ether's summary of Jaredite history, which is in Mulekite hands, is turned over to Mosiah, who adds it to the Nephite library of records.

This means that the historians who come after Mosiah are familiar with all three migrations and their descendants. The balance—indeed, the bulk—of the story outlines events that concern the Nephite-Mulekite society, including their interactions with the Lamanites.

These events are sometimes peaceful, reflecting times of trade and prosperity, but often bloody, describing periods of war and destruction, usually involving conflict with the Lamanites. The most significant event is the appearance of Jesus Christ as the resurrected Lord following his ascension into heaven from Jerusalem. This event has a profound effect on all who experience it, bringing about a peaceful era that lasts for close to two hundred years.

When the effect of Christ's visit finally wears off, there is a reappearance of brutal warfare. All who believe in Christ are targets of destruction by those who do not. A man named Mormon is commanded by God to abridge the Nephite records into a single volume, summarizing the most important aspects of their history with the primary emphasis being on their religious experiences. The purpose is to keep these experiences from being lost to future generations.

Mormon engraves his account on metal plates so that they will not fade over the centuries. He is killed in battle in 385 C.E. and the plates pass to his son, Moroni. He adds comments of his own as well making an abridgment of Ether's work, thus adding a summary of the Jaredite records to the Nephite summary made by his father. He buries the plates in the ground to keep them from being destroyed.

That is the framework of the Story we will examine.

THE NARRATIVE TEXT

Even though it is named after Mormon, the book is not put forward as a single effort by a single author. Rather, it claims to be a collection of the works of many authors, men whose writings, passed down through the centuries, provided source material that Mormon and Moroni abridged.

Richard Bushman, in *Joseph Smith: Rough Stone Rolling*, describes the book's claim of multiple sources this way:

> One gets a picture of Mormon surrounded by piles of plates, extracting a narrative from the collection, and not

completely aware of all there is. At various points while hurrying through the records, he interjects a comment about how much he is leaving out, as if overwhelmed by his abundant sources. . . . The entire Book of Mormon is an elaborate framed tale of Mormon telling about a succession of prophets telling about their encounters with God.[2]

The complexity of the claims does not stop there. The book contains a "book within a book," a series of first-person accounts attributed to people unconnected to Mormon.

Here's the background for that claim. After he had completed his compilation, Mormon says that he came across a set of plates that provided a "small account of the prophets" (Words of Mormon 1:3). These plates contained a first-person account written by two of Lehi's sons, Nephi and Jacob, with a few additions by Jacob's descendants. They recount the travails of those who followed Lehi out of Jerusalem as well as the visions they saw and the sermons they gave. Because the historical period described in these small plates was already covered in Mormon's narrative, he might well have ignored them.

But he didn't. He said the information on the small plates was "pleasing" to him and inserted them into his own record without any further comment (Words of Mormon 1:4).

Adding Nephi and Jacob to Mormon and Moroni as record keepers whose first-person accounts were written directly on the plates means that the overall book claims four primary authors; their contributions break down statistically as follows:

Mormon—71 percent
Nephi—13 percent
Moroni—8 percent

Jacob—4 percent

Isaiah—4 percent

Others—less than 1 percent

I put Isaiah on the list because Nephi and Jacob both quote him extensively.

There is also another complication. All of Mormon's material is taken from the records of the Nephites, so his narrative presumably began with Lehi's decision to leave Jerusalem in 600 B.C.E. But the first 116 pages of Mormon's abridgment were lost—I shall describe in a later chapter the circumstances in which this happened—which means that Mormon's narrative in the book as currently published begins around 130 B.C.E. and runs to the date of Mormon's death in 385 C.E.

That is why the small plates are important. By preserving them intact, Mormon made them available as a "book within a book": The first-person accounts of Nephi and Jacob, taken from the small plates, serve as substitutes for the missing 116 pages of Mormon's work.

Adding this narrative to the writings attributed to Mormon and Moroni means that the four different authors have written three different Stories. Here they are, listed by author, in the order in which they appear in the book as it is now published:

STORY ONE

Attributed to Nephi, Jacob, and Jacob's descendants, it covers approximately 470 years, although most of the action is limited to the first 180 years. It describes events that take place both in the Middle East and on the American continent.

Story Two

Attributed to Mormon, it is what is left of Mormon's abridgment after the loss of the 116 pages and covers events from around 130 B.C.E. to 385 C.E., all of which take place in the Americas.

Story Three

Attributed to Moroni, it was written in 421 C.E., well after his father's death, and contains a summary of the history of the Jaredites along with a few additions of his own.

Because each of these three stories is claimed to be a stand-alone effort, it is appropriate to apply the basic tests for forgery to each individually, and that is what we shall do, arriving at whatever conclusions are possible with regard to each one. Then we will apply the tests to the entire Story as a whole.

Before we embark on that effort, however, I need to make three important points.

First, I am a believer in the authenticity of the book, as the Prologue makes clear. Nonetheless, my repeated readings of it, as well as my reading commentary regarding it—for and against—have shown me that there are legitimate issues with respect to it, and I have done my best to be fair to those issues rather than hide them. That may make other believers a bit uncomfortable, as they see these issues laid out, but it is the premise of this work that any conclusion regarding the origins of the Book of Mormon requires a leap of faith. No one should make that leap without having heard all sides of the argument.

Second, this book will break no new ground; I do not pretend to be a scholar of high academic standing. However, I am competent enough to understand and weigh the arguments of those who are, and I take the role of commentator, reporting and weighing the strength of both sides. Those who want to check on my objectivity are encouraged to go to the Sources, where I have included works that are critical as well as supportive, and read the source material themselves.

Finally, the standard disclaimer: This is entirely my own work, neither commissioned nor sanctioned by the Church.

With that, let us turn to a discussion of how forgers work, after which we will look at the circumstances under which the Book of Mormon came to light in the nineteenth century.

2

THE PROCESS OF FORGERY

My credentials in the area of forgery are, to put the matter simply, based on my experience.

"Up close and personal," as the saying goes, I was directly involved with two of the more celebrated forgeries of the last quarter of the twentieth century, albeit from a position outside the forgeries themselves. Both were associated with the late reclusive billionaire Howard Hughes, for whom I was working at the time the forgeries were produced.

Later on, like most Latter-day Saints, I followed with great interest the controversies and excitement that surrounded the bogus documents foisted on the Church in the 1970s and '80s by the forger-murderer Mark Hofmann. My interest in the Hofmann murders was heightened by the fact that I was personally acquainted with some of the principal participants in that series of tragic events, including one of Hofmann's murder victims, with whom I went to school.

Let's go through each one of these attempts at forgery in some detail, starting with the first one to enter my life in the early 1970s—"The Autobiography of Howard Hughes"—and see what they teach us about the process of forgery.

Largely forgotten now—although a movie was based on it, entitled *Hoax*—the announcement that Howard Hughes had written his memoirs created an enormous stir when it was made. The press release describing the book reported that Hughes had done it with the help of a novelist named Clifford Irving. McGraw-Hill, the prestigious publishing house that had made the deal to bring it to market, paid Hughes, through Irving, an advance totaling three-quarters of a million dollars— a huge, perhaps record-breaking, sum for a book at the time. It was considered the publishing coup of the decade, if not the century.

I had never heard of Irving before the story broke in the press; most people had not. However, no less an institution than Time, Inc., vouched for the authenticity of Irving's work. They paid handsomely for the privilege of printing excerpts from it in *Life* magazine. When McGraw-Hill executives were challenged by skeptics to prove that Hughes had really been in-volved, they produced several cancelled checks that had cleared a Swiss bank, endorsed in Hughes's handwriting. All seemed in order.

In fact, Irving had never met Hughes. He created the auto-biography out of whole cloth with the help of a researcher-writer associate named Richard Suskind. It was a blatant forgery, but there were reasons why he thought he could pull it off.

First, Howard Hughes was a true eccentric who had disap-peared from public view in the 1950s. (Not exactly in the way the movie *Aviator* would suggest, however.) At the time of Irving's attempt to create a biography for him, Hughes had not been seen in public for roughly twenty years. Irving was sure that Hughes's reclusiveness would continue. He conceived the idea for a fake autobiography after a crisis within the Hughes corporate empire had given rise to an incredible amount of public hue and cry but still produced no sign of Hughes himself. His only communication with the outside world had been a handwritten letter in which he said that he had known what was going on and approved it.

Irving decided that Hughes would not surface to discuss the book, either, if he (Irving) made it a sympathetic effort. Irving was sure readers would accept his descriptions of Hughes's behavior as reasonable, given their perceptions of the hermit billionaire. He expected that the executives of Hughes's company would disavow it, but he wrote into the book a "Hughes" statement that he had met with Irving without telling them. Irving bet his career on the belief that any flurry of denials from Hughes executives would ultimately be swept aside in the face of some manufactured "evidence" that he had really met Hughes.

To create such evidence, he took a copy of the Hughes letter mentioned above and practiced duplicating Hughes's handwriting, which was eerily similar to his own. When he was satisfied that the two were interchangeable, he started forging notes, in "Hughes's" own hand, to prove that he and Hughes had been in contact with each other. But Irving had more.

Unbeknownst to anyone, he had gained access to the unpublished writings of Frank McCulloch, a *Time* reporter who had interviewed Hughes at some length during the years when

Hughes was still giving interviews. Irving put information he had found in the unpublished McCulloch manuscript into the autobiography, assuming—correctly—that McCulloch would be one of the people called upon to examine his work for accuracy. When he was consulted, McCulloch at first believed Irving was a phony, but after he read through Irving's work and discovered his own information in it, he wrongly assumed that no one other than Hughes himself could have given this material to Irving. When McCulloch corroborated the Irving effort as genuine, his opinion carried great weight with both Time, Inc., and McGraw-Hill.

Even so, McGraw-Hill officials wanted to be absolutely sure they were dealing with the real thing. They submitted Irving's handwritten "Hughes" notes to Osborn, Osborn, and Osborn, the most prestigious handwriting experts available. After careful analysis, these experts certified that the notes had in fact been written by Howard Hughes. Both McGraw-Hill and Time, Inc., were satisfied. The royalty advance checks were delivered to Irving and were cleared through a Swiss bank. The publication date was set.

When the story broke, the vigorous public denials by Hughes officials and employees, one of whom I was, were largely dismissed, just as Irving had hoped. The public really did believe that Howard Hughes was weird enough to do something like this. But the Hughes organization was certain that a fraud had been perpetrated, denounced the book, and launched its own investigation.

Time, Inc., and McGraw-Hill stood firm, sure they had covered everything. When I told an investigative reporter from *Life* magazine that there was absolutely no way Clifford Irving could ever have met Howard Hughes, he replied, "Maybe not. I agree with you that Irving is probably lying about how he got the manuscript. But the manuscript itself is genuine—the internal evidence is too strong, and the holographic evidence [referring to the handwriting samples] is overwhelming."

The project moved forward, controversy or no.

It never got to the bookstore shelves because the investigators working for Hughes broke open the scheme by focusing on the money McGraw-Hill had given Irving.

Howard Hughes had a circle of aides around him, at least one of whom was with him at all times, twenty-four hours a day. These aides kept logs of everything Hughes did, and they knew he had never slipped out of their sight for hours at a time to confer with Clifford Irving or anybody else. Armed with this certainty, Hughes's agents went to Switzerland to convince the relevant bank officials of that fact. Once the bankers became suspicious that something might be amiss, they let the American investigators know that the H. R. Hughes into whose accounts the McGraw-Hill checks had been deposited was a woman.

No one had paid much attention to the fact that Irving had told executives at McGraw-Hill to make the checks payable to H. R. Hughes instead of Howard R. Hughes—seemingly an insignificant difference—but that was the key element in Irving's plan to keep the money for himself.

His wife had gone to a Swiss bank and introduced herself as Helga R. Hughes. She furnished a signature card with "H. R. Hughes" on it, written by Irving. When the same "H. R. Hughes" signature appeared as endorsement of the McGraw

Hill checks, it naturally matched the card exactly. The bank treated it as a routine transaction.

As the story of the true identity of "Helga" was unraveling behind the scenes in Europe, the Irvings received another blow, this one in public, in America. The real Howard Hughes surfaced—albeit only by telephone—to denounce the autobiography as fake, in his own voice. It was a scene fully consistent with the legend of Howard Hughes, as television cameras showed a group of reporters sitting around, staring at and conversing with a speakerphone.

These men had been chosen for the interview because all of them had met and interviewed Hughes before he went into hiding and could be relied upon to recognize both his voice and his manner.

The interview began with some friendly chitchat, complete with some reminiscing, to help determine whether or not this was the real Howard Hughes talking. Then they got down to business:

How about this new book, Howard?

It's a fake, guys.

Hughes made it very clear that he had never met Irving and that the whole thing was a fraud.

After Hughes hung up, the reporters all said that they were sure they had been talking to the real Howard Hughes. Scientific voice-print analysis confirmed that, and McGraw-Hill finally had to admit that they had been bilked. The firm became the butt of jokes on the late night talk shows after someone noticed that their new office was located in the building of the Irving Trust Company. Irving and his collaborators all went to jail.

During Irving's trial, he was asked by a prosecutor if he really had been the one who forged Hughes's handwriting so perfectly. To demonstrate that he had, he picked up a yellow legal pad, wrote out a letter to the prosecutor, signed it "Howard R. Hughes," and handed it over. Several of the other lawyers in the room asked him to do one for them as well, which he did. One prosecutor had his framed and hung it on his office wall.

Needless to say, the whole episode did not provide good publicity for the handwriting experts at Osborn, Osborn, and Osborn.

Now to the second Hughes forgery—the fake Hughes "will." This time, there would be no telephonic press conference to denounce it because Hughes was dead.

This document would have enriched, among others, one Melvin Dummar, a service station attendant in Utah who claimed to have once met Hughes in the Nevada desert. It was a far clumsier effort than Irving's, but it got more headlines and over a longer period of time. It was taken so seriously in Hollywood, where producers are seldom inclined to let the facts get in the way of a good story, that they made a movie about it, entitled *Melvin and Howard,* with Jason Robards as Hughes. It won two Academy Awards, one for best screenplay written directly for film and the other for best supporting actress, Mary Steenburgen.

The "will" contained many references to things considered known items of Hughes lore. Two examples: It named Noah Dietrich as executor of the Hughes estate and directed that the

Spruce Goose, Hughes's most famous airplane, be given to the city of Long Beach.

Dietrich had been Hughes's chief executive for many years, and the plane had been housed in a Long Beach hangar for more than three decades, so, for many reporters, these two provisions seemed logical and demonstrated that Hughes had, in fact, written the will. Their stories treated it as genuine.

For those of us who worked for the Hughes companies and knew the history, however, either one of these stipulations demonstrated conclusively that Hughes had *not* written the "will." He and Dietrich had had a serious falling out, and Dietrich was fired in a bitter parting. He would have been the last man Hughes would have named to handle his estate.

As for the airplane, neither Hughes nor anyone close to him ever called it the *Spruce Goose.* The title had been made up by the press because the plane was made almost entirely of wood (metal materials were scarce in the Second World War), and Hughes hated the name, considering it a trivializing insult to a serious effort. He would never have written a will referring to the plane as anything but the *Flying Boat* or its formal designation, the HK-1.

The "will" was a clumsy enough forgery that it was thrown out of every court where it was introduced, but the story of its finding was romantic enough that it was widely accepted, even defended vigorously, by many people, including some who didn't stand to get anything from it. It stayed in the news for months and, as I said, even made it onto the silver screen. I still run into people who think there must have been something to it.

Finally, there were the Hofmann forgeries of "found" Mormon historical documents. Their history is far better known than either of the Hughes forgeries, so I won't go into many of the specifics; several excellent books on this subject are available to those who want all the details. For those who may not be familiar with Hofmann's history, I shall simply summarize.

Mark Hofmann is a man who devoted his entire career to forgery, thereby earning an adequate living for himself and his family for years. His works were examined by experts for proper content and, since they were supposedly old, were also subjected to careful scrutiny of the physical evidence. They always passed both tests. How did he do it?

Basically, because he took it very seriously and worked at it very hard. He did his homework and was careful to use the right inks and paper, devising various ways of aging documents in his basement. After practice, he proved to be every bit as good at faking handwriting as Clifford Irving. The experts who examined all aspects of Hofmann's "discoveries" were fooled completely by the quality of his work.

Also, as his early efforts were accepted, he reaped the benefit of the inertia of success. The more he was established as a reliable source of old documents, the less his new discoveries were challenged. In marketing terms, he "built the brand"—If it comes from Hofmann, it has to be real.

On the content side, Hofmann did something akin to Irving's poaching of material from Frank McCulloch. He knew which experts would be called in to examine his works for historical accuracy, so he attended their symposia, jotted down their theories, and then put those theories in the "newly discovered" historical documents, thus giving the experts an opportunity to see their own research validated by evidence. Hofmann knew that the experts' egos would urge them to embrace such validation; not expecting a massive effort at fraud, they were open to being conned by an expert con man. And they were.

It all blew up, literally, when he couldn't deliver a promised manuscript and was confronted by an angry customer who had become suspicious. He moved outside his area of expertise—forgery—into one where he was a neophyte—murder. He planted several bombs, including one in his own trunk, perhaps in the hope that this would create investigations that would divert suspicion from himself as well as explain where the nonexistent papers had gone. A much clumsier murderer than forger, he is now serving a life sentence in prison.

LESSONS LEARNED

What do we learn from all this? A series of things:

A forger will salt his work with information that others would either hope or expect to find there.

Irving salted his manuscript with the McCulloch material, the author of the Hughes "will" used information that appeared in Hughes's obituary, and Hofmann "confirmed" the scholarly theories that were current at the time his discoveries appeared.

During the 2004 presidential campaign, the forger who produced faked Texas Air Guard memos that "exposed" President George W. Bush's failure to do his duty as a Texas Air Guardsman was believed at CBS because he was furnishing proof of rumors that CBS producers had been chasing for years.

Having something in it that contemporary readers would want to find there is not only the first but perhaps the best tool of a forger.

The more detail a forger goes into, the more he exposes himself to detection.

Irving's detailed descriptions of his many meetings with Howard Hughes made even the *Life* reporter suspicious. Hofmann escaped detection by keeping things simple and sticking to short efforts—usually one or two pages.

A forgery reflects the attitudes that are current at the time when it appears.

Irving wrote his book while the publicity that surrounded the upheaval in the Hughes corporate structure was still fresh, which meant that his scheme resonated with public perception at the time. The Hughes "will" mirrored the printed reviews of Hughes's life that were current at the time of its discovery. Hofmann's documents dealt with issues that were being discussed in Mormon scholarly circles at the time he forged them. As we look at them now, outside the setting in which they appeared, all three efforts seem much less believable than they did when they first came to light.

The fact that a document is tied to the time and culture in which its author lived applies to any creative effort, not just a forgery. Orson Scott Card, a successful writer of science fiction, says that one can tell, simply by reading it, whether a work of that genre was produced in the 1950s, 60s, or 70s, because it will be filled with the conventions of the decade in which it was written.

A forger will always have a motive that influences the resulting product. For starters, "follow the money."

Irving's "lark," as he called it, would have made him an instant millionaire. Melvin Dummar was in the Hughes "will" as a beneficiary, which makes him the prime suspect as the forger. Hofmann was able to make a decent living and support his family for years.

Important as money is, however, there are often other considerations as well. Irving's writing career would have skyrocketed if his work had been accepted as genuine. Hofmann harbored a deep desire to destroy the LDS Church, and his forgeries were designed to discredit some of the Church's most important history. The author of the Texas Guard memos had no monetary motive; he—or she—desperately wanted President George W. Bush to be defeated in the election.

Start with money, but don't ignore the fact that other motives may well be in play.

When examining possible forgeries, experts, even ones with the best credentials, can be fooled if they have a predisposition to believe one way or the other.

Irving fooled the handwriting experts and the executives at McGraw-Hill in part because they wanted to believe they had the deal of the century on their hands; the Hughes "will" fooled the reporters because they loved the nuttiness of the story; Hofmann fooled the scholars because they saw their pet theories validated; the forger of the Texas Air National Guard memos fooled the producers at CBS News because they hated George W. Bush.

Experts also miss things because they are under time pressure to give a definitive answer too soon, because they are sloppy or, as was the case with Hofmann, because the forger is, in fact, very, very good. Or any combination of the above.

A potential forgery should be looked at in a total context.

The *Life* reporter was so focused on the strengths of the McCulloch material and the handwriting experts that he shrugged aside the inconsistencies of Irving's overall story as minor irritants. Scholars who validated Hofmann's efforts one by one failed to ask the big question, "How does he keep coming up with this stuff at just the right times?" One must consider not only the work itself but all aspects that surround it.

Finally, time is not on the forger's side.

There is an old saying: "Truth is the daughter of time." The farther one gets from the date of the appearance of the forgery, the easier it is to apply all the lessons we have outlined.

These are the lessons we will keep in mind as we search for forgery in the Book of Mormon.

3

DISCOVERY

IN THE FALL OF 1829, TWO young men went to a printer in Palmyra, in upstate New York, with a manuscript they said they wanted printed under the title Book of Mormon. It was in the handwriting of one of them, Oliver Cowdery, but they said that it had been dictated to Oliver and a few other scribes by the other, Joseph Smith, known to his neighbors as a local farmer.

The printer was understandably dubious. A book written by a man who lived in the fourth century C.E, talking about an appearance by Jesus Christ in the Western Hemisphere in the first century, translated into English by a twenty-five-year-old farmer in the nineteenth century?

Very curious. Where did Joseph claim to have gotten it?

From an angel.

Even more curious. How did it happen?

Joseph said that the angel's name was Moroni, the last person to have possession of the plates in life. Joseph claimed that Moroni appeared to him in 1823 and led him to the place where the plates were buried and then came back again, several times through several years, to give Joseph additional instructions and prepare him for the time when the plates would be turned over to him for translation. That supposedly happened in September 1827, when Joseph began translating the writing on them into English.

He said he was able to do this because, along with the plates, which had "the appearance of gold," Moroni had given him a set of interpreters, a unique instrument called the Urim and Thummim, words which appear in the Old Testament.[1] This instrument enabled him to receive by divine revelation an understanding of the meaning of the engravings on the plates. In addition to the Urim and Thummim, he said, he also possessed a seer stone that emitted light and provided additional information when it was needed.[2]

No wonder the printer refused to go forward with the job unless he saw the money up front.

Regardless of how preposterous this story sounds, however, the manuscript exists, so there had to have been some source for its creation. Let's begin our search for such a source by looking at the details of Joseph's tale, starting with those elements of his story that are undisputed.

He began work on the book almost immediately after the date he claimed to have obtained the plates, in September 1827. By July 1828, he had dictated 116 pages of manuscript, using his wife, Emma, and a neighbor, a prosperous farmer named Martin Harris, as two of his scribes. Harris was so impressed with what was on the 116 pages that he asked for permission to take them home to show his wife, who had originally been fascinated by Joseph's story but then became extremely skeptical of the entire enterprise. At first, Joseph refused, because he was afraid the pages would be lost. But Harris was persistent, and finally Joseph reluctantly agreed. His worst fears were realized when the pages disappeared. Believing they had fallen into the hands of someone who would alter them and then use them to try to discredit him, Joseph was afraid to retranslate them.

So, he didn't. He decided that the information available on the small plates that Mormon had discovered at the end of his work would be a sufficient substitute for the missing narrative. After this experience, however, Joseph not only stopped using Martin Harris as his scribe but stopped translating altogether.

Then, in April 1829, he met Oliver Cowdery, a local school-teacher, who became convinced that Joseph had indeed received a divine calling. With Oliver in the role of chief scribe—there were others who relieved him from time to time—translation resumed.

The time needed to dictate the manuscript that was taken to the printer was approximately sixty-five days, which means they moved at a very rapid pace. (Oliver is reported to have tried to translate some himself, but he couldn't do it.) Joseph would sit at one end of a table and Oliver at the other, with Joseph talking and Oliver writing everything down in long-hand. Joseph did not make things up as he went along, because he never asked where they were, asked for anything to be read back to him, or lost his train of thought. When they broke for meals or the end of the day and then resumed later on, he simply began right where he had left off.

The resulting physical product was a manuscript that had no punctuation. Oliver and his relief scribes—there were several of them, whose handwriting is evident on the original manuscript—just wrote down words as Joseph spoke them.

When the dictation was completed, Oliver copied it all onto a second manuscript, which was taken to the printer a few pages at a time. It was the printer who separated it into paragraphs, provided the punctuation, and, where necessary, corrected the spelling. There have been efforts made over the years to detect and correct any errors that may have crept into the printed version as a result of the printer's misreading Oliver's handwriting or Oliver's failure to understand Joseph's pronunciation of certain words.

Portions of the original manuscripts still exist and are available for examination, but the plates are not. Joseph Smith says he translated only a third of the material on them before returning them to Moroni. The other two thirds, he said, were "sealed," containing prophecies for which the world was not yet ready (Joseph Smith–History 1:65). He said they would be made available at some unknown future time.

That is Joseph and Oliver's description of how the first edition of the Book of Mormon came to be. The physical details—the description of the table at which they sat, the times of their work, and so forth—have been corroborated in the journals of others who were in the house they occupied.

The most significant aspect of this account is the time frame in which they completed their task.

We know how people create books and how long it takes, and sixty-five days is much too short a time for a forger to have produced a document that filled 584 pages when put in printed form. Mark Hofmann took months to research and then forge documents that were just a few pages long, spending night after night in his basement, alone. Clifford Irving did not act alone, but he still took a lot of time. He and his researcher went through the McCulloch manuscript carefully, read all they could about Hughes from other sources, and took turns "being" Howard Hughes, dictating to each other ideas they thought Hughes would have. They then patched, edited, and rewrote. They were both competent writers, experienced in their craft, and it took them over a year to produce a work much less complex than the Book of Mormon.

The requirement for more time than sixty-five days applies even to a fiction writer who is not engaged in forgery. In 2007, the country was consumed with Harry Potter mania, in anticipation of J. K. Rowling's final book about the boy wizard she had created. No one knows the world of Hogwarts School better than she does, and yet it still took her at least a year, and many rewrites and many arguments with her editor, to produce a five-hundred-page book on the subject.

So, because the time frame of sixty-five days for production of the Book of Mormon by a pair of amateurs is consistent with the claim of divine assistance, is that enough internal evidence to prove conclusively that Joseph was telling the truth about where it came from?

No. All it proves conclusively is that, as he spoke, Joseph was not composing; he was reading. While one cannot *create* such a book in sixty-five days, one can certainly *read it out loud* in that time, even going slowly enough for Oliver to take it all down in longhand. The real question, then, is—what was he reading from?

Believers accept his claim that, with God's help, he was dictating the impressions he got while looking at either the interpreters he had received from Moroni or the seer stone that he used as a substitute. However, if we look around for other scenarios that could be internally consistent with the known facts, two other possibilities fit. The first is that he was reading from a text that he had previously written out himself; the second is that he was reading from the work of someone else. Let's examine both of these alternatives.

JOSEPH SMITH AS THE AUTHOR

Joseph Smith started talking about the plates in 1823, claimed to have them in his possession in September 1827, began the work that produced the first 116 pages, and then stopped dictating in 1828, resuming when Oliver Cowdery arrived in April 1829.

Okay, let's do some math.

Assume that he conceived the project in 1823, when he first mentioned the plates to his family. That means that by 1827, the year he said he finally had the plates in his possession and started his dictation, he would have had almost four years in which to think it through and work on it.

Suppose that, after dictating the 116 pages, he decided it was still somewhat clumsy and needed more work. He seized upon the loss of the 116 pages in 1828 as an excuse to start over in secret, to reorganize and rewrite the entire book. Martin Harris could even have been part of a conspiracy to "lose" the 116 pages and cover up an initial failure. That additional year, in which he could have polished his earlier effort and composed the book as we have it, makes five years in all. In this scenario, the book's claim that there were two sources for the first part of the story—the plates originally available to Mormon and the small plates attributed to Nephi and Jacob—is a convenient way for Joseph to cover up the shift from the first effort to the later one.

In 1829, with changes made and a gullible Oliver at hand, he would have been ready to begin dictation again, pretending to read from sacred interpreters while actually reading from his own manuscript. This ruse would lend credence to his claim that he was translating and fool Oliver into believing that he had a gift from God. It would also explain why Oliver couldn't translate when he looked at the interpreters—or whatever Joseph showed him—as he made his own attempt.

Thus, with respect to the short time period in which Joseph dictated the book to Oliver, the internal evidence that applies to Joseph's story is as consistent with the possibility that the book is a forgery written entirely by Joseph Smith as it is with the claim of divine intervention.

SOMEONE ELSE AS THE AUTHOR

Suppose that someone I shall call Third Party—a person (or persons) unknown—had written the book and given it to Joseph; alternatively, suppose that Joseph discovered Third Party's work and stole it. Either way, with such a manuscript in his possession, Joseph could easily have then dictated the entire work to Oliver in the time described.

Having Third Party in the picture not only solves the time problem connected with the book's creation but also explains why Joseph, "an untutored farm boy," could have dictated something this complex at such an early age. Third Party could have taken years to concoct the scheme and do considerable research into the subjects it covers. If you assume a Third Party with skills and resources far beyond anything that Joseph possessed, you have a logical answer to the question of how such a young and uneducated man could have produced such a large and complex manuscript.

With three possible candidates for the book's authorship—Mormon, Joseph Smith, and Third Party—and each one arguably passing the timing test with regard to the book's creation, we must ask, "Which is the most likely?"

Each has its problems.

For those who believe Joseph and say that the book was put together by Mormon, there is the obvious question of the existence of angels. One must accept the idea that Moroni actually lived, first as a man and then as an angel, and then, equally fantastic, the idea that God would arrange such an elaborate scheme, one that took many centuries to unfold, just to get the information of the book before the modern world.

There is also the convenient return of the plates to Moroni. If there were no plates in the first place, it would be essential for a forger to offer a reason why they were not available for others to examine. Joseph does that with his statement about a portion of the plates being "sealed" and therefore not to be translated until later.

Was there any contemporary evidence that the plates ever actually existed, aside from Joseph's claims?

Just enough to give believers something to cling to but certainly suspect enough to make doubters scoff. He said he showed the plates to at least eleven men, all of whom signed statements that they had seen them, "hefted" them—a good nineteenth-century word—and satisfied themselves that Joseph was telling the truth about them. I say at least eleven because there are journal entries that suggest that members of the household in which Joseph and Oliver worked saw the plates while the work of the translation was in progress; the house was quite small, by today's standards, and it would have been impossible for family members to go about their daily activities without looking in on the two men. Emma Smith, Joseph's wife, says she handled the plates, although she says they were covered by a linen cloth when she did so. So, including Joseph himself, there were thirteen people who claimed firsthand knowledge of their existence, and very likely more. Three of them—Oliver Cowdery, Martin Harris, and David Whitmer—swore that they had also seen and talked with Moroni and that the voice of God had told them that the plates were genuine and the translation correct.

Believers take comfort in the fact that none of these three ever disavowed his affirmation, although all of them became disenchanted with Joseph for a time. David Whitmer's break with Joseph and the Church was perhaps the most dramatic because it was the only one that was permanent; still, he went to the trouble and personal expense of publishing a formal written statement, reaffirming his experience with Moroni and the plates, after Joseph Smith was dead. All the witnesses stood by their statements about the plates, regardless of their later experiences, good or bad, with Joseph.

At this distance in time it is impossible for us to evaluate how reliable their testimonies may have been. In Joseph's day, those who wanted to believe him accepted the witnesses as trustworthy, and those who chose to reject him dismissed them as either dupes or participants in a conspiracy. Even if we credit the witnesses as being honest men, however, acceptance of Joseph's version of how the manuscript was produced requires a huge leap of faith.

Most of today's commentators outside the Church agree among themselves that Joseph created the manuscript all by himself. But when coming up with a reasonable explanation of how he did it, the consensus dissolves; there are a number of different, often conflicting, theories.

Some say he was simply a brilliant charlatan and con man who made it up as he went along, Clifford Irving style.

Others suggest that Joseph had some sort of mental disturbance—something like an epileptic seizure, perhaps—that produced visions and similar surrealistic events. Those who hold this view speculate that he may even have believed that what he was saying came from God, thus removing the con man stigma even as they brand his product a fraud.

Then there is the idea that he was neither mentally unstable nor a con man but a true religious genius.

There is admiration in that phrase. It suggests that Joseph combined a fantastic imagination with a deep understanding of religion to produce a truly significant book, worthy of serious study. That would mean it is not a true history, of course, but, for these commentators, that really doesn't matter. After all, the ancient Greek myths are not true histories either, but they are worthy of serious study; we should give Joseph the same reverence we have for, say, Homer.

Of course, even this favorable view still means there were no angels and no plates.

Whatever their different explanations, the bottom line for today's critics is always the same: Joseph did it by himself, and the book is a combination of his own personality and his exposure to the religious fervor and political issues of his time.

A significant problem with accepting Joseph as the sole author of the book, whatever his mental condition, is that it is done from the perspective of almost two centuries after the fact. As we look back at Joseph now, we see a man who, at the time of his death, had accomplished significant things and was acknowledged as one of the dominant figures of his era: mayor of the second largest city in his state, author of a significant body of religious literature, prolific sermonizer, and confident leader of a growing church.

That view can mislead us with respect to his abilities with regard to the production of the Book of Mormon. Though all of those things were true of him in 1844, the year of his death, none was true in 1829, the year the book was produced. In 1829, he was, indeed, still a very rough stone.

If we could go back to 1829 and ask his contemporaries, "Which of the three possibilities was most likely to have written the book—Mormon, Joseph Smith, or Third Party?"—it is likely that Joseph would be the last one they would choose. Friends and foes alike saw the creation of the Book of Mormon, or any book, for that matter, as far beyond Joseph's capability as a twenty-four-year-old.

Starting with his wife, Joseph's friends all said his literary skills in 1829 were bad—she said he could barely compose a common English sentence at the time. As far as his foes went, affidavits filed by many of his neighbors describe him as lazy, shiftless and ignorant, hardly the attributes of a creative and studious type. During his growing-up years, he also had to earn his living by common labor, which would have made it hard for him to closet himself and compose, without anyone knowing he was even working on it, 700 pages of complex text: the 584 that composed the first edition plus the 116 that were lost. If he had either the skills or the opportunity needed to create the Book of Mormon prior to 1829, both were well hidden from anyone who knew him then.

On the issue of his writing abilities at the time, we are not entirely at the mercy of the surviving opinions of his supporters and detractors. We have a formal paragraph that undisputedly was written by him in 1830 and printed in the first edition of the Book of Mormon. Here it is, in its entirety:

> To the reader—As many false reports have been circulated respecting the following work, and also many unlawful measures taken by evil designing persons to destroy me, and also the work, I would inform you that I have translated, by the gift and power of God, and caused to be written, one hundred and sixteen pages, the which I took from the Book of Lehi, which was an account abridged from the plates of Lehi, by the hand of Mormon; which said account, some person or persons have stolen and kept from me, notwithstanding my utmost exertions to recover it again—and being commanded of the Lord that I should not translate the same over again, for Satan had put into their hearts to tempt the Lord their God, by altering the words, that they did read contrary from that which I translated and caused to be written; and if I should bring forth the same words again, or, in other words, if I should translate the same over again, they would publish that which they had stolen, and Satan would stir up the hearts of this

generation, that they might not receive this work: but behold, the Lord said unto me, I will not suffer that Satan shall accomplish his evil design in this thing; therefore thou shalt translate from the plates of Nephi, until ye come to that which ye have translated, which ye have retained; and behold ye shall publish it as the record of Nephi; and thus I will confound those who have altered my words. I will not suffer that they shall destroy my work; yea, I will shew unto them that my wisdom is greater than the cunning of the Devil. Wherefore, to be obedient unto the commandments of God, I have, through his grace and mercy, accomplished that which he hath commanded me regarding this thing. I would also inform you that the plates of which hath been spoken were found in the township of Manchester, Ontario County, New York.

Those familiar with Joseph's later sermons will see similarities between them and this overlong paragraph; his style remained the same even as his syntax improved as he matured. However, the question is not whether this paragraph resembles Joseph's other writings but whether this paragraph resembles the prose in the Book of Mormon. It does not. We'll talk more about that later on.

Now, as for the "he-may-have-thought-it-came-from-God-but-it-was-really-some-form-of-hallucination" theory, we know about people who have mental disturbance. It comes involuntarily, often at inconvenient times. Manifestations of it remain throughout a person's life. It is unpredictable and, unless subject to modern medical treatment, often uncontrollable.

Some commentators who support this theory have compared Joseph Smith to Muhammad. Their reasoning goes this way: Muhammad was an illiterate Arab, and he produced a significant religious book; why couldn't an illiterate Joseph Smith do the same thing?

Neat parallel at first glance, but, in fact, the difference between Muhammad's reported experiences and Joseph Smith's is stark. In her book *Islam: A Short History,* Karen Armstrong describes how Muhammad awoke from sleep during the time of Ramadan "to find himself overpowered by a devastating presence, which squeezed him tightly until he heard the first words of a new Arab's scripture pouring from his lips."[3] He kept quiet about this for two years, confiding only in his wife and her cousin. Later he began to preach, but he did not suggest that he was writing a book. He was reciting scripture—the Arab word *quran* means recitation—and Armstrong says, "The Quran was revealed to Muhammad verse by verse, *surah* [chapter] by *surah* during the next twenty-one years, often in response to a crisis or a question that had arisen in the little community of the faithful. The revelations were painful to Muhammad, who used to say, 'Never once did I receive a revelation, without thinking that my soul had been torn away from me.'"[4]

Nothing even close to this behavior ever surfaced in Joseph's life.

Also, it is noteworthy that Joseph Smith did not do it again. He did claim to translate other ancient documents, but the results were nothing like the Book of Mormon in their breadth and complexity. He lived a very active, very public life, giving many sermons, writing many letters, and meeting with many people, but he never, ever, secluded himself and produced a sequel. If he was given to mental conditions that caused the creation of the Book of Mormon in the first place, why did those conditions cease with the book's publication? On the other hand, if he was a Hofmann-like cynic who deliberately fooled a good many people, why didn't he repeat his triumph when the need and occasion arose?

He had plenty of motive to do it again—at several points in the Church's history, he was beset with dissatisfaction on every side. What better way to bring everyone back into the fold than to come forth with some more material from the "sealed" portion of the plates, the two-thirds of the total book that Joseph said he had returned to Moroni? There were certainly no people more anxious to know what was in the sealed portion of the plates than those who had believed Joseph in the first place. If he was a forger, why didn't he give them what they wanted, reestablishing himself in their minds as the undisputed link with God? Doing so would have immediately solved internal Church difficulties and would have been logical behavior for a forger in trouble with his followers. It is certainly something Hofmann would have done.

Again, his contemporaries, friends and foes alike, would say he didn't do it because he couldn't do it, because he hadn't written the book in the first place. Believing that he had requires a significant leap of faith, which is much easier for critics to make now, more than a century and a half after the fact, than it was for those who knew him.

Which brings us to our final possibility—Third Party—as the book's creator. Taken through the facts we have laid out so far, Third Party emerges as a strong contender, because this theory requires less of a leap of faith than either of the other two.

With Third Party as the author, we can assume that Joseph

was as unlearned as his friends said, as lazy and stupid as his foes said, as unaffected by hallucinations and as busy with farm labor as his life story says, and still be the con man who foisted a forgery on his gullible followers. Under this option, he doesn't have to be able to write a book; all he has to do is be able to copy one. This idea is much easier to accept than the notion that Joseph acted alone.

That is why, during Joseph's lifetime and for many decades after his death, those who condemned the book endorsed the Third Party option virtually unanimously. They were even sure they knew who Third Party was.

Sometime before 1829, a former Presbyterian minister named Solomon Spaulding was known to have written a novel called "The Manuscript Found," in which a fictional narrator describes events that took place in America before Columbus. Joseph's detractors focused on the similarity between this plot line and the story of the Book of Mormon and insisted that Joseph was simply a plagiarist. Somehow, they say, he had come across the Spaulding book and stolen it for his own purposes.

The theory started in 1834 and grew in scope and detail over the years. Its final version was laid out in the book *New Light on Mormonism,* by Mrs. Ellen E. Dickinson. In the preface, to establish her credentials, Mrs. Dickinson reports "that the Rev. Solomon Spaulding, the author of the romance called 'The Manuscript Found,' from which the 'Book of Mormon' was formulated, was my mother's uncle by marriage."[5] I assume she is telling her readers that she is a credible source because she is family.

She talks of visiting Spaulding's daughter and only child, who "made a sworn statement as to her father's authorship of the work which has been used with such disastrous effect by crafty men."[6] Her book, she says, "is the only attempt of the Rev. S. Spaulding's relatives to set this matter in its proper light."[7]

In her first chapter she describes Spaulding's novel as "an account of the peopling of America by the lost tribes of Israel, the tribes and their leaders having very singular names; among them, *Mormon, Moroni, Lamenite,* and *Nephi*—names found nowhere else in literature. So much interest was awakened by this romance, and it was such a distinction, at the time, to write a book, that he determined to publish it."[8]

She tells how Spaulding took his novel to a publisher named Patterson. "A young printer, named Sidney Rigdon, was in Mr. Patterson's printing house; . . . he had followed Mr. Spaulding from Conneaut, . . . and having heard him read 'The Manuscript Found,' . . . devised a treachery toward both author and publisher, which the world has reason to remember. This same Sidney Rigdon figured prominently twenty years later as a preacher among the Mormons."[9]

That's the theory, and it has a grain of truth in it: Sidney Rigdon was in fact once employed as a printer. In 1829, he was a minister in another faith, but he converted to The Church of Jesus Christ of Latter-day Saints in the first year of its organization and brought a good portion of his congregation with him. He quickly became Joseph's trusted counselor.

If the entire scheme had been arranged between the two of them, it is logical that Sidney would have wanted to wait on the sidelines to see if the book would catch on before associating himself with it. That way, if it failed, it would not embarrass him. If it succeeded, however, he could show up as a convert and then, later on, maybe even supplant the unlearned Joseph as the head of a successful new church. That he was ambitious for position is demonstrated by his contesting the leadership succession issue in the Church after Joseph was killed.

Spaulding/Rigdon as Third Party solves all the problems.

It validates the claim that Joseph was as incapable of producing the work by himself as his contemporaries thought. It explains why he was unable to produce a sequel—Spaulding was dead—and why his writing and sermon styles differed markedly from the book. Sidney Rigdon's presence in the scheme provides an acceptable source for the religious material in the book; the doctrines he taught before joining the Mormons were similar to those Joseph taught, and he was acknowledged as a more skillful preacher than Joseph was.

Thus there are no time problems, no angels, no hallucinations, and no genius. No leap of faith required. And, with an irony that was almost too perfect, the original Spaulding manuscript was lost, unavailable for checking, just like the plates. It is easy to understand why the Spaulding theory was accepted as the final word on the issue by critics for nearly half a century, appearing as the settled explanation for the book's origin in an article in *Encyclopedia Americana*.

No more. Spaulding's actual manuscript turned up, after all, and ruined everything. In 1884 it was found and placed in the library at Oberlin College, Ohio, where it is still available for examination; it has been circulated in printed form, and I have gone through it. It bears no resemblance to the Book of Mormon at all, with none of the Book of Mormon names in it, as Mrs. Dickinson claimed, and no religious content whatsoever. The Spaulding theory, once the staple of all commentary on the book offered by critics outside the Church, rarely comes up anymore. Even Fawn Brodie says it is nonsense.[10]

When the critics abandoned the Spaulding theory, they also abandoned the whole idea of Third Party, but it should not be dismissed so lightly. Just because Solomon Spaulding wasn't Third Party doesn't mean that Third Party didn't exist. It is still a reasonable theory; more reasonable, perhaps, than the other two because it requires less of a leap of faith than either of them.

The primary problem with it is that the trail of possible candidates for the title has long since grown cold. We cannot go back to search for a new Third Party now—or can we? In many current books and websites, a new candidate has been identified, one that supposedly emerged from an unlikely source—research conducted within the Church itself.

As the centennial of the publication of the book approached, Church leaders asked one of their own, B. H. Roberts, to review it against whatever scholarship had become available since its printing to see what, if anything, could be said to those who insisted that it was a forgery.

This was a logical choice, because Roberts was one of the best scholars in the Church. Along with considering possible anachronisms and other normal tests, Roberts looked around for Third Party. Was there anyone else out there, other than Solomon Spaulding, who could have had an influence on Joseph Smith in the 1820s?

Yes. Roberts came across the work of Ethan Smith, a clergyman who lived in Poultney, Vermont (Joseph Smith's birth state), and published in 1823 (the year of Joseph Smith's first claim of angelic visitation) a book called *View of the Hebrews*.

Knowledge of *View of the Hebrews* was certainly available to Joseph and his contemporaries; it was successful enough that it went through multiple printings. Further, Oliver Cowdery had lived in Poultney until 1825, while the book was still in circulation, and members of his family were members of Ethan Smith's church.

B. H. Roberts's work was submitted to Church authorities but not circulated by them. It remained unknown to the public until his papers were published posthumously in 1985. His typewritten comparison between *View of the Hebrews* and the Book of Mormon ran eighteen pages long. At the end of his work on this subject, he wrote the following, which some modern critics have seized upon with great glee:

> In the light of this evidence, there can be no doubt as to the possession of a vividly strong, creative imagination by Joseph Smith, the Prophet, an imagination, it could with reason be urged, which, given the suggestions that are to be found in the "common knowledge" of accepted American antiquities of the times, supplemented by such a work as Ethan Smith's *View of the Hebrews,* would make it possible for him to create a book such as the Book of Mormon is.[11]

Tantalizing. I read through *View of the Hebrews* and was struck by several things that quickly jumped out of it with regard to the Book of Mormon:

First, its main thesis is that the American Indians are the lost ten tribes of Israel. That satisfies one test for forgery— timing of a current topic. Tying Indians to the Book of

Mormon, which Joseph did, deals with an issue in which Joseph's contemporaries were interested.

Second, it goes to great lengths to prove similarities between the Indians' religious practices and those of the "Hebrews." That corresponds to the Book of Mormon claim that its first family brought scripture with them to preserve their religious practices for their posterity.

Third, it is full of quotations from Isaiah, as are the writings from the "small plates." This would have been appealing to nineteenth-century readers.

Fourth, there is discussion of warfare among Indian tribes. The Book of Mormon too is full of descriptions of warfare.

Finally, the timing and location of its publication fits nicely with the timing and location of the appearance of the Book of Mormon.

So, even though Solomon Spaulding is no longer in the picture, we should not automatically dismiss Third Party as a possibility for the book's authorship. Many current critics place Ethan Smith's name at the head of the list as a possible, if unwitting, candidate for that title, even though there are many differences between the Book of Mormon and *View of the Hebrews,* as we shall see. The former is full of intricate stories, lengthy sermons, and strange names; the latter has none of these things in it. It is strictly an analytic treatise, with many more differences from the Book of Mormon than similarities to it.

Now, let us turn from the question of how the material was created to the question of the existence of the plates from which it was supposedly taken. The idea that ancient people used metal plates for record keeping was one of the most scoffed at

Courtesy The Oriental Institute, University of Chicago, Chicago, Illinois

The Darius plates

portions of Joseph's story when he told it, but that is no longer true. Archaeological discoveries in the Middle East support his claim.

The most dramatic of these discoveries occurred in the early 1930s in Iran in the ruins of the ancient city of Persepolis, the ceremonial capital of ancient Persia, where King Darius I reigned. Not much remains of that city, which was presumably built beginning in 516 B.C.E., because it was looted by Alexander the Great roughly two centuries later. However, digging in the foundations of some of the grand buildings that had been built, archaeologists found in each of the four corner-stones two gold plates and two silver plates, covered with writing. These plates were taken to the Persian Museum of Antiquities in Tehran.

The dimensions and appearance of the Darius plates match Joseph's description of the plates he said he received from

Moroni. The stone box in which they were placed for burial also conforms almost exactly to Joseph's account. The only difference is that the Darius plates are slightly larger. This is solid confirmation of the idea that ancient desert peoples wrote on metal plates and then buried them for the benefit of later generations, and it significantly bolsters the credibility of the eleven witnesses who described what they said were Moroni's plates.

The Darius plates are not unique, nor were they the first plates to have been found. The first discoveries of ancient metal plates and scrolls with writing on them began several decades after Joseph's death, with subsequent findings continuing to this time. The number of known sets of ancient plates now exceeds one hundred. As knowledge of the existence of ancient plates has grown, so has understanding of what is written on them and in what languages. A thin gold plate found in Sicily has now been shown to have been written in Hebrew; translations of the copper scrolls found in Cave IV at Qumran disclose that the writings were considered sacred and "hidden away" so they would not "be desecrated by profane use."[12]

Thus, it is now beyond dispute that ancient peoples living in the Middle East during the time Nephi is said to have lived wrote things they considered to be sacred on metal plates, sometimes put them in stone boxes, and buried them in the ground, just as Joseph claimed. It is also beyond dispute that no forger living in America in the 1820s would have known that. Joseph Smith certainly did not, nor did B. H. Roberts, a century later. (*View of the Hebrews* makes no mention of plates.) If either one had, he would surely have steered critics toward such information.

In their book *Mormon America,* Richard and Joan Ostling

discuss B. H. Roberts's comments about Ethan Smith and *View of the Hebrews:* "Most Mormons are either unaware of these scholarly finds or unperturbed by them," implying a state of denial on the part of the book's believers.[13] The same charge can be made against the critics on the subject of the plates. I have never read an article or book by critics of the Book of Mormon that mentions either the Darius plates or the other examples of the ancient practice of using plates. This means, using the Ostlings' phrase, those commentators "are either unaware of these scholarly finds or unperturbed by them."

If the book's critics don't know about the practice of ancient writing on plates, that means their scholarship is bad. If they do know but don't want their readers to know, that means their claim of objectivity is compromised. The external evidence that bears on Joseph's and Oliver's story of its origins says that their insistence on the existence of gold plates is fully credible.

Now let's talk about motive. Why would any of our three possibilities want to create the Book of Mormon? What would he gain?

Mormon's stated motive is clear—he says he wrote the book because God told him to. He would get his reward in heaven. Noble, but uncheckable.

Because the existence of Third party is speculation, Third Party's possible motives are necessarily all speculation as well and therefore equally uncheckable. Anything we suppose about Third Party's motives is just that: supposing.

That leaves us with Joseph Smith. Whether he wrote it or stole it, what might have been his motive, as a forger, for publishing it? If he did it for money, he was disappointed, because he never made any money out of the book, nor did anyone else in the Church. Indeed, Martin Harris had to mortgage part of his farm to pay the printing bill and lost it as a result. But that doesn't put Joseph in the clear on the issue.

The publication of the book played an essential part in launching both the Church and Joseph on the road to success. Even an "unlearned farm boy" in 1830 would know that being acknowledged as the force behind the production of a significant literary effort in a time when books were relatively rare would be a great boost for his reputation. Whether the effort was financially rewarding or not, Joseph had a reason to do it if he was, in fact, a con man.

SUMMARY

The Book of Mormon is a large and complex work, originally comprising some seven hundred pages, attributed to several different primary authors. It covers a wide variety of history and doctrine over a very long period of time. It surfaced as a manuscript written by Oliver Cowdery, who says it was dictated to him and a few relief scribes by Joseph Smith in sixty-five days in 1829. That means that someone, a real person or persons, created the book before that time.

There are only three possibilities for that someone—Mormon, Joseph Smith, and an unknown Third Party.

Internal analysis shows that all three possibilities can be advanced as consistent with existing facts that bear on the book's production. Which one you choose to believe depends on which assumptions you are willing to make. Joseph's claim is the hardest to swallow, however, because he insists on the existence of angels.

External evidence corroborates Joseph's description of both the appearance and purpose of the metal plates he claims to have found and thus supports Mormon as the author. No one in America in 1830 was aware of the ancient practice of writing on metal plates and burying them in the ground.

On the *question of motive,* unless we accept the idea that God was directing the entire project, Joseph is the only one who derived any benefit from the book's publication.

Now it is time to read it.

THE STORIES

4

STORY ONE

STORY ONE, FROM THE "small plates of Nephi," is the "book within a book" that Mormon inserted into his own account.[1] It has three distinct sections, which I have labeled Nephi, Jacob, and the Transition Verses, attributed to Jacob's descendants.

Before we get into each of these three, a few style notes apply here and in the chapters to follow:

When I am summarizing the narrative, it appears in normal type, like this.

When I am commenting on the narrative, it appears in italics, like this.

When I use quotation marks, I am taking words directly from the Book of Mormon, as in previous chapters.

The book is all in the language of the King James Version of the Bible, which is the way a forger would have written it to impress nineteenth-century readers.

NEPHI

Nephi begins with a formal introduction of himself. He says that he was taught in the learning of his father, makes a solemn affirmation of the truthfulness of the record he is writing, and then launches into the story.

It is 600 B.C.E., just a few years before Babylon will invade and carry the inhabitants of Jerusalem into captivity. Nephi's father, Lehi, comes into the family circle and announces that he has had a vision, given him in answer to prayer, in which it is made clear that Jerusalem will be destroyed if its inhabitants do not repent—*essentially the same message that Jeremiah, the Old Testament prophet who is Lehi's contemporary, has been preaching.*

After recording the details of the vision, Nephi says that "the Jews did mock him [Lehi] because of the things which he testified of them," that they "were angry with him," and that "they also sought his life" (1 Nephi 1:19–20). Understandably, Lehi leaves town, as he is commanded to do by the Lord in a dream. "He departed into the wilderness. And he left his house, and the land of his inheritance, and his gold, and his silver, and his precious things, and took nothing with him, save it were his family, and provisions, and tents, and departed into the wilderness" (1 Nephi 2:4).

This passage suggests that Lehi was wealthy and experienced in traveling in the desert. Moroni will tell us later that the language used on the plates was "reformed," or altered, Egyptian, which implies that Lehi did enough business there to have learned the language.

A link between a Jewish businessman and Egypt was not unusual in biblical times—the two countries were tied by much more than the Moses story. Jeremiah speaks of Egypt in his writings and, according to tradition, was taken to Egypt after the Babylonian captivity and was killed there. It would be perfectly normal for Lehi's family to have had an Egyptian connection.

Lehi's two oldest sons, Laman and Lemuel, start "murmuring"—*the Book of Mormon word for whining*—almost immediately. They refuse to believe that Jerusalem is in any jeopardy and require a strong rebuke from their father to keep them in line. Nephi, on the other hand, offers prayers of his own and receives his own witness of the propriety of his father's actions. Thus convinced, he speaks to his next older brother, Sam, and convinces him as well.

This is our first introduction to an obvious teenage sibling rivalry between the boys, particularly Laman and Nephi.

Nephi goes to his father's tent, where he is told that Lehi has had another dream. In this one, he was instructed to send his sons back to Jerusalem to the house of Laban, a man who is a relative of Lehi's—*the exact relationship is not disclosed*—who has a "record of the Jews and also a genealogy of my forefathers, and they are engraven upon plates of brass." Lehi promises Nephi that he will be "favored of the Lord, because thou hast not murmured" (1 Nephi 3:3, 6).

The boys go back to Jerusalem on this assignment and, on the outskirts of the city, draw lots to see which one should go to call on Laban. The lot falls to Laman, but when Laman goes into the city and tells Laban what he wants, Laban promptly throws him out, threatening to kill him. Laman returns to his brothers and reports his failure, after which the older boys want to return to their father.

Nephi says no. He gives his brothers a sermon about the importance of keeping God's commandments, one of which he considers this assignment to be. "It is wisdom in God," he says, "that we should obtain these records, that we may preserve unto our children the language of our fathers; and also that we may preserve unto them the words which have been spoken by the mouth of all the holy prophets . . . since the world began, even down unto this present time" (1 Nephi 3:19–20).

From this speech, as well as information given later on, we learn that the brass plates of Laban contained much of what we would call the Old Testament, as it had been compiled up to that time.

The boys decide to try to buy the plates, since Laban wouldn't part with them just for the asking. They go to Jerusalem and gather up the riches that had been left at their home when the family departed for the wilderness. Alas, once Laban sees how much "gold, and . . . silver, and . . . precious things" (1 Nephi 3:24) they have brought, he not only throws them out again but sends his servants after them to kill them, so that he can keep their riches. They escape with their lives but are forced to leave their possessions behind.

The recriminations between the brothers become truly heated once they are safely beyond the grasp of Laban's men. Nephi reports that Laman and Lemuel "did speak many hard words unto us, their younger brothers, and they did smite us even with a rod." An angel intervenes and, after stopping the beating, promises that the third trip into Jerusalem will produce results—"the Lord will deliver Laban into your hands" (1 Nephi 3:28–29). With his brothers hiding just outside the walls of the city, this time Nephi creeps into the streets, alone. It is now nighttime.

As he wanders through the dark and deserted streets, he comes across a man, fully clothed in armor, who has fallen into a drunken stupor. On close examination, Nephi discovers that it is Laban himself and is "constrained by the spirit that I should kill Laban." He shrinks from this command—"Never at any time have I shed the blood of man"—but the instructions from the Spirit of God are firm: "Slay him, for the Lord hath delivered him into thy hands; behold the Lord slayeth the wicked to bring forth his righteous purposes. It is better that one man should perish than that a nation should dwindle and perish in unbelief" (1 Nephi 4:10, 12–13).

After agonizing over this decision, Nephi kills Laban with Laban's sword and then puts on his armor. He goes to Laban's treasury as if he were Laban.

This particular incident has given rise to much criticism, if not derision. What sort of religious record has a supposed prophet begin his career with a murder? If we are looking for forgery, however, we must look at it from the other end of the question—why would a forger put his main character in such a position? It puts a jarring note in the opening chapters of a religious book, which is something a forger would be unlikely to do, and it is unnecessary as far as the point of the action is concerned. If the only purpose of the story were to tell how Nephi got into Laban's house, it would work just as well if Nephi had found Laban already dead when he came upon him. That would have been a more convenient way to tell it for American audiences in the 1830s.

On the way to Laban's house he meets Zoram, Laban's servant, who, seeing both the armor and sword of his master, assumes that Nephi *is* Laban. Zoram, on Nephi's command, gives him the brass plates Nephi has come for and then follows Nephi outside of the walls of the city, where the brothers are waiting.

When Laman and the other brothers see Nephi, dressed as Laban and accompanied by Laban's servant, they are "exceedingly frightened" (1 Nephi 4:28) and start to flee, but Nephi calls to them in his own voice. This reassures them, but now terrifies Zoram, who turns to rush back towards Jerusalem.

Nephi, being "large in stature" (1 Nephi 4:31), grabs Zoram and prevents his escape, at the same time swearing an oath that, if Zoram will listen to them, they will spare his life and allow him to stay with them as a free man. *Presumably he was under some sort of indenture to Laban, so freedom could have been attractive to him.* Zoram stops trying to escape and agrees to accompany the brothers into the wilderness, swearing an oath of his own that he will remain with them. Taking both the records and Zoram with them, the boys then return to their father. Nephi notes that having Zoram come with them means that no one in Jerusalem will be aware of the facts surrounding Laban's death and attempt to pursue them in the wilderness.

When the boys are safely in camp with the brass plates, their mother, Sariah, who had been sure that they would all be killed, is both comforted and reassured that Lehi has a true prophetic calling. Lehi settles down to read the plates and makes prophecies concerning them and the effect their possession will have on his posterity.

Then comes another instruction from the Lord. It is not good, Lehi is told, for the boys to go forward on this journey without wives. They are to go back again to Jerusalem, this time to the house of a man named Ishmael, and bring him and his family into the wilderness to join with Lehi and his group. "The Lord did soften the heart of Ishmael, and also his household," and they come out to Lehi's camp (1 Nephi 7:5). *We are not told any of the names or the exact number of people in Ishmael's family.*

Two of Ishmael's sons and two of his daughters soon rebel against the whole project. They want to go back to Jerusalem, and Laman and Lemuel readily agree. Nephi gives them a sermon, urging them to obey the Lord, but it only makes them all the more angry, and they tie him up. He prays and his bonds are loosened—presumably by divine power—which makes them even angrier. They are about to beat him when one of the daughters of Ishmael, along with her mother and one of her brothers, pleads for Nephi's life. The rebels relent and agree to stay. The now enlarged group moves on into the desert.

Although he is the youngest of the adult sons, Nephi emerges as the primary supporter of his father. When Lehi has a new vision in the form of a dream, Nephi prays for his own understanding of the dream and receives it in vision, with an angel as his narrator. The dream is Christ-centered; among many other things Nephi is shown "a virgin, most beautiful and fair above all other virgins" and is told, "The virgin whom thou seest is the mother of the Son of God" (1 Nephi 11:15, 18). *The full description of the vision takes up fourteen pages. It is the first of a continuing series of mentions of Christ.*

Nephi and his brothers, along with Zoram, take daughters of Ishmael as their wives.

Lehi is given a miraculous instrument to guide them, a ball-shaped device somewhat like a compass, called the Liahona. Nephi is the primary hunter who brings in the food, and when his bow breaks, the others despair, because their own bows have "lost their springs" (1 Nephi 16:21). There is plenty of murmuring because they are sure that they will now die of starvation.

Nephi makes himself a new bow, arms himself with stones and a sling, and asks his father, "Whither shall I go to obtain food?" Lehi prays and is told to "look upon the ball, and behold the things which are written." Following the directions written on the Liahona, Nephi goes to the top of a mountain and finds beasts to hunt, which provide the food they need to survive. Their joy over the food is cut short by Ishmael's death. His daughters "did mourn exceedingly, because of the loss of their father, and because of their afflictions in the wilderness" (1 Nephi 16:23, 26, 35). They again want to go back to Jerusalem.

Laman and Lemuel and the sons of Ishmael talk of killing both Lehi and Nephi. Nephi reports that "the voice of the Lord came and did speak many words unto them, and did chasten them exceedingly; and after they were chastened by the voice of the Lord they did turn away their anger, and did repent of their sins, insomuch that the Lord did bless us again with food, that we did not perish" (1 Nephi 16:39).

After this, they turn eastward as they continue their journey. All in all, their wandering goes on for eight years, during which time the routine sets in so that "they began to bear their journeyings without murmurings" (1 Nephi 17:2). Sariah has two more sons, who are named Jacob and Joseph.

Then they come to "the land which we called Bountiful, because of its much fruit and also wild honey," and they "exceedingly rejoiced when we came to the seashore." In this place of vegetation, the Lord summons Nephi to a mountaintop and gives him a new assignment—"Thou shalt construct a ship, after the manner which I shall show thee, that I may carry thy people across these waters" (1 Nephi 17:5–6, 8).

When Nephi reports this, his brothers' reaction is predictable: "Our brother is a fool, for he thinketh that he can build a ship; yea, and he also thinketh that he can cross these great waters" (1 Nephi 17:17).

There is another angry confrontation, with an attempt on Nephi's life. He responds, "In the name of the Almighty God, I command you that ye touch me not, for I am filled with the power of God, even unto the consuming of my flesh; and whoso shall lay his hands upon me shall wither even as a dried reed; and he shall be as naught before the power of God, for God shall smite him. . . . And now, if the Lord has such great power, and has wrought so many miracles among the children of men, how is it that he cannot instruct me, that I should build a ship?" Nephi says, "I stretched forth my hand unto my brethren, and . . . the Lord did shake them, even according to the word which he had spoken" (1 Nephi 17:48–51, 54).

Thus chastened, the brothers accept Nephi's leadership and agree to help with the ship, which Nephi builds "after the manner which the Lord had shown unto me." When it is done, the others are sufficiently impressed with the result that "they did humble themselves again before the Lord." The Lord then speaks to Lehi, and, on his command, the family gathers the necessary provisions for the voyage to come, loads the ship, and sets out, "driven forth before the wind towards the promised land" (1 Nephi 18:2, 4, 8).

The tensions of the wanderings in the desert reassert themselves on board, with more angry confrontations between Nephi and his brothers, one of which requires divine intervention in the form of a violent storm to humble the dissenters and restore Nephi to his place of prominence. Finally, the group arrives in the "promised land"—*presumably somewhere on the coast of Central or South America.*

They pitch their tents, till the earth, plant seeds that "did grow exceedingly; wherefore, we were blessed in abundance. . . . There were beasts in the forests of every kind, both the cow and the ox, and the ass and the horse, and the goat and the wild goat, and all manner of wild animals, which were for the use of men. And we did find all manner of ore, both of gold, and of silver, and of copper" (1 Nephi 18:24–25).

This is an issue we need to test for forgery. The list appears to name animals that Joseph Smith was familiar with rather than those that were pre-Columbian species.

Nephi uses the available ore to make metal plates, on which he writes prophecies and relevant passages that he has read from the brass plates. He expounds the scriptures to his brothers in a comprehensive way.

Having grown old, Lehi gathers the group around him, counsels and blesses his posterity, and then dies (2 Nephi 4). *We are not told exactly how many years they have been ashore when this happens, so we cannot be sure of his age, but he was possibly in his late sixties.*

With Lehi gone, it doesn't take long for the old antagonisms to reassert themselves. Laman and Lemuel "murmur" once again, with a familiar refrain. "Our younger brother thinks to rule over us; and we have had much trial because of him; wherefore, now let us slay him, that we may not be afflicted more because of his words. . . . For it belongs unto us, who are the elder brethren, to rule over this people" (2 Nephi 5:3).

Warned by the Lord of his brothers' intent, Nephi takes his family and flees into the wilderness, along with "Zoram and his family, and Sam, mine elder brother and his family, and Jacob and Joseph, my younger brethren, and also my sisters, and all those who would go with me" (2 Nephi 5:6). *The implication here is that most of Ishmael's sons and their descendants stay with Laman and Lemuel.*

After a trek of "many days" they find a place to pitch their tents and "call themselves the people of Nephi," a phrase that is soon shortened to "Nephites." They call the other group, from which they have fled, "Lamanites" (2 Nephi 5:7, 9, 14).

The Nephites are busy. They plow and plant and soon begin "to prosper exceedingly, and to multiply in the land." They build buildings, among them a temple "after the manner of the temple of Solomon" (2 Nephi 5:13, 16). *Another possible forgery issue, as some scholars insist that true Israelites would never construct or honor a temple outside Jerusalem.*

They also prepare for the possibility of war. Using the sword of Laban as his template, Nephi "did make many swords, lest by any means the people who were now called Lamanites should come upon us and destroy us; for I knew their hatred towards me and my children and those who were called my people" (2 Nephi 5:14).

The Nephites seek to make Nephi their king, but he insists they should not have a king. He does, however, serve in the king-like role of protector and anoints a king in his stead as he nears death. Those who hold this position after him are called Nephi II, Nephi III, etc.

The Lord puts a curse upon the Lamanites to make them loathsome to the Nephites so that the Nephites will not want to mingle with them and become corrupted by their sinful ways. The sign of this curse is "a skin of blackness" (2 Nephi 5:21).

Apart from its racist overtones that are repugnant in a religious work, this phrase appears to represent a racial view that would have been common in Joseph Smith's time, and therefore is considered yet another indication of forgery. It did not arouse outrage in Joseph's original American audience, but it is one of the most controversial statements in the book for current readers.

Nephi records that forty years after they left Jerusalem *(which could put him in his mid-fifties in age),* wars with the Lamanites begin. Fifteen years later, or fifty-five years after their departure, he turns the task of keeping the record over to Jacob. *Nephi would then be around seventy; Jacob, in his early fifties.*

JACOB

Jacob records no history other than reporting Nephi's death and mentioning continuing difficulties with the Lamanites. However, with his own doctrinal expositions and those he quotes as having come from Nephi, along with quotations from the brass plates of Laban—primarily passages from what we recognize as the book of Isaiah—he fills up seventy pages of our current printed version of the book. Sparse as it is on history, Jacob's section is an important part of the book, with heavy emphasis on the mission of Christ.

THE TRANSITION VERSES

After Jacob's death—*we don't have the date, but if he lived into his late sixties, it would be about 530 B.C.E.*—the plates are handed down through his posterity, mainly from father to son, for the next four hundred years. Little of historical significance is added during this process. Each recipient of the plates simply records his name as he passes the plates along. Then, as the "book within a book" comes to its end, the final entries take a curious turn.

In 130 B.C.E., the last of Jacob's descendants to handle the plates, Amaleki, says he has no children. That means he has no posterity to whom he can give the plates, so he turns them over to Benjamin, the then-current Nephite king, whom Amaleki describes as "a just man before the Lord" (Omni 1:25).

Amaleki tells how Benjamin's father, Mosiah, had led the Nephites out of their land as a result of a warning from the Lord. "Led by many preachings and prophesyings" and "the power of [God's] arm," they came into a land called Zarahemla, which was heavily populated (Omni 1:13). *The descendants of Lehi thus discover that they are not the only Israelites to have migrated from Jerusalem to the promised land.*

"Mosiah discovered that the people of Zarahemla came out from Jerusalem at the time that Zedekiah, king of Judah, was carried away captive into Babylon. And they journeyed in the wilderness, and were brought by the hand of the Lord across the great waters, into the land where Mosiah discovered them; and they had dwelt there from that time forth" (Omni 1:15–16).

By the time Mosiah discovered them, "they had become exceedingly numerous. Nevertheless, they had had many wars and serious contentions, and had fallen by the sword from time to time; and their language had become corrupted; and they had brought no records with them; and they denied the being of their Creator. . . . Mosiah caused that they should be taught in his language. And . . . after they were taught in the language of Mosiah, Zarahemla gave a genealogy of his fathers, according to his memory. . . . The people of Zarahemla, and of Mosiah, did unite together; and Mosiah was appointed to be their king" (Omni 1:17–19).

So, roughly 470 years after Lehi's arrival, the Nephites meet and unite with a people whose population is larger than theirs, with whom they had unknowingly been sharing a portion of the continent all that time. If Zarahemla's ancestors had left Jerusalem at the time of the Babylonian invasion and sailed to America directly, they could have arrived almost at the same time as Lehi, whose family wandered in the desert for eight years before starting the building of their own ship.

Amaleki tells of a large stone "with engravings on it" that the people of Zarahemla took to Mosiah, which he interpreted "by the gift and power of God" (Omni 1:20). It referred to another group of people that had lived in the Americas for centuries. Their last survivor, Coriantumr, had been discovered by the people of Zarahemla before Mosiah and the Nephites appeared on the scene.

We will meet Coriantumr and learn the full background of his ancestors, the Jaredites, in Story Three.

After Amaleki's account, Mormon appears on the pages of the book for the first time. Speaking in the first person, he tells us how he found "these plates" (Words of Mormon 1:3) and offers the comments quoted in Chapter 3, in which he says he was so pleased with Nephi's and Jacob's writings that he decided to put them in his own book without abridgment or commentary. He then says he will "proceed to finish out my record" (Words of Mormon 1:9) and switches to the third person, *presumably picking up where the lost 116 pages had left off.*

With that, the Transition Verses are over, and so is Story One.

5

COMMENTARY ON STORY ONE

BECAUSE THE BOOK STARTS WITH Nephi's narrative instead of whatever introductory material Mormon may have written on the lost 116 pages, casual readers of the Book of Mormon assume that all of its players are descendants of Lehi and that all of the history that follows is the saga of an extended family quarrel between Nephites and Lamanites. In fact, things are nowhere near that simple, as the Transition Verses make clear. There are other peoples involved who make up the bulk of the population; when Mosiah's people unite with the people of Zarahemla, the latter group is the majority.

It is easy to miss this fact because Mormon seldom refers to them by name. Following the Book of Mormon practice of identifying a people by the name of their leader, Amaleki calls them the people of Zarahemla, their leader at the time the Nephites ran into them (Omni 1:14). But Mormon simply refers to all members of the newly formed society as Nephites (Mosiah 25:13). In modern terms, the Nephites took the naming rights of the combined nation because their king was chosen as its king.

Later on, Mormon says that Zarahemla is descended from
Mulek, a son of King Zedekiah (Mosiah 25:2). This raises additional questions because the Bible says that all of Zedekiah's
sons were killed by the Babylonians. Is this something the
forger simply didn't know?

No. In Story Two, Mormon quotes Helaman, a Nephite
prophet, as saying specifically that all of Zedekiah's sons were
killed *except* for Mulek. That means the designation of Mulek
as a survivor of the slaughter of his family is a deliberate insertion.

Why would a forger do such a thing? The story would unfold the same way if there were no claim regarding Mulek's
background. Why open the subject and then later offer what
some consider a lame excuse? Why not just leave it out of
any mention of his parentage? That would be a more logical
thing for a forger to do. Instead of being a problem, as some
commentators have insisted, the claim that Mulek was a
son of Zedekiah just as easily suggests that the history is
genuine.

Back to the main point, the merger of the Nephites with
the Mulekites (to describe the latter group in typical Book of
Mormon terms). If they were real people, the Mulekites
would not have suddenly changed their culture just because
they agreed that Mosiah should be their king. Human nature
being what it is, most if not all of the Mulekite practices that
were in place before they met the Nephites would have continued afterward. That means that the traditions that had
produced the "wars and serious contentions" among them
would infect the Nephites as well, particularly since there were
more Mulekites than Nephites in the resulting new society.

The presence of the Mulekites in the record complicates it significantly.

So, again, why are they there, if this is a forgery? The primary reason for introducing a new element in a forgery is to make the overall work more believable. It's hard to see how this new twist in the account accomplishes that goal.

Now let's apply the tests.

INTERNAL ISSUES

Is the work consistent within itself? Is it consistent with its purported origin? Are there any loose ends—items or stories that start off in one direction but end up somewhere else—indicating that the forger, in his invention, lost track of where he was? What does the work tell us about the person who wrote it?

Whoever wrote Story One had a good deal of talent. Well constructed and tightly written, it does not ramble. There are no loose ends. Good as it is, however, it is short enough and simple enough that the task of creating the overall framework for it would not be too big a challenge for a competent and imaginative writer.

But it does contain a significant challenge to a forger's skill that goes beyond the routine, and that is the challenge of speaking in different voices.

In Story One, Nephi and Jacob both speak in the first person. So does Lehi, when he is giving his instructions to his sons just before his death. So does Zenos, a prophet whom Jacob quotes, about whose background we are told nothing. Each one of these speakers covers at least half a dozen pages.

Quoting four different individuals at such length in the first person means that a single writer, to be convincing, must be creative enough to make sure that those individuals do not sound like each other, something very hard to do. The matter is worth pursuing.

We've heard a little from Nephi; let's turn to Lehi. Because it is Nephi who is the author of the record, Lehi's descriptions of the visions he receives are summarized in Nephi's words. It is not until Lehi is ready to die and gathers his family around him to give them a father's instructions and blessing that we hear him speak at length in his own voice. When he does, he comes through as a stronger figure than the Lehi whom we met only through Nephi. He sounds like a man who was fully equal to his role as the patriarch of this clan, one who could keep Laman and Lemuel in line despite their murmuring—something Nephi couldn't do.

He is also rather eloquent. Here are some excerpts:

> Hear the words of a trembling parent, whose limbs ye must soon lay down in the cold and silent grave, from whence no traveler can return; a few more days and I go the way of all the earth.
>
> But behold, the Lord hath redeemed my soul from hell; I have beheld his glory, and I am encircled about eternally in the arms of his love.
>
> And now that my soul might have joy in you, and that my heart might leave this world with gladness because of you, that I might not be brought down with grief and sorrow to the grave, arise from the dust, my sons, and be men, and be determined in one mind and in one heart, united in all things, that ye may not come down into captivity;

That ye may not be cursed with a sore cursing; and also, that ye may not incur the displeasure of a just God upon you, unto the destruction, yea, the eternal destruction of both soul and body.

Awake, my sons; put on the armor of righteousness. Shake off the chains with which ye are bound, and come forth out of obscurity, and arise from the dust. (2 Nephi 1:14–15, 21–23)

Let's compare that statement with a sermon attributed to Jacob, who was born in the wilderness after the family had left Jerusalem and thus was untainted by the kinds of experiences that formed Laman and Lemuel. He was raised in the Western Hemisphere under Nephi's tutelage and presumably had a great deal of time to study the material on the brass plates of Laban. All of this means that he should have a style much more pedantic and scholarly than his father's. Readers can make their own judgments about how the following meets that requirement:

Wo unto him that has the law given, yea, that has all the commandments of God, like unto us, and that transgresseth them, and that wasteth the days of his probation, for awful is his state!

O that cunning plan of the evil one! O the vainness, and the frailties, and the foolishness of men! When they are learned they think they are wise, and they hearken not unto the counsel of God, for they set it aside, supposing they know of themselves, wherefore, their wisdom is foolishness and it profiteth them not. And they shall perish.

But to be learned is good if they hearken unto the counsels of God.

But wo unto the rich, who are rich as to the things of the world. For because they are rich they despise the poor, and they persecute the meek, and their hearts are upon their treasures; wherefore, their treasure is their god. And behold, their treasure shall perish with them also.

And wo unto the deaf that will not hear; for they shall perish.

Wo unto the blind that will not see; for they shall perish also.

Wo unto the uncircumcised of heart, for a knowledge of their iniquities shall smite them at the last day.

Wo unto the liar, for he shall be thrust down to hell.

Wo unto the murderer who deliberately killeth, for he shall die.

Wo unto them who commit whoredoms, for they shall be thrust down to hell.

Yea, wo unto those that worship idols, for the devil of all devils delighteth in them.

And, in fine, wo unto all those who die in their sins; for they shall return to God, and behold his face, and remain in their sins.

O, my beloved brethren, remember the awfulness in transgressing against that Holy God, and also the awfulness of yielding to the enticings of that cunning one. Remember, to be carnally-minded is death, and to be spiritually-minded is life eternal. (2 Nephi 9:27–39)

In addition to Nephi, Lehi, and Jacob, Story One also contains a long, convoluted allegory attributed to a prophet named Zenos, whose writing presumably was on the brass plates obtained from Laban. It bears no resemblance to anything else in the book. I won't quote it because it is much too long even to be summarized, but those who want to go through it will find it in chapter 5 of the book of Jacob.

So, to summarize the point: Story One has four principal first-person speakers: Nephi, Jacob, Lehi, and Zenos. Each one speaks enough to give us a significant sample, and each one has a distinctively different style. That means that if the book is forged, it was done by an author who was not afraid of the challenge of creating such different voices, something that is very hard to do.

Those looking for a link with Joseph Smith should place the excerpts quoted here next to the paragraph written by him and quoted in Chapter 3 to see how close they come to Joseph's style. I see no connection whatsoever, but computer analysis is available to reduce the guesswork on this subject. Such analysis confirms that the different passages attributed to different writers in the Book of Mormon were, indeed, written by different people and that Joseph Smith was not one of them.

Professional analysis can be wrong—Osborn, Osborn, and Osborn said that Howard Hughes was the only person who could have written the notes that Clifford Irving forged, and they were wrong—but the fact that the book is good enough to pass such a computer test demonstrates that the skill level required to forge it would be extremely high.

Now let us turn to some internal details, because even the best of forgers get tripped up when they put in too many specifics, and Story One is full of specifics. They open the door for some fairly obvious questions.

How many people were on the boat?

This is relevant because the group needs to be big enough

to have been the foundation of not one but two subsequent societies, the Nephites and the Lamanites. Let's count.

Lehi and Sariah make two; their four sons and their wives
add eight more, making ten; Zoram and his wife make twelve.
At one point in the record Nephi refers to his sisters, unnamed
and unnumbered but plural, which means at least two more.
Two of Ishmael's sons are mentioned, which makes sixteen; if
they had wives other than Lehi's daughters, as the record implies, that would make eighteen. If Ishmael had other sons who
married Lehi's daughters, that would take us to twenty. Because
we don't know how many more children Ishmael may have had,
the total could have been as many as twenty-five or even thirty,
but let's stay with twenty as the size of the initial party, for the
sake of being conservative.

The group was in the wilderness for eight years, during
which time Ishmael died, so I haven't counted either him or his
wife. However, Sariah had two additional children—that makes
twenty-two—and an unspecified number of babies were born
to the married children. A minimum of seven couples were
involved—Lehi's four sons, Zoram, and Ishmael's at least two
sons—all of whom had wives. If each couple had an average of
three children each during the eight years of wandering, the
total would then be forty-three. There is no mention of servants, but Lehi was certainly rich enough to have afforded
some, and leaving out their names would be consistent with the
attitude of the time. (After all, Nephi left out the names of his
own sisters.) The narrative thus supports a total of more than
forty and possibly as many as sixty or more at the time they
boarded the ship.

What ages were they?

When they left Jerusalem for the wilderness, the boys were old enough to be married, but none of them was. That means that Nephi, the youngest, had to be at least fourteen—because he was "large in stature" (1 Nephi 4:31) when he grabbed Zoram, sixteen is more likely—which suggests that Laman, the oldest, would be at least twenty.

Sariah, their mother, was still of childbearing age. She had two more sons, Jacob and Joseph, during the eight years of desert wandering. If Laman were twenty at the beginning of the narrative, and if Sariah had married at fourteen and borne him when she was fifteen, that would put her at age thirty-five when they left, still capable of bearing two more children. Putting Laman much older than twenty-one would raise the question of why he was not already married and push Sariah to an age at which two additional births in the desert would be unlikely.

Unfortunately, beyond referring to them in the plural as his sisters, Nephi does not give us any of the names of any women in the family other than his mother, so we don't know how many there were or where they came in the family birth order. Given Sariah's age limits for childbearing, however, it is reasonable to assume they were younger than the boys. That would mean they would be available to Ishmael's younger sons as wives, because the group was in the desert long enough for them to come to marriageable age.

All of this suggests that Sariah had borne at least six children—more, if she had more than two girls—before the family left Jerusalem, and at least two more after, with an age difference of more than twenty years between the births of the first child and the last. That would not be unusual for that time and culture.

Is this initial band big enough and young enough to be the foundation of the two groups that spring up after Lehi's death?

Maybe, maybe not. The eventual population of Pitcairn's Island, empty of humans until the mutinous crew members from *HMS Bounty* arrived there with their young Polynesian wives, shows that it is possible. Also, the wars between the two groups don't start until forty years after Lehi left Jerusalem, which is enough time for two more generations of young men of fighting age to be born. It's possible.

It is equally possible, however, that there were other indigenous peoples present in the areas where Lehi's descendants settled, peoples whose existence didn't make it into the record that Nephi and Jacob kept. If we had the 116 pages on which Mormon supposedly wrote more detail about their history, we would have a better picture of what the early settlements were like. I will have more to say on this in later chapters.

So the book appears to pass these tests of detail. Where it does not appear to pass is in the list of Jacob's descendants who handled the plates. The Transition Verses say that the plates were passed down from father to son for a period of some four hundred years. Assume that each son outlived his father by an average of thirty years during this time; at that rate, how many father to son combinations would be required to cover four hundred years? The math is clear—the book would have to list at least thirteen such transfers.

It records only seven.

It gets specifically worse than that. Enos, described as Jacob's son, says that he "began to be old" 179 years after Lehi had left Jerusalem (Enos 1:25). "Began to be old" indeed—if Enos was fathered when Jacob was thirty, he would have to have lived to be more than 140 to still be alive at that time. The numbers work if Jacob fathered the boy when he was near ninety and gave him the plates as a newborn, with Enos then living into *his* nineties, but that seems pretty farfetched.

One possible explanation is that *son,* as used throughout the Bible, has two meanings. The first is the obvious one—the physical male child of a set of parents—but the second denotes lineage rather than immediate issue. The Bible never uses the terms *grandson* or *great-grandson,* as we do; any direct descendant is a son regardless of how distant the relationship is in time. Jesus is referred to as the Son of David, and Book of Mormon writers Benjamin and Mormon, for example, refer to their predecessors as "our father" or "our fathers" when the writers clearly are not literally first-generation sons (Mosiah 1:4, 5–7, 13–14, 16).

If we use the second definition of *son,* Enos could have been a very young great-grandson of a very old Jacob when he received the plates; Jacob would not have to have been fathering children in his extreme old age in order to make the record an accurate one. Believers can cling to that as critics can claim they have found an internal problem.

EXTERNAL ISSUES

Is there evidence external to its claims that either corroborates or contradicts those claims? Do the things that it says fit with facts that have come to light since its publication? Are there any anachronisms that its original readers may have missed but that are now obvious?

As noted in Chapter 3, B. H. Roberts attempted to find external evidence for the book in the 1920s and was unable to do so. I presume that is why the book's critics now quote him so enthusiastically. But B. H. Roberts cannot be taken as the final word on external issues because he has been dead for more than half a century. A great deal of new information is now available. Most of Nephi's story takes place in the wilderness between Jerusalem and the Red Sea, lands that have not changed appreciably from that time to this, and this area is now more open to Westerners than it has ever been before. That means we can check on the details Nephi mentions, something that Roberts could not do. A few examples:

THE PRESENCE OF WATER

Nephi says the family camped in a valley, three days' journey from Jerusalem, in which there was a river flowing continually to the Red Sea. It is from this site that he and his brothers went back to Jerusalem to fetch the brass plates from Laban. This statement has raised considerable skepticism because Saudi Arabia, which is presumably where such a campsite would have been, is known as one of the few countries on Earth that has no rivers. For many years, the book's supporters had no answer for this discrepancy. Now, some of them think they have.

Some Western scholars were in Arabia in 1996 on a search for the biblical Mount Ararat. As they talked with local Arabs about ancient geography, they were referred to an area known as the Waters of Moses, a site where water comes out of the ground. It was reputed to have been the spot where Moses struck a rock with his staff to provide water for the thirsty Israelites in the wilderness. The Americans went there more for curiosity than anything else.

When they arrived in the area, they found, not far from the Waters of Moses, a stream running through a valley all the way to the Red Sea. There was every indication that it ran year-round, and, like most of the topography of the region, had been there for centuries, if not millennia.[1] Those familiar with the Book of Mormon began to wonder if they had, in fact, found the river of which Nephi spoke, even though one would be hard pressed to call this stream a river in terms of the mighty rivers of the world.

The valley through which this river runs is seventy-five miles south of Jerusalem, which puts it within the three days' journey that Nephi mentions. It is unknown and unmarked on any Western maps. Whether it is or isn't the place spoken of by Nephi is open to debate, but its discovery demonstrates that Nephi's story is plausible on this point.

And it is in a place that no Westerner knew about before 1996.

ARCHAEOLOGY AND THE ROUTE OF THE MARCH

Nephi says that the party proceeded in a southeastern direction. The narrative is specific, very specific, about where they went in a desert where conditions have not changed over the millennia. Nephi's description is so precise that it is possible to reconstruct a map of the possible wanderings of the family.

That means Nephi's description of the journey can now be tested against current conditions and locations in the area, and

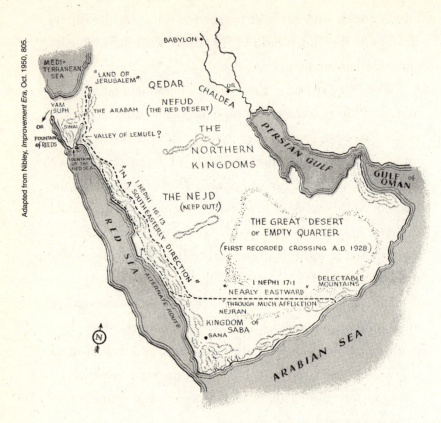

Adapted from Nibley, *Improvement Era*, Oct. 1950, 805.

A suggested route for Lehi's travels, taken from the specifics in Nephi's account

it must meet a very rigorous standard with respect to its archaeology.

It does.

In just the past few years, believing scholars have traveled
along the route suggested by the map above and discovered
some interesting things:

The route closely approximates what is known as the
Incense Trail, a route followed in the ancient world by those
trading in incense and other goods. One location on that trail
was a mining site from which a great deal of precious metal—

primarily gold—was taken. Many archaeologists believe this site was the one known as King Solomon's Mines.

Nephi said that he himself made the plates on which his narrative was engraved. This stop along the route supposedly followed by Lehi's party is a logical source from which the gold he used could have come.

Beyond the mines, the route goes by what was once an important city, one whose ruins have only recently been discovered. Modern archaeologists have found that the name of the city, engraved in stone, was NHM, a word written without vowels as was the Hebrew tradition in the centuries before Christ.

Nephi's narrative records the death of Ishmael and identifies the place where he was buried as "Nahom." Archaeologists working in NHM have found a significant burial ground that contained both Egyptian and non-Egyptian graves. Putting name and function together, a believing scholar calls the discovery of NHM/Nahom "an archaeological bull's-eye" in support of Nephi's story.[2]

Toward the end of their eight-year period in the desert wilderness, the record says, they reached a land so rich with vegetation that they named it Bountiful. Nephi says that they did this after turning eastward; previously they had been traveling in a southeasterly direction. One Church leader, John A. Widtsoe, in a 1950 article entitled "Is Book of Mormon Geography Known?" says that the turn eastward occurred at the nineteenth parallel. He quotes Joseph Smith himself as the source of this information.[3]

Turning directly east on the nineteenth parallel would have taken Lehi's family to a geographical location on the Arabian

Peninsula that fits perfectly Nephi's description of Bountiful: the Qara mountains. In his book *Arabia Felix*, Bertram Thomas describes them:

> What a glorious place! Mountains three thousand feet high basking above a tropical ocean, their seaward slopes velvety with waving jungle, their roofs fragrant with rolling yellow meadows, beyond which the mountains slope northwards to a red sandstone steppe. . . . Great was my delight when in 1928 I suddenly came upon it from out of the arid wastes of the southern borderlands.[4]

Thomas is reported to have been one of the first Europeans to see this location, a century after Joseph Smith. I have searched through books on Palestine that were current in the 1820s to see if either Joseph Smith or Third Party could have had a contemporary source for this knowledge, and I have not been able to find a similar description. The first recorded Western discovery of similar mountains in what is now Oman, on the twenty-fifth parallel, came in 1838, too late to have been available to a forger in 1829.

All of this is important because one of the most persistent criticisms of the Book of Mormon is that it fails the test of archaeology: it does not give any recognizable descriptions of landmarks that have been uncovered in pre-Colombian America. Richard and Joan Ostling make quite a bit out of the fact that many believers do not understand that and frequently bombard the Smithsonian Institution for confirmation of the urban legend that archaeologists exploring the ruins of Central and South America use the Book of Mormon as their guide. Indeed, the level of such inquiries is high enough, and persistent enough, that Smithsonian officials have developed a form letter to send out in response, patiently repeating over and over that the book is not being used in this way.

That is not as big a problem for the book as the Ostlings suggest because it cannot be held responsible for the ignorance or overenthusiasm of its supporters. A careful reading of it makes it clear that it is never specific enough in its description of places in the Western Hemisphere to justify anyone saying for certain, "This is a Book of Mormon site." There are Latter-day Saint archaeologists who insist that they *have* found Book of Mormon sites or artifacts, but, as the Ostlings point out, no archaeologist who is not a believer agrees with them. That doesn't mean that the believing archaeologists are wrong, only that their enthusiasm does not have enough evidence behind it to convince an outside observer.

In the Middle East, however, as we have seen, the situation is much different. Whoever wrote the portion of the "book within a book" attributed to Nephi knew the geography of the Arabian Peninsula very well—better than anyone in America in Joseph Smith's time (or B. H. Roberts's time a century later, for that matter). I have not been able to find any published challenges to believers' claims regarding the specificity of locations described in Story One.

I have taken the map shown on page 90, as well as a good portion of the information in this chapter, from Dr. Hugh Nibley, whose first book on the subject, *Lehi in the Desert and the World of the Jaredites,* was originally published in 1952, roughly two decades after B. H. Roberts did his work. Nibley was the inspiration for the generation of scholars who went into the Arabian desert and found the items I have mentioned.

One critic of the Book of Mormon rebuked me for paying attention to Nibley. He put forth the same argument used to discredit LDS archaeological efforts in pre-Columbian America, saying, "No one agrees with him."

That set me back a bit. Although Nibley's academic credentials are impeccable, he is a believer, so he is, by definition, a special pleader, and one should be wary of relying too much on his conclusions.

Then I realized something. When it comes to his research on cultural activities and geography in the ancient Middle East, no one *disagrees* with him, either. Nibley has been challenged on many other fronts by scholars who take issue with some of his other conclusions—indeed, I took issue with him myself, on his political beliefs—but on the items I cite here, I cannot find any articles or books that challenge the information he puts forward. Also, in every instance he cites a work or author other than himself as his primary source. In political terms, Nibley is "running unopposed" regarding the items listed herein; with respect to them, he has no challengers. Until such appear and make their case, I will continue to cite his work.

AGRICULTURAL PRACTICES

I mentioned that Jacob quotes an extensive allegory attributed to the prophet Zenos (Jacob 5). It likens the house of Israel to an olive tree; in it, the branches of the tree are separated from the original roots, yet they still survive, because they are grafted onto other trees. In time, they are grafted back onto the original one.

Olive trees do not grow in New England. They are, however, an essential, even life-giving, part of the agricultural economy of the Middle East. They require enormous patience and time and skill before they will bear edible fruit. Zenos's description of olive culture, offered to make the point of his allegory, runs on for nearly seven pages. It is given in excruciating detail, with so many prunings, plantings, graftings, and re-graftings in it that the Western reader gets completely lost trying to follow it all. Nonetheless, as I have traveled in the Middle East, I have been told by those who know the olive culture that such a regime of prunings and graftings is completely authentic.

What are the odds that Joseph Smith, or anyone in his neighborhood, would have known the intricacies of how olives were grown and cared for, centuries before Christ?

Also, why would Joseph or any forger put such a thing in this book? As I said, for many readers, Zenos's description of olive farming is absolutely impenetrable. If you are a forger, you don't want to insert something into your narrative that will baffle your audience; the far more logical thing to put forward would be a parable tied to something with which they are likely to be familiar.

DESERT POETRY

Poetry is an art form that is always unique to the culture in which it is found, and it is often strange to the eyes and ears of those from a different culture. For example, Westerners have come to know of a Japanese poetic form known as haiku that has no counterpart in English. Is there a comparable poetic form that would have been indicative of Nephi's time, which neither Joseph nor Third Party could be expected to know?

Yes. It is called a *qasida,* and it has several specific elements, which Nibley outlines: "The standard pattern is a simple one:

(a) the poet's attention is arrested by some impressive natural phenomenon, usually running water; (b) this leads him to recite a few words in its praise, drawing it to the attention of a beloved companion of the way and (c) making it an object lesson for the latter, who is urged to be like it." Nibley notes that where possible, one such poem should be followed by its "'brother,'" a second one very like the first.[5]

With this description in mind, we turn to Nephi's account of Lehi's actions after he and the family had "traveled in the wilderness in the borders which are nearer the Red Sea" and "pitched his tent in a valley by the side of a river of water" (1 Nephi 2:5–6).

"He called the name of the river, Laman, and it emptied into the Red Sea. . . .

" . . . He spake unto Laman, saying: O that thou mightest be like unto this river, continually running into the fountain of all righteousness!

"And he also spake unto Lemuel: O that thou mightest be like unto this valley, firm and steadfast, and immovable in keeping the commandments of the Lord!" (1 Nephi 2:8–10).

In these few verses from the Book of Mormon, their author perfectly captures a form of desert poetry that was authentic to Nephi's time but unknown to the Western audience that received the book in the 1830s. It was obviously unknown to B. H. Roberts in the 1920s as well. Believers didn't learn about it until Nibley published it in 1952.

CREDIBILITY OF DETAIL

The only incident described in any significant detail is Nephi's adventure in Jerusalem, when he killed Laban, entered his chambers, and safely got out of the city with the brass plates. This incident has given rise to a great deal of comment, but it has not been consistent, because readers have reacted out of their own cultures.

To illustrate, at one point in his teaching career, Dr. Nibley had some Arabic students in his class on the Book of Mormon. When they got to the story of Nephi's sortie into Jerusalem at night, they were very much disturbed by it. They said, "This can't be right."

"Why not?" Nibley asked.

Because, they said, Nephi *hesitated* in killing Laban. No true Middle Easterner would have done that. If Nephi was a real person, with real Middle Eastern roots, they said, he would have dispatched Laban without a second thought.[6]

That's an interesting counterpoint to Western critics of the incident who say that Nephi could not have been a real prophet because he *did* kill Laban.

For me, Nephi's story about finding Laban lying drunk in the street has the ring of truth, on several levels.

First, the record in which it is told is put forward as a memoir, written at least thirty years after the fact, rather than a contemporary journal, written as it happened. As they write their memoirs, older men, even while talking in lofty terms about lofty things, often think back and reminisce about the particularly memorable deeds they did in their youth. My father did it, and I find that I am now doing it as I talk with my children and grandchildren.

Nephi was a teenager when he pulled off a feat that his brothers—all older—had told him he could not possibly do. Succeeding where his brothers had failed must have pleased him a great deal, both at the time it happened and as he reflected on it in later years. The way in which this incident is related strikes me as an authentic memory of a youthful triumph that an older man writing for his posterity would want to report in detail.

Next, the setting for this adventure fits an experience I had a few years back. With several other Senators, I was in Fez, Morocco, with my wife. We went into the ancient quarter of the city, a strange and exotic place that has remained essentially unchanged for hundreds of years. Many of the streets, if they could be called that, are about eight feet wide, and the walls of the buildings on either side of the streets go straight up, often for as many as three stories. That meant that when a fully loaded donkey came down the street we had to step into a shop door to let the donkey pass—the saddle bags it carried nearly touched the walls on both sides of the street at once. It was like being in a tunnel or a maze without a roof, with the high walls blocking any view of any sort of a landmark or even a view of the position of the sun. Side streets came from every different direction, seemingly at random, and we were instantly lost. That's why we were not allowed to go in there without a guide.

I imagined what it would be like at night in such a place, before the invention of electric lighting, with all the doors bolted shut and windows covered. Deserted. Very dark.

Standing there looking at this ancient place suddenly made the entire Nephi-Laban story seem totally plausible to me. Going to Laban's house in such a city would have meant darting down these narrow streets completely unobserved by anyone—a perfect setting for a chance encounter with a drunken man, a quick sword thrust, and a change of outer clothes. Nephi's account seems very strange if set in an American town in nineteenth-century New England, but it would be perfectly at home in this city of the ancient world.

Back to Nibley, who puts the finishing touch on the final portion of the Laban episode, the decision of Zoram to join the sons. Quoting from his book *Lehi in the Desert*:

When Zoram, the servant, discovered that it was not his master with whom he had been discussing the highly secret doings of the elders as they walked to the outskirts of the city, he was seized with terror, as well he might be. In such a situation there was only one thing Nephi could possibly have done, both to spare Zoram and to avoid giving alarm—and no westerner could have guessed what it was. Nephi, a powerful fellow, held the terrified Zoram in a vice-like grip long enough to swear a solemn oath in his ear, "as the Lord liveth, and as I live" (1 Nephi 4:32), that he would not harm him if he would listen. Zoram immediately relaxed, and Nephi swore another oath to him that he would be a free man if he would join the party: "Therefore, if thou wilt go down into the wilderness to my father thou shalt have place with us."

. . . What astonishes the western reader is the miraculous effect of Nephi's oath on Zoram, who upon hearing a few conventional words promptly becomes tractable, while as for the brothers, as soon as Zoram "made an oath unto us . . . that he would tarry with us from that time forth . . . our fears did cease concerning him."

The reaction of both parties makes sense when one realizes that the oath is the one thing that is most sacred and inviolable among the desert people. . . . But not every oath will do: to be most binding and solemn an oath should be by the *life* of something, even if it be but a blade of grass; the only oath more awful than "by my life" or (less commonly) "by the life of my head," is the *wa hayat Allah,* "by the life of God," or "as the Lord liveth." . . . So we see that the one and only way that Nephi could have pacified the struggling Zoram in an instant was to utter the one oath that no man would dream of breaking, the most solemn of all oaths to the Semite: "as the Lord liveth, and as I live."[7]

Although Nephi's encounter with Laban and, subsequently, Zoram is exotic enough that it has been dismissed as clear proof that Joseph Smith simply made it up, evidence since Joseph's time suggests otherwise.

OTHER FORGERY ISSUES
IN STORY ONE

I noted Nephi's reference to the building of a temple. A *temple,* in the Old Testament tradition, is a place where sacred ordinances are carried out by the temple priests, dedicated to their holy orders. Because of the special and sacred place that temple worship holds in Jewish theology, some scholars have insisted that Nephi's reference to its taking place in the Western Hemisphere represents clear proof of forgery. There is only one spot for the temple, they say, and that is in Jerusalem. If they were real Israelites, and as steeped in Jewish religious history as the book says they were, the sons of Lehi would have known this.

On this point, translations of the Dead Sea Scrolls and other documents discovered since Joseph Smith's death now come into play. They indicate that there were, indeed, temple rites performed in places and buildings other than the one in Jerusalem. Ruins that appear to have been temples have been found along the Incense Trail in the Arabian Peninsula, including one at NHM. Nephi's account is consistent with these new discoveries.

A more serious problem for the book stems from the extensive quotations that both Nephi and Jacob take from Isaiah. The source for these quotations was supposedly the brass plates Nephi obtained from Laban in 600 B.C.E., which was prior to the Babylonian captivity. Biblical scholars are convinced that only portions of the book of Isaiah in our Bibles were written by that time, because the book also makes reference to events that took place *after* the Babylonian captivity. This proves, they say, that there were at least two Isaiahs and possibly more. Since some of the passages cited by Nephi and Jacob are now attributed to the second, or Deutero-Isaiah, the one who is said to have lived long after Lehi had supposedly left Jerusalem, the book is open to serious challenge on this point.

The scholarly determination that there were at least two Isaiahs was not reached until after Joseph Smith's death. A forger in the 1820s, lifting passages from the Bible of the time, would not have known about it.

Believers respond by insisting that scholars are wrong in trying to put a strict chronological straitjacket on the writings of Isaiah. After all, they say, if Isaiah accurately described the birth, mission, and crucifixion of Jesus centuries before the fact, couldn't he do the same thing with the Israelites under the Babylonians? They claim that his statements about things that happened after the Babylonian captivity were the result of his prophetic ability to see these events, not personal experience. Naturally, critics scoff at this as rationalization.

In the light of new information about the Bible that has come from translations of the Dead Sea Scrolls and other similar discoveries, a few scholars are now backing away from the Deutero-Isaiah theory, and a few others never accepted it in the first place. While this latter group is still a small minority, believers in the Book of Mormon must hope that they are right.

CONCLUSIONS ABOUT STORY ONE

I said in the Introduction that we would try to come to some conclusions about each of the three stories, as we examined them one by one. As a framework for doing so, I will use the legal concepts that became familiar to Americans as a result of the O. J. Simpson murder case.

Simpson was first tried in a criminal court, where the legal standard of certainty required was "beyond a reasonable doubt." Members of the jury that heard the case concluded they could not find him guilty when the evidence was measured against that standard, so he was set free. However, in a subsequent civil case where the legal issue focused on where the "preponderance of evidence" lay, jury members decided, on the basis of this slightly lower standard, that he had, indeed, killed his former wife.

So, given the evidence we have reviewed, can we conclude that Story One is authentic beyond a reasonable doubt? Believers are quick to say yes. Nibley wrote that anyone who said that the Book of Mormon was a fraud would have to throw out its first forty pages.

I would not go that far. While there is much support for its authenticity, as we have seen, there are enough unresolved issues that "beyond a reasonable doubt" is a bit of a reach.

But "preponderance of evidence" is not. Whoever wrote the story of Lehi's family and the Transition Verses that follow it had these attributes:

1. Sufficient writing skill to construct a coherent narrative line of the story of the family's migration to the New World.

2. An accurate understanding of the geography of the Arabian Desert, one that was not available in any American library in the 1820s but that has been confirmed by archaeological discoveries in the last half century.

3. A deep familiarity with ancient Middle Eastern culture and poetry, as well as enough experience with its agricultural practices to give a complete description of the proper care of olive trees.

4. A solid knowledge of the Old Testament, with special emphasis on the Messiah passages and prophecies in Isaiah.

5. The capacity to record—or create—a number of lengthy sermons, visions, and expositions of religious doctrine.

6. The ability to speak in different voices when writing under different names.

7. The willingness to complicate things by speaking of additional peoples who were unrelated to the main characters.

Which possibility for authorship is most likely to fit this profile?

A Western forger, writing in America in the 1820s? Or someone born in the Eastern Hemisphere in pre-Christian times?

The preponderance of evidence clearly says it is the latter. Because the book claims just such an authorship, that strongly argues that this portion of the Book of Mormon—Story One—is authentic.

That is not enough to validate the entire book—the McCulloch material in Irving's book didn't mean that it wasn't a forgery—but it is well worth keeping in mind.

6

INTRODUCTION TO
STORY TWO

REMEMBER: STORY TWO IS supposed to be missing its first 116 pages. Stepping into it should be like going into a movie twenty minutes after it has started—and it is. It is quite confusing. If it weren't for the brief material in the Transition Verses, where Mormon tells of finding the plates that record Story One, we wouldn't even know the author's name, let alone who he is.

So, who is he?

The answer to that question doesn't come until the end of Story Two, where Mormon describes his own life in proper chronological sequence. Because we need to know his background if we are to judge whether the work attributed to him is consistent with it, I bring his personal history forward here, to the beginning. This is what the record says about him:

Mormon was born in 310 C.E., somewhere north of the city of Zarahemla. When he was ten years old, Ammaron, the keeper of the plates at the time, went to him and said:

"I perceive that thou art a sober child, and art quick to observe;

"Therefore, when ye are about twenty and four years old

I would that ye should . . . go to the land Antum, unto a hill which shall be called Shim; and there have I deposited unto the Lord all the sacred engravings concerning this people.

"And behold, ye shall take the plates of Nephi unto yourself, and the remainder shall ye leave in the place where they are; and ye shall engrave on the plates of Nephi all the things that ye have observed concerning this people" (Mormon 1:2–4).

Quite an assignment for a ten-year-old.

The next year, Mormon's father took him to the land of Zarahemla, where "the whole face of the land had become covered with buildings, and the people were as numerous almost, as it were the sand of the sea" (Mormon 1:7).

The descendants of Lehi and Mulek were now a large civilization indeed.

Mormon had another significant religious experience at age fifteen, when, he says, "being somewhat of a sober mind, . . . I was visited of the Lord, and tasted and knew of the goodness of Jesus. And I did endeavor to preach unto this people, but my mouth was shut, and I was forbidden that I should preach unto them; for behold they had wilfully rebelled against their God" (Mormon 1:15–16).

Something else happened to him at fifteen. He reports, "Notwithstanding I being young, was large in stature; therefore the people of Nephi appointed me that I should be their leader, or the leader of their armies" (Mormon 2:1).

Some critics of the book take this double reference to the age of fifteen as an indication of forgery. Their reasoning is that Joseph Smith was fifteen when he first started talking about having visions; the statement that Mormon's career began at the same age—just as Nephi's did, in Story One—is considered to be, perhaps unconsciously, an autobiographical insertion on Joseph's part.

Mormon was not successful, at least at first. He does not record a significant victory until 331 C.E., when he would have been twenty-one. From that time forward, he served with enough distinction to keep his command. The level of warfare was high, and he was fully engaged in it, year by year.

When he was thirty-five, with his people gathered in the city of Shem, Mormon urged his forces to "stand boldly before the Lamanites and fight for their wives, and their children, and their houses, and their homes." They responded, and his army of thirty thousand Nephites fighting against fifty thousand Lamanites "did stand before them with such firmness that they did flee from before us" (Mormon 2:23, 25).

"Nevertheless," he says, "the strength of the Lord was not with us; yea, we were left to ourselves . . . ; we had become weak like unto our brethren" (Mormon 2:26). A treaty was signed, dividing the land, and there were no attacks for ten years.

When he was fifty years old, the Lamanites came in force; Mormon's armies prevailed. The Lamanites came back the next year; Mormon's armies won again. As a result of these victories, the Nephites became boastful and vowed that they would attack the Lamanites in their own territory.

Mormon was appalled at such a lust for war. He "did utterly refuse from this time forth to be a commander and a leader of this people, because of their wickedness and abomination. . . . Thrice have I delivered them out of the hands of their enemies, and they have repented not of their sins" (Mormon 3:11–13).

"I did stand as an idle witness to manifest unto the world the things which I saw and heard, according to the manifestations of the Spirit which had testified of things to come" (Mormon 3:16).

After another series of terrible battles, he says, "It is impossible for the tongue to describe, or for man to write a perfect description of the horrible scene of the blood and carnage which was among the people, both of the Nephites and of the Lamanites; and every heart was hardened, so that they delighted in the shedding of blood continually. And there never had been so great wickedness among all the children of Lehi, nor even among all the house of Israel, . . . as was among this people" (Mormon 4:11–12).

The Lamanites came back again when Mormon was sixty-five. This time the Nephites "began to be swept off by them even as a dew before the sun" (Mormon 4:18). He went to the hill Shim and gathered all the records hidden there by Ammaron, to prevent them from falling into Lamanite hands. He repented of his oath not to lead the Nephites in battle and again took command of their armies, "for they looked upon me as though I could deliver them from their afflictions. But behold, I was without hope, for I knew the judgments of the Lord which should come upon them; for they repented not of their iniquities" (Mormon 5:1–2).

Although there were some battles in which the Nephites repelled the attacks, by the time Mormon was seventy "we did . . . take to flight, and those whose flight was swifter than the Lamanites' did escape, and those whose flight did not exceed the Lamanites' were swept down and destroyed" (Mormon 5:7). The stage was set for the final confrontation.

"I, Mormon, wrote an epistle unto the king of the Lamanites, and desired of him that he would grant unto us that we might gather our people unto the land of Cumorah, by a hill which was called Cumorah, and there we could give them battle" (Mormon 6:2).

The Lamanite king agreed. It took four years to get everyone there, and Mormon, at seventy-four, finished his record and hid it in the hill Cumorah, "save it were these few plates which I gave unto my son Moroni" (Mormon 6:6).

In the final battle, Mormon was wounded and left on the field for dead; the Nephites were utterly destroyed. In 385 C.E, he wrote his farewell, lamenting the fate of the Nephites and then addressing himself to the "remnant of this people who are spared, if it so be that God may give unto them my words" (Mormon 7:1). He tells them that they are of the house of Israel, that they must repent if they are to be saved, that they must "delight no more in the shedding of blood," and that they must "believe in Jesus Christ, that he is the Son of God" (Mormon 7:4–5).

His death was recorded by Moroni, his son and the author of Story Three.

That's the purported autobiography of the author who is represented as being responsible for writing Story Two—a precocious child who grew into a deeply religious, physically imposing, gifted military commander, one who viewed the Nephite records through the prism of sixty years of experience with his nation and concern for it.

What sort of final product should we expect to get from such a man?

Certainly it would not be a novel. I make that point because one of Fawn Brodie's criticisms of the Book of Mormon is that it has in it no dialog attributed to women, as a good novel should.[1]

But it was not put forward as a novel. Story Two claims to be an abridgment of records originally written by men who were prophets and then summarized by Mormon, a military commander as well as a prophet himself. It originally covered roughly a thousand years, from Lehi's departure from Jerusalem in 600 B.C.E. to Mormon's death around 385 C.E.; even with 116 pages missing, its narrative still spans more than five hundred years. If it is genuine, it would be a mixture of historical, religious, and military accounts, with some commentary on governmental structures as well—and that is exactly what it is.

We would see that clearly if we went through it with the same level of detail provided in summarizing Story One, but I will not do that because I'm afraid I would lose all but the most dedicated of Book of Mormon aficionados if I did. It often bogs down in excruciating detail.

So, although its bulk and complicated narrative are part of the forgery question—is it logical to believe that Joseph Smith was capable of writing this big and complex a work?—we will try to get an adequate understanding of Story Two by dipping into it at various places, by taking core samples, if you will. The danger is that we will miss things that are important, but the advantage is that we will not be overwhelmed by the sheer mass of it and miss even more.

Because it is so long, I have divided it into two parts. The first is filled with a series of events, which I call the History of Story Two, and the second concentrates on specific events surrounding the visit of Jesus Christ to the Western Hemisphere, which I call the Climax of Story Two. I devote both a chapter and a commentary to each, but when we have examined them both, I will put them back together and analyze all of Story Two as a single unit.

7

The History of Story Two

THE FIRST PORTION OF STORY TWO contains the following:

- A substantial and tightly integrated narrative that includes flashbacks, side accounts, narratives, and individual stories, covering 130 years
- A large number of sermons, prophecies, letters, and lengthy personal blessings, all given in first person
- Detailed descriptions of war—battle tactics, behind-the-scenes spy activity, supply challenges, and defensive fortifications
- An outline of the machinations of a corrupt secret society
- A chronology of changing forms and actions of the Nephite government

Such a bundle of items represents a significant amount of exposure; remember, the longer and more complicated the forgery, the more difficult it is to write and the more likely it will be to contain clues to its true author. The length and complexity of the History of Story Two make it fertile ground for forgery testing.

Let's start with only the barest of background information, just enough to provide a framework for the three core samples I have chosen to describe in detail.

When we step into this narrative, the year is 130 B.C.E. and King Benjamin is on the throne in Zarahemla. He is the son of the King Mosiah described by Amaleki, the last writer whom we met at the conclusion of Story One. Mormon records Benjamin's valedictory sermon at the end of his life and the changes in Nephite society as a result of it. Then he spends a great deal of time, through several flashbacks, on the historical background of a prophet named Alma, who grew up away from Zarahemla, outside the mainstream of Nephite society.

Alma knows nothing about King Benjamin. He is converted by another prophet, named Abinadi. After significant travels and turmoil, he does end up in Zarahemla, where he is made the head of the church by the son of Benjamin, a new king named Mosiah after his grandfather.

Alma has a son, also named Alma, who rebels against his father, as do four of Mosiah's sons. The younger Alma has his own dramatic conversion experience with an angel while out on the road seeking to destroy the Church. Like Paul, who was converted on the road to Damascus, this second Alma emerges from his conversion with enough zeal to become the most prolific sermonizer in the book. *Brodie says that Joseph Smith simply cribbed the whole thing from the King James Bible.*[1]

CORE SAMPLE ONE

Our first core sample of the History of Story Two is the story of Ammon, one of Mosiah's sons who was with Alma the Younger at the time of the appearance of the angel. Fully converted himself as a result, Ammon went with his brothers to preach among the Lamanites. I choose his story because it demonstrates the sweep of the narrative and also contains details that show how much of a leap of faith is required of those who choose to believe it. This is a story that believers like to tell and critics like to ridicule:

Upon entering Lamanite territory, Ammon is captured, bound, and taken before the Lamanite king, named Lamoni, who has the option of killing, enslaving, or exiling him. Ammon tells Lamoni that he wants to live among the Lamanites for a time and maybe even for the rest of his life. Lamoni is so impressed that he not only sets Ammon free but offers him one of his (Lamoni's) daughters as a wife.

Ammon demurs: "Nay, but I will be thy servant" (Alma 17:25). He is allowed to take a place in the king's household.

Three days later, Ammon is in the fields with other servants, driving the king's flocks to "the place of water" (Alma 17:26). Other Lamanites who are there to water their own flocks scatter the king's flocks, sending the animals in every direction.

The king's servants start to weep for fear of being executed by the king for their failure to protect his flocks from this sort of vandalism. Ammon sees this as an opportunity to show his loyalty to the king. He tells them, "My brethren, be of good cheer and let us go in search of the flocks, and we will gather them together and bring them back unto the place of water; and thus we will preserve the flocks unto the king and he will not slay us" (Alma 17:31).

The king's servants do as Ammon suggests and are

successful. He then goes out to meet those who had scattered them in the first place.

These men have no fear of Ammon as they see him approaching because they are sure that any one of them could kill him without much difficulty. But Ammon starts to pelt them with stones from his sling, killing some. *(Another lift from the Bible, this time the David and Goliath story?)* Enraged, they rush Ammon, wielding clubs.

As they swing their clubs at him, he attacks them with his sword, cutting off "not a few" of their arms. At the end of the fight, after Ammon has killed six with his sling and the leader of the group with his sword, they "flee before him" (Alma 17:38, 37). He returns to his fellow servants, and they return the flocks to the pasture, carrying the arms that have been cut off as proof of what has happened.

The servants tell Lamoni everything. When they finish describing the events of the day, he is "astonished exceedingly" and exclaims, "Surely, this is more than a man. Behold, is not this the Great Spirit who doth send such great punishments upon this people, because of their murders?" (Alma 18:2). The servants say that they don't know if Ammon is the Great Spirit or not; all they know is that he can't be slain by the enemies of the king.

Lamoni asks where Ammon is. He is told he is tending to the king's horses, in preparation for the king's journey to a great feast that is to be given by Lamoni's father. Lamoni is further astonished, saying, "Surely there has not been any servant among all my servants that has been so faithful as this man" (Alma 18:10). He desires to talk with Ammon, but, now convinced that Ammon is the Great Spirit, dares not summon him.

Ammon finishes his work and enters the king's chambers. Realizing that something is different, he turns to leave, but one of the king's other servants hails him as a powerful king and tells him that Lamoni wants him to stay. Ammon does, and he asks the king what he wants. But Lamoni cannot answer (Alma 18:10–15).

Inspired, Ammon knows what to say. He asks Lamoni if the incident with the men who scattered the king's flocks is what has caused his "marvelings." If so, he says, "What is it, that thy marvelings are so great? Behold, I am a man, and am thy servant; therefore, whatsoever thou desirest which is right, that will I do" (Alma 18:16–17).

This impresses Lamoni even more—Ammon can read minds. He asks, "Who art thou? Art thou that Great Spirit, who knows all things?" (Alma 18:18).

Ammon's answer is a simple "I am not" (Alma 18:19). He then begins a dialog in which he teaches both the king and his servants about God. He goes all the way back to Adam, discusses the workings of God with their forebears, including Lehi, and tells them of the Christ that will come. The king believes and is so overcome that he falls to the earth in a stupor. Unable to revive him, his servants put the king on his bed, where he lies as if dead for two days. Preparations are made to bury him (Alma 18:24–43).

The queen sends for Ammon. She says she believes her husband is still alive and asks that Ammon go see him. Ammon is glad, knowing that Lamoni is not dead but under the care of God, in the process of having "the dark veil of unbelief . . . cast away from his mind" (Alma 19:6).

When he and the queen see the king, Ammon tells her, "He

is not dead, but he sleepeth in God, and on the morrow he shall rise again; therefore bury him not" (Alma 19:8). They watch together until the next day, when Lamoni revives, praising God and describing the things he has seen and learned during the time he has lain "as if he were dead" (Alma 18:42).

Lamoni is so overcome with the joy of the moment, as is his wife, that they both "[sink] down, being overpowered by the Spirit." Ammon rejoices, falls to his knees to pray, and he, too, is "overpowered with joy." That makes three of them "sunk to the earth," that is, lying inert as if dead (Alma 19:13–14).

The servants of the king are truly frightened now—as the ones who had told the king that Ammon was a prophet, they feel some responsibility for all this. They begin to pray and are likewise overcome, falling to the earth alongside the other three.

Except for one. A Lamanite woman named Abish, who is a servant to the queen, has been a secret convert to the Lord for years because of a remarkable vision of her father—*no details are provided*. Aware that the power of God is responsible for this situation, she runs from house to house to tell the people what has happened. They assemble themselves in the king's quarters, where they see the king, queen, and their servants all lying as if dead, along with a Nephite in the same condition.

They begin to argue about what has happened. Some say this "great evil" (Alma 19:19) is because the king tolerated the presence of a Nephite in the land. Others say the king has been struck down because he killed so many of his servants over the issue of the scattering of his flocks. Still others, related to the men who did the scattering, focus their anger on Ammon because he killed their kinsmen as he defended the flocks. One of this group draws his sword to strike the recumbent Ammon, to make sure he is dead, but falls dead himself.

"Fear came upon them all" (Alma 19:24). They begin a new debate about what is going on. Some say that Ammon is the Great Spirit, others that he has been sent by the Great Spirit, and others that he is a "monster . . . sent from the Nephites to torment them." The bickering becomes "exceedingly sharp" among them (Alma 19:26, 28).

Abish, the woman who has brought them all together, bursts into tears at this point. Hoping to rouse her queen, Abish takes her by the hand, whereupon the queen stands up and cries out, "O blessed Jesus, who has saved me from an awful hell! O blessed God, have mercy on this people!" (Alma 19:29).

The queen takes the king by the hand, and he arises as well. Seeing the contention among his subjects, he begins to teach them the things Ammon has taught him. Some believe him and become converted; others refuse to listen. Those who do believe are baptized, and a church is set up among them. Mormon comments: "And thus the work of the Lord did commence among the Lamanites; thus the Lord did begin to pour out his Spirit upon them; and we see that his arm is extended to all people who will repent and believe on his name" (Alma 19:36).

Quite a story.

A king offering his daughter to a total stranger from an enemy tribe just because he said he wanted to be the king's servant?

One man alone in a fight with a number of foes armed with clubs, who succeeds by cutting off their arms?

Survivors of the battle gathering up the arms to take back to show others what had happened?

People swooning and appearing to be dead for days and

then rising up and preaching sermons that instantly convert nearly everyone around them?

Sounds like an old Cecil B. DeMille movie. No wonder critics say, "Come on! This is *Arabian Nights* stuff—clearly outside any actual human experience."

Believers say in response, "These things may sound far-fetched, but they are not physically impossible—there are no magic flying carpets or genies. Put this story in the context of the entire book, which is packed full of connecting history and flashback explanations, and it all fits together perfectly. Whoever wrote it was a person with skills far beyond anything either Joseph Smith or Oliver Cowdery ever demonstrated."

Some recent commentaries suggest that in the culture of Mesoamerica, religious swooning was not uncommon. Further, there is evidence that, in some pre-Columbian tribes, arms, not scalps, were taken off the battlefield by victorious warriors as proof of their triumph. Believing scholars who have done the research on these topics say that critics who are looking at the account of Ammon's exploits through the lens of their own society should remember that what is unusual to our time may not have been in previous times.

Maybe, but accepting that reasoning requires quite a leap of faith.

CORE SAMPLE TWO

For our second core sample, I go to a narrative that significantly raises the bar for a forger.

After the death of Alma and his contemporaries, Mormon gives us what I call the war chapters, more than fifty pages of detailed description of decades-long battles between the Nephites and the Lamanites. The primary criticism of the Book of Mormon is that it all came from Joseph Smith's own background, the religious fervor of his time, and the stories he had heard around his home. Mormon's meticulous and often tedious description of battle tactics gives us a chance to test that idea. What follows is a highly abridged, small portion of that narrative:

"In the eleventh month of the nineteenth year, on the tenth day of the month, the armies of the Lamanites were seen approaching towards the land of Ammonihah" (Alma 49:1).

The Lamanite armies choose Ammonihah as their objective because they expect it to be the most vulnerable. In previous fighting, it has been almost completely destroyed. They are surprised to discover that the Nephite commander, named Moroni, has fortified the city extensively with earthworks as well as with troops. *It is this military leader Moroni after whom Mormon names his son.*

"The chief captains of the Lamanites were astonished exceedingly, because of the wisdom of the Nephites in preparing their places of security."

The Nephite fortifications are built "in a manner which never had been known among the children of Lehi" (Alma 49:5, 8)—*Mormon describes the earthworks in some detail*—which leaves the Lamanite leaders at a loss as to what to do.

Mormon says that if Amalickiah—*a Nephite traitor who has, through treachery and murder, supplanted the Lamanite king*—had been at the head of the army, he would have attacked, because he had no regard for casualties. The Lamanite captains on the scene, however, retreat back into the wilderness. They head to the land of Noah, thinking it the next most vulnerable spot. On the way, they swear an oath that this time they will destroy the city. But Moroni has anticipated this move also, knowing that the city of Noah had previously "been the weakest part of the land" (Alma 49:15). It is now just as well prepared as Ammonihah is.

Nonetheless, because they have sworn an oath to attack, the Lamanites bring up their armies and concentrate all their force on the entrance, because the earthworks around the rest of the city give the Nephites high ground from which to repel attempts from anyplace else. The Nephites drive them back, "insomuch that they were slain with an immense slaughter" (Alma 49:21).

The Lamanites try a new tack. They start to "dig down their banks of earth that they might obtain a pass to their armies, that they might have an equal chance to fight" (Alma 49:22). The Nephites, from the top of their barricades, stop this effort as well. All the Lamanite captains are killed in the process. Leaderless, the Lamanite troops flee into the wilderness and make their way back to inform Amalickiah what has happened. Amalickiah, furious, curses God and swears an oath that he will drink Moroni's blood (Alma 49:27).

Moroni does not relax his preparations. He has earthworks built around all the Nephite cities and adds timber frames on top of the earthen ridges, "strong and high," providing a place from which Nephites "could cast stones from the top thereof, according to their pleasure and strength" (Alma 50:3, 5).

The description of cities built of earth and wood is noteworthy. If true, that would make it difficult for modern archaeologists to find any traces of them, as wood and earthen buildings disappear quickly over the centuries. Elsewhere in the Book of Mormon we find references to cement buildings, but the stated reason for building them is that there was not enough timber available where they were built. The book is clear that wood was the preferred Nephite building material.

With the cities properly fortified, Moroni leads his armies against Lamanites that are camped in the wilderness, driving them back to their own lands. Then he has some of the inhabitants of Zarahemla occupy the places from which the Lamanites have been cleared, and he erects fortifications to protect them. Additional cities are built, and the Lamanites are bottled up in their own territory.

The account goes on in this same vein for many pages, with full detail of the feints, stratagems, and forced marches that are employed by both sides. Then, with the momentum of the war seesawing back and forth, there is trouble on the home front.

Certain elements of Nephite society rebel against Pahoran, the chief judge. That gets sorted out by means of an election, but the losers don't abide by the decision. They continue to undermine the legal authority. Faced with an attack from without and dissension from within, Moroni is "exceedingly wroth because of the stubbornness of those people whom he had labored with so much diligence to preserve" (Alma 51:14). He seeks authority from Pahoran to force dissenters to defend the country on penalty of death. This authority is granted, and he leads his army against them. Some four thousand are killed, with others imprisoned; the balance—*Mormon doesn't give us a number*—sign up to help defend the cities.

As a result of Moroni's preoccupation with these internal challenges, the Lamanites move through Nephite territory more easily, taking city after city. They are finally stopped by an army headed by Teancum, who checks the Lamanite advance and then harasses Amalickiah's army until nightfall. Both armies pitch their tents and the Lamanites fall asleep, "overpowered . . . because of their much fatigue, which was caused by the labors and heat of the day" (Alma 51:33).

With a servant, Teancum slips into the Lamanite camp, finds Amalickiah's tent, and puts a javelin through his heart, killing him so quietly that none of his guards is aroused. Teancum then returns to his own camp and tells his men what he has done.

The Lamanites awake to find their leader dead, and they select Ammoron, Amalickiah's brother, as their new leader. He orders the Lamanites to maintain the cities they have taken. He also instructs his commanders in the captured cities to venture out and harass the Nephites to the degree that they can.

"And thus were the Nephites in . . . dangerous circumstances in the ending of the twenty and sixth year of the reign of the judges over the people of Nephi" (Alma 52:14).

There are more than fifty pages of this sort of thing, covering decades of battles and intrigue, with full details of the attacks on the various cities—the forced marches through difficult terrain, the strategic maneuvers, point and counterpoint, etc. While it can be extremely difficult for the first-time reader to follow, it all fits together carefully, in timing, battleground position, and overall location. Tedious or not, whoever wrote it took great care to get it right.

Nothing in Joseph Smith's background would have equipped him to write such a detailed and lengthy description of warfare and internal political bickering. The tactics used in the war chapters bear no resemblance to either the American Revolutionary War or the War of 1812, the two conflicts that would have produced veterans with whom Joseph might have been acquainted. Nor do they resemble the descriptions of war he might have read about in the military histories of his time, if, indeed, he ever spent time with such books. There is no evidence that he did.

This section of the Book of Mormon was jarring for me, when I first read it as a young man, for that very reason; it did not conform to *my* ideas of what war and politics were all about. I was born between World Wars I and II. While I knew that the Lamanite wars would not have been waged like those wars, I couldn't quite swallow the series of shifting alliances and rapid transitions from peace to fighting and back again, the occupation, liberation, and reoccupation of cites in a relatively short time. This portion of the book seemed open to the charge of being the result of a wild imagination, no matter how well it was done.

Also, for me, the wars between the Nephites and Lamanites went on much too long. In my mind, wars were over in about a half dozen years. That was the case with the American Revolutionary War, the Civil War, the two World Wars, and, later on, Korea. I could not envision such continual fighting, regrouping, slaughter, and internal dissension going on for decades, and then, after a brief peace, breaking out yet again.

So, if this lengthy and detailed description of war strikes such a discordant note to a modern reader, why would the author, be he Mormon or forger, have put it in?

If the book is genuine, there are several possibilities.

Mormon's source for much of the war account was the

writing of Alma's son Helaman, who played a significant part in the fighting. Perhaps Helaman was so preoccupied with these battles that he didn't write about anything else, giving Mormon little with which to work outside the battle story.

Or perhaps Mormon chose to go into such detail about war because he believed that a full understanding of its destructive force in Nephite society was necessary for the reader to understand the depths to which the Nephites had sunk before the coming of Jesus.

Or—my own favorite theory—perhaps Mormon's own military background made him so much at home when he found himself reading Helaman's military history that he couldn't resist dwelling on it, lingering over details that were interesting to him on the assumption that they would be equally as interesting to everybody else.

Or perhaps a bit of all three. If the book is genuine, there are plenty of reasons why these chapters are in it.

If the book is a forgery, however, the question of why this section is in it is harder to answer.

It is not clear how its detailed description of continuing war would serve a forger's purpose, and producing it would require a significant military and historical background with respect to how wars were fought in ancient times. It also creates a great deal of exposure, which most forgers would want to minimize.

It handles that exposure rather well; the picture it paints is much more authentic than it appears at first glance. I refer readers to a book called *The Crusades through Arab Eyes,* by Amin Maalouf. As the title indicates, it is a history of the battles that took place in the Middle East at the time the European Crusaders, primarily Frenchmen, invaded the Holy Land.

What I had not understood before reading this book was that Arab resistance to the Crusaders was neither universal nor constant among the Arab leaders at the time. Rather, there was a series of shifting alliances. As one Arab prince would decide to stop fighting the Crusaders in order to get their help in unseating his cousin (or half-brother, or brother-in-law, or whomever), another Arab prince who had been the Crusaders' ally would break with them to try to make some other deal. Double-crossing of relatives, wholesale slaughter of entire populations of besieged towns, almost continuous conflict—that was the pattern, and all the local Arab warlords engaged in it. It went on for decades. It was not until later on that the Arab tribes finally decided to unite and drive the Crusaders out.

As I read Maalouf's book, it struck me as being much like Mormon's description of the wars between the Nephites, Lamanites, and Mulekites, the ancestors of whom came from the same part of the world this book described.

One last comment before moving on. The war chapters highlight what some commentators call the Nephite cycle, a histori-cal pattern that repeats itself again and again throughout Story Two, thus:

When the Nephites are righteous and humble before God, he blesses them. They prosper, temporally as well as spiritually, in fulfillment of Lehi's prophecy about their status in the promised land. As they become wealthy, they become proud. Then they are beset with troubles, usually in the form of a Lamanite invasion. Because of these troubles, they are "brought down" in sorrow. This causes them to repent in humility, and they are delivered from their difficulties. They praise the Lord for such deliverance and return to righteousness and humility. When

God blesses them for their repentance, they return to prosperity, and the cycle starts all over again.

Most of Mormon's side comments during the History of Story Two bemoan the inability of the Nephites to learn from this repeated experience and stay valiant in their righteousness.

CORE SAMPLE THREE

For our third core sample, I focus on a different challenge to Nephite stability—the emergence of internal secret plotters against both the government and the church.

Mormon talks of the rise of a "band of robbers," a covert society headed by a man named Gadianton that employs terrible oaths and "secret combinations" to infiltrate both Nephite and Lamanite society (Helaman 2:10; 3:23). They operate entirely in the dark, employing a system of code words to maintain their anonymity until they succeed in taking over in certain areas, after which they are quite bold in their demands. They are completely corrupt; their only pursuit is for money and power. Their activities dominate a good part of the second half of Story Two. Their inclusion in the book has given rise to much comment by skeptics, including Fawn Brodie, who is perhaps the primary critic on this point.

She insists that the Gadianton robbers were not an ancient conspiracy at all but an obvious and contemporary nineteenth-century one. She says they were Joseph Smith's version of Freemasons, disguised by a funny name. Her discussion on the subject:

The country [the United States] was seized by a swiftly spreading fear that the Republic was in danger. The terror

began in western New York in September 1826, when the
Book of Mormon had barely been conceived, and it
swelled to cover eight states before the book reached the
press late in 1829.

In Batavia, on the road to Buffalo, a printing press was
burned and its owner beaten by a group of masked men.
In the press office were fresh proofs of a new book, an ex-
posé of the secret rites and oaths of Freemasonry. The author, William Morgan, was abducted some days later and
carried to Canandaigua, nine miles from Joseph Smith's
home, for a mock trial. He was then taken secretly to Fort
Niagara on the Canadian border, where he disappeared.

Five prominent Masons in Canandaigua were tried
for his murder in January 1827. The whole countryside
moved in to hear the proceedings. When three were ac-
quitted and the other two received sentences of less than a
year, the public felt cheated. Further trials were held in
February, and anti-Masonry spread with each acquittal.
Morgan and the Masons became the standing theme of
conversation in field and tavern. Ancient suicides, long
buried and forgotten by everyone save the coroners who
had sat upon them, were raked up in all their lurid details
and the Masons were found to have murdered them all.
The skulls, it was said, served as tankards in the lodges.

Churches dismissed pastors who would not renounce
Masonry, and deacons who would not resign their mem-
bership were forbidden the sacrament.[2]

Brodie reports widespread interest in the subject, political
as well as religious, and then says: "So it happened that Joseph
Smith was writing the Book of Mormon in the thick of a
political crusade that gave backwoods New York, hitherto

politically stagnant and socially déclassé, a certain prestige and glory. And he quickly introduced into the book the theme of the Gadianton band, a secret society whose oaths for fraternal protection were bald parallels of the Masonic oaths, and whose avowed aim was the overthrow of the democratic Nephite government."[3]

In a footnote in her book, Brodie refers to an unpublished manuscript by a Professor J. H. Adamson of the University of Utah. "There is good evidence that Joseph Smith was familiar with Masonic literature even before the murder of William Morgan." She says that Adamson "analyzed in detail Smith's use of the Masonic legends of Enoch and Hiram Abiff," which include stories of an engraved golden plate, a brass pillar holding a metal ball with magical qualities, and treasure found while excavating the foundation for Solomon's Temple.[4]

Hiram Abiff, "'the widow's son,'" is an important Masonic figure who dies rather than reveal the secret to evil men, and his followers kill one of his murderers in his sleep.[5] *(Is this where Joseph Smith got the idea for the exploits of Teancum?)* King Solomon rewards them by putting all of the treasures, along with the Urim and Thummim, in the temple.

Brodie concludes: "Joseph Smith's adaptation of these myths will be obvious to any student of the *Book of Mormon* and the history of its writing. Engraved golden plates, brass plates, a magical ball called the 'Liahona,' the Urim and Thummim, and the treasure cave in the hill, were all incorporated into his story and into his book."[6]

For those looking for indications of forgery, these are classic examples.

The timing is right—people in the 1820s were interested in the subject of secret societies.

The location is right—the murder of William Morgan happened less than ten miles from Joseph's home, as did the subsequent trials, so Joseph undoubtedly knew about the fear of secret societies they created.

The details are right—Masonic myths discussed plates, magical balls, and the Urim and Thummim, all of which are mentioned in the Book of Mormon.

This is as good as it gets in tying material in the book to Joseph's own background. Score a big one for the critics.

Believers do have a few defenses. We now know that the Hebrew word meaning "robber" denotes more than just a thief; a "robber" in ancient Hebrew is a terrorist, or gangster, seeking power, which is a perfect description of the Gadianton band. Thus, the term is correctly used here, even if it seems odd at first to American readers. The book at least got that one right.

Next, believers say that the real question should not be, "Were discussions of these things *present* in Joseph's time?" but, rather, "Were discussions of these things *exclusive* to Joseph's time?" And the answer to that is no.

If the Book of Mormon had come from Europe, this part of it could be said to have been inspired by the anti-Semitic descriptions of a Jewish conspiracy to take over the world, outlined in the fraudulent *Protocols of the Elders of Zion*. If it had appeared in San Francisco during the late 1800s, when tong wars were going on among Chinese immigrants there, one might say that the Gadianton robbers were based on journalistic reports of the activities of Chinese gangs. If it had appeared in the 1970s, one might say that this part of the book was a thinly veiled version of the *Godfather* books and movies. Secret societies and the fear of them have been with humans for a long time, in many cultures.

There is no reason why the Nephites should have been any different.

And, as Brodie should have known, the mention of brass and gold plates in the Masonic myths is, in fact, not an indication of forgery. We saw in Chapter 3 that the ancients actually used both metals in the making of plates that were reserved for sacred writings. Joseph's statement about them is completely consistent with the facts.

So, did Joseph get the idea of plates from the myths and just get lucky? Did the mythmaker make it up and get lucky? Are the myths and Joseph's story completely independent of each other and any similarity just coincidence, or are they somehow based on some unknown ancient reality?

No way to know.

The uncertainty arising from these questions does not mean that the Gadianton robbers were *not* patterned after Freemasonry and that believers can simply dismiss the notion out of hand, but it does mean that we can't be quite as sure about it as Fawn Brodie was. Also, their inclusion in the book shows that, if they were invented, the forger had both a fertile mind and a firm confidence in his own capacity to weave their story into the larger narrative. That is not an accurate description of Joseph Smith in 1829.

8

COMMENTARY ON THE HISTORY OF STORY TWO

THE HISTORY OF STORY TWO describes a large battleground on which believers and critics joust. I have placed the opposing points of view on two lists, one labeled Proofs and the other, Problems. Some of what we will cover will be from the core samples we have examined, but most of it will be new ground, taken from parts of the history that we have skipped.

PROOFS

NAMES

We have seen a few strange names in our samples, and the Book of Mormon as a whole is full of them, which is a good thing for analysis.

Names are a reliable source of information about a person's roots. We know that McGregor is Scottish, and O'Reilly is Irish; Kohl is German, and Gonzales is Spanish. All Italian names end in vowels; Japanese names do too, with two exceptions—*h* and *n*. Russian names end in *sky* while Polish ones are spelled *ski*. Names are the first indication of tribal affiliation.

Oliver Cowdery said that the names were the only words of the book that Joseph did not speak in English. When he came to a name neither he nor Oliver recognized, he simply dictated the spelling. That means the names are claimed to be in their original language, which provides a significant test for forgery. To be genuine, all of the names in Story Two must be consistent with the claim that their owners descended from people who were led to the New World from the Old by either Lehi or Mulek. Because both of those families had their roots in Jerusalem, one might expect their descendants to have Hebrew names, and a lot of them do.

But many of the names in the book are obviously not Hebrew. More than 150 of them have spellings so strange that critics say that they are gibberish, that the forger simply created a bunch of nonsense words to use as names.

We now know that such critics are wrong. Most of the strange non-Hebrew names have been determined to be Egyptian, and those which are not are tied to the society we will meet in Story Three.

In Story One, I mentioned the possibility that Lehi had dealings with the Egyptians. Mormon says that the language used to write the plates was "reformed"—that is, altered—Egyptian, because writing in Hebrew would take up too much space. Therefore, under the heading of internal tests, it would be a mark against the book if there were *not* Egyptian names in it.

Let's start our test with the question of frequency. That is logical because in every society some names appear more often than others. For example, in 1830, the most common surname in England was Smith, and in Wales, Jones. So, what is the most common name in the Book of Mormon? Ammon. And what was the most common name in Egypt, in 600 B.C.E.? Ammon.

That information also comes from Dr. Hugh Nibley, the only authority who has written on the subject. He fills four pages of his book with comparisons of Book of Mormon (BM) names with Old World (OW) ones.[1] Here are just a few:

Aha (BM), son of the Nephite commander in chief.

Aha (OW), a name of the first Pharaoh; it means "warrior" and is a common word.

Cezoram (BM), Nephite chief judge.

Chiziri (OW), Egyptian governor of a Syrian city.

Hem (BM), brother of the earlier Ammon.

Hem (OW), means "servant," specifically of Ammon.

Himni (BM), a son of King Mosiah.

Hmn (OW), a name of the Egyptian hawk-god.

Korihor (BM), a political agitator who was seized by the people of Ammon.

Kherihor (also written Khurhor, etc.) (OW), great high priest of Ammon who seized the throne of Egypt at Thebes, cir. 1085 B.C.

Manti (BM), the name of a Nephite soldier, a land, a city, and a hill.

Manti (OW), Semitic form of an Egyptian proper name.

Nephi (BM), founder of the Nephite nation.

Nehi, Nehri (OW), the name of famous Egyptian noblemen.

Paanchi (BM), son of Pahoran, Sr., and pretender to the chief-judgeship.

Paanchi (OW), son of Kherihor, a) chief high priest of Amon, b) ruler of the south who conquered all of Egypt and was high priest of Amon at Thebes.

Pahoran (BM), a) great chief judge, and b) son of the same.

Pa-her-an (OW), ambassador of Egypt in Palestine.

Pacumeni (BM), son of Pahoran.

Pakamen (OW), Egyptian proper name meaning "blind man."

Sam (BM), brother of Nephi.

Sam Tawi (OW), Egyptian "uniter of the lands," title taken by the brother of Nehri upon mounting the throne.

The last two are favorites of mine. Who in 1800s America knew that "Sam" was an authentic Egyptian name rather than just a New England shortening of the Hebrew "Samuel"?

Nibley comments: "It will be noted that the names compared are rarely *exactly* alike, except in the case of the monosyllables *Sam* and *Hem*. This, strangely enough, is strong confirmation of their common origin, since names are bound to undergo some change with time and distance, whereas if the resemblance were perfect, we should be forced to attribute it, however fantastic it might seem, to mere coincidence. There *must* be differences; and what is more, those differences should not be haphazard but display definite tendencies."[2]

He shows how the book fulfills all the requirements of the "definite tendencies" he describes. I have looked for commentary on this subject from someone other than Dr. Nibley, for some expert who will challenge his conclusions, and, as I have said, I cannot find any.

So, throughout several hundred pages of rich and highly specific history, including accurate detail about ancient methods of war-making, the author of Story Two uses more than 200 names (at least 150 of which are strange to us) that all have either Hebrew or Egyptian roots.

Poetry

We saw in Story One that Lehi was a master of the poetry of the desert. In the multitude of sermons offered in Story Two, is there a similar example?

Yes. Mormon records the use of the highly religious, almost sacred, Hebrew poetic form known as chiasmus.

Chiasmus gets its name from the Greek letter chi, which is a cross—X—symbolizing a top-to-bottom mirror image. It involves the repetition of a pattern of words, arranged so that the words "go in" to the central phrase in one order and then "come out" in reverse order. For example, the phrase "Truth is beauty, and beauty, truth" is a simple chiasmus, involving only two words; however, the repetition and the placement of the words make the point more powerfully than would otherwise be the case.

The Old Testament contains a lot of chiasmus, although not every prophetic writer uses it. However, Isaiah, the Old Testament writer most quoted in the Book of Mormon, is one that uses it a great deal. The following is from Isaiah 6:10, with the repeated words in bold:

(a) Make the **heart** of this people fat,

   (b) and make their **ears** heavy,

      (c) and shut their **eyes;**

      (c') lest they see with their **eyes,**

   (b') and hear with their **ears,**

(a') and understand with their **heart,**

      and convert [return], and be healed.

There is no doubt that chiasmus is used in the Book of Mormon. The following chiasmus is taken from King Benjamin's speech, which was written down and circulated rather than given extemporaneously:

(a) Whosoever shall not take upon him the **name** of Christ

  (b) must be **called** by some other name;

    (c) therefore, he findeth himself on the **left hand** of God.

      (d) And I would that ye should **remember** also, that this is the **name**

        (e) that I said I should give unto you that never should be **blotted out,**

          (f) except it be through **transgression**;

          (f') therefore, take heed that ye do not **transgress**,

        (e') that the name be not **blotted out** of your hearts.

      (d') I say unto you, I would that ye should **remember** to retain the **name**

    (c') written always in your hearts, that ye are not found on the **left hand** of God,

  (b') but that ye hear and know the voice by which ye shall be **called**,

(a') and also, the **name** by which he shall call you. (Mosiah 5:10–12)

There are more, but that is enough to demonstrate the form. The most significant example of chiasmus in the book comes from the blessings that Alma, like Lehi just before his death, gave to his sons. The giving of such sacred instructions by a father to a son was an occasion important enough not to be handled extemporaneously, so it is logical that Alma not only constructed his statements carefully but put them in writing so that the sons would have a permanent record. It is a logical place for us to find chiasmus, if the book is genuine, and we do.

The following is taken from chapter 36 of the book of Alma, from Alma's statement to his son Helaman. It is offered here in summary form, with the verses in which each element appears shown in parentheses at the end of each line:

(a) My son, give ear to my **words** (1)

  (b) as ye shall **keep the commandments** of God ye shall **prosper in the land** (1)

   (c) **do as I have done** (2)

    (d) in **remembering the captivity** of our fathers (2);

     (e) for they were in **bondage** (2)

      (f) he surely did **deliver** them (2)

       (g) **trust** in God (3)

        (h) supported in their **trials, troubles,** and **afflictions** (3)

       (i) shall be lifted up at the **last day** (3)

        (j) I **know** this not of myself but of **God** (4)

        (k) **born of God** (5)

         (1) I sought to destroy the church of God [action] (6–9)

         (m) **my limbs** were paralyzed (10)

         (n) fear of being in the **presence of God** (14–15)

         (o) **pains** of a damned soul (16)

          (p) **harrowed up by the memory of my sins** (17)

          (q) I remembered **Jesus Christ,** a **Son of God** (17)

          (q') I cried, O **Jesus,** thou **Son of God** (18)

          (p') **harrowed up by the memory of my sins** no more (19)

         (o') joy as exceeding as was my **pain** (20)

         (n') long to be in the **presence of God** (22)

         (m') my **limbs** received their strength again (23)

         (l') I labored to bring souls to repentance [action] (24)

        (k') **born of God** (26)

        (j') therefore my **knowledge** is of **God** (26)

        (h') supported under **trials, troubles,** and **afflictions** (27)

       (g') **trust** in him (27)

      (f') he will **deliver** me (27)

       (i') and raise me up at **the last day** (28)

     (e') as God brought our fathers out of **bondage** (28–29)

    (d') retain in **remembrance their captivity** (28–29)

   (c') **know as I do know** (30)

  (b') **keep the commandments** and ye shall **prosper in the land** (30)

(a') this is according to his **word** (30).

The (i') element is out of place, but believing scholars have explanations for that. Even with that defect, this appears to be a remarkable example of a carefully constructed poetic form.

Nonbelievers, however, say that this is not a chiasmus at all. They claim that the words and phrases are in order by coincidence, not planning.

To prove the point, an anonymous critic on the Internet has taken a modern computer manual—a work that uses certain words in a repetitive manner—and highlighted those words in a way that "demonstrates" chiasmus in a situation where it was obviously not intended. He says the chiasmus pattern described above is just as contrived and is nothing more than "Jack Welch's wishful thinking." Jack Welch is the Mormon scholar who first discovered chiasmus in the book in 1969, four decades after B. H. Roberts was looking for external evidence and couldn't find any.

Once again, we turn to the computer. Boyd Edwards and Farrell Edwards set up a computer model as a test to determine the odds that a particular chiasmus structure came by accident or design. They tested Leviticus (as a control), Alma, some other writings of Joseph Smith's, and the proffered computer manual. Their work is cited in the Notes to this book for those who want to check out their methodology, but it is their conclusion that there is a high likelihood that chiasmus in both Leviticus 24:13–23 and Alma 36 appears by design. Their scores are virtually identical.

They say: "These results rule out, with 99.98 percent certainty, the claim that Alma 36:1–30 is simply an arrangement of words that happen to fall into chiastic order by chance. . . . Our results do not prove that the Book of Mormon is a translation of an ancient document, but they do establish that chiastic passages in the Book of Mormon likely appeared . . . by the deliberate application of the chiastic form by the author(s) of these passages."[3]

With respect to the chiastic form taken from the computer manual, as well as claims that chiasmus appears in Joseph Smith's other writings, they say that the form "could easily have emerged from random rearrangements of their literary elements." They conclude: "Our results do not rule out the possibility that Joseph Smith knew about the chiastic style . . . but do rule out the use of chiasms in [Joseph's other writings] as possible evidence of that knowledge."[4]

So, computer tests say that chiasmus is in the Book of Mormon by design, not coincidence, and that it is not in Joseph Smith's other writings.

Could a forger in America in 1829 have known about chiasmus? Possibly, because the form is ancient—as demonstrated by the passages in Isaiah and Leviticus—but very unlikely. Only a few examples of it turned up in American literature before 1830.

Remember, from our discussion in Chapter 2, that the first tool of a forger is to salt his work with things that will be familiar to his audience, things they either would expect or even hope to find there. If Joseph Smith put chiasmus in the Book of Mormon for this purpose, he would have pointed out its presence to his critics when they attacked his work in 1830. If B. H. Roberts had known about it, he would have mentioned it a century later. As we have noted, no believer knew about it until Jack Welch came across it in 1969.

MORE "DIFFERENT VOICES"

In Story One, we saw four first-person speakers: Nephi, Lehi, Jacob, and Zenos. In Story Two, there are seven more plus Jesus. Here they are, by length:

- Benjamin—1 sermon, covering 12 pages
- Abinadi (the prophet who converted Alma)—1 sermon, covering 7 pages
- Alma the Younger—8 sermons, covering 22 pages; 3 detailed blessings, 1 per son, filling 16 more pages
- Amulek (missionary companion of Alma the Younger)—2 sermons, covering 6 pages
- Samuel the Lamanite (about whom we will hear in Chapter 9)—1 sermon, covering 7 pages
- Jesus—description of his appearance, including his sermons, covering 36 pages
- Zeniff and Helaman—historical rather than religious writings, covering another 13 pages

Thus, roughly a third of Story Two—more than 100 pages—consists of words attributed to men other than Mormon. (There are still more "different voices" to come in Story Three.)

As noted in Story One, computer analysis has been used to determine whether these insertions were, in fact, written by different persons. The computer tests says that they were, indeed—and that Joseph Smith was not one of them.[5]

GOVERNMENT

In the beginning of Story Two, the Nephite system of government is a hereditary monarchy, with Benjamin on the throne. However, when his grandsons all refuse to take the throne at the impending death of their father, Mosiah, Mosiah delivers a lecture on the evils of monarchy and urges the Nephites to adopt a system of judges instead. They do, electing the first judges by popular vote. Some critics have identified this as sign of forgery, an effort by Joseph Smith to make the work attractive to nineteenth-century Americans who remembered the Revolutionary War.

But the system the Nephites embrace is not a reflection of American democracy in any way. Ascension to the chief judgeship is often hereditary, with the voters playing only a ratifying role—there are few examples of actual elections where there are competing candidates. It is a unique system, described in meticulous detail. In the next chapter, we will see other governmental changes, ones that are consistent with political history in other societies.

If all of this is forged, it was done with significant creativity.

MONEY

At one point, Mormon describes the Nephite system of coins in complete detail. It appears quite strange to us because it is not on the decimal system we're familiar with, but "it has been shown by mathematicians to be the most efficient system possible; . . . it requires fewer 'coins' . . . than any other system devisable, including our own."[6] What nineteenth-century farm boy could have invented such a system?

PROBLEMS

Now it is time to hear from the critics.

INCONSISTENCIES IN THE NARRATIVE

There are differences between the Nephite society described

in Story Two and the one whose founding was outlined in Story One. For example, in Story One, Jacob says that the leaders after Nephi used his name as their official title and ruled as Nephi II, Nephi III, etc. By 130 B.C.E., however, the kings are named, instead, Mosiah, Benjamin, and Mosiah again.

There is no explanation as to why the earlier practice was abandoned. Isn't this a structural blunder?

The Lamanites compose the majority of Lehi's descendants, but there is no description of their society, government, religion, or leaders, except when they intrude upon the Nephites.

This is supposed to be a record of all of Lehi's descendants. Isn't that a bit odd?

While Story One told us that the Lamanites were given dark skins to keep the Nephites from associating with them, Story Two describes frequent contact between the two nations, including years when there is free travel and regular trade between them. For instance, there is a time when "Nephites did go into whatsoever part of the land they would, whether among the Nephites or the Lamanites. And . . . the Lamanites did also go whithersoever they would, whether it were among the Lamanites or among the Nephites; and thus they did have free intercourse one with another, to buy and to sell, and to get gain, according to their desire. . . . They became exceedingly rich, both the Lamanites and the Nephites; and they did have an exceeding plenty of gold," crops, and other goods (Helaman 6:7–9).

When and why did the Nephite leaders decide to stop shunning the Lamanites on the basis of skin color and begin trading with them? Isn't this a significant internal mistake?

CREDIBILITY OF EVENTS

I've already commented on the fantastic nature of some of the internal stories—the exploits of Ammon, the swooning and recovery of the Lamanite king, the similarity between the Gadiantons and the Freemasons, etc.—so I will not repeat them here. Taken together, however, they are an important argument for critics of Story Two: its specifics are simply too improbable to be credible.

LANGUAGE DIFFICULTIES

There is no linguistic connection between the languages and dialects of American aboriginals and either Hebrew or Egyptian. B. H. Roberts found this particularly troubling. If the pre-Columbian Americans were in fact the descendants of the Lamanite survivors of the final wars, as Joseph Smith claimed they were, there should be at least some hint of a connection that could pass muster with nonbelieving scholars.

Now the big one, on which the critics rely most heavily:

PRE-COLUMBIAN ARCHAEOLOGY

The Nephites are constantly building, modifying, and moving in and out of cities, with Zarahemla being the one constant. No archaeologist who is not a believer has ever looked at a pre-Columbian ruin in Central or South America and said, "This is a Nephite city." On the contrary, such specialists have been quite explicit in saying there are no ruins that could conceivably be such a city.

There are also no connections the critics can accept between pre-Columbian religious practices and either Hebraic or

Christian traditions. The pre-Columbians practiced human sac-rifice and had other traditions that are anathema to both Christians and Jews. If the Nephites existed, they left no trace of their religion behind.

REBUTTAL DIALOG

Believers first, with the critics' responses following.

The information regarding shifts in Nephite governmental practices and contacts with the Lamanites was lost with the missing 116 pages. Regarding the paucity of Lamanite infor-mation, Mormon had only Nephite records available to him; he failed to quote from Lamanite records simply because there were none.

Maybe, but that is also very convenient as a way for the forger to save himself some work—instead of fixing the record, create a big gap in it to explain things away.

On the fantastic nature of the specifics, they are not as fan-tastic as some of the stories in the Bible.

True, but for those who find the Bible stories themselves hard to swallow—the Flood, perhaps, or Jonah and the fish—not persua-sive.

With respect to the ruins (or lack thereof), remember what was noted during the extended description of war, in which Mormon describes in some detail how the cities are fortified for battle with earthworks and wooden barriers. Because wooden walls disappear rather quickly, that is one reason why there are not many cities for the archaeologists to uncover.

But the book's description of Zarahemla makes it clear that it was a city obviously big enough to have been built with more than just wood, and it is not the only one. You are trying to have it both ways—you use the "wood and earth" explanation as a reason why there are few ruins and then embrace the claims of your own archaeologists when they insist that they have found some.

Until an undisputably Book of Mormon site is discovered in the New World, as solid in its credentials as the discovery of NHM/Nahom is in the Old, pre-Columbian archaeology will remain one of the strongest sources of objection to Story Two.

SUMMARY

Old World names, Hebrew poetry, multiple different voices, meticulous details—there are many things in the record that say that Story Two is genuine history.

Gaps in the history, convenient excuses about why things are not there, lack of archaeological evidence, fantastic stories—there are many things in the record that say that it is not.

The case for authenticity in Story Two is strong but not as strong as the case for Story One. An honest observer can still have reasonable doubts.

9

THE CLIMAX OF STORY TWO

THE BOOK OF MORMON HAS both a theme and a climax. The theme is the divinity and mission of Jesus Christ as the Hebrew Messiah. The climax is Christ's appearance on the Western Hemisphere after his crucifixion and resurrection. The key event heralding that climax is the appearance of a prophet named Samuel the Lamanite, so we start this second portion of Story Two with him.

First, however, another style note.

After Mosiah, the Nephites abandoned the monarchy and started to be governed by a system of judges. As they did so, they changed their calendars. Instead of reckoning time by the number of years passed since Lehi left Jerusalem, they started doing it by using the number of years passed since the governmental change. Mormon carefully noted every single year, by number, after that time. For example, he tells us that Samuel the Lamanite came in the eighty-sixth year of the judges, which corresponds to our 6 B.C.E.

In this chapter, I shall follow Mormon's practice of recording each year as it passes, to give a sense of the chronology and context for the events described, but I will use our calendar numbers instead of his.

6 B.C.E. While "the Nephites did still remain in wickedness . . . the Lamanites did observe strictly to keep the commandments of God" (Helaman 13:1). A new prophet appears, named Samuel, who is a Lamanite, *which is appropriate, because at that time the Lamanites are the more righteous group.*

Samuel preaches in Zarahemla, where his message is rejected by the Nephites. As he prepares to "return to his own land," the voice of the Lord comes to him and instructs him to go back and "prophesy unto the people whatsoever things should come into his heart" (Helaman 13:2–3). Denied access to the city itself, he mounts the wall that surrounds it and gives his sermon.

He warns that "heavy destruction awaiteth this people." Nothing can save them except "repentance and faith on the Lord Jesus Christ, who surely shall come into the world, and shall suffer many things and shall be slain for his people" (Helaman 13:6).

Samuel prophesies the final destruction of the Nephites in four hundred years if they do not repent. He preaches to them about their sins and what will happen in the future and then makes specific prophecies about the life of Jesus Christ, whose birth, Samuel says, is five years away (Helaman 14:2).

The birth of Jesus Christ will be marked by a remarkable display of light in the heavens. There will be a day and a night and a day, in sequence, in which there is no darkness. The sun will go down, but the heavenly display will keep it light until the sun rises the next morning. This time of light will be the sign of the birth of Christ.

Samuel then gives them the sign of Christ's death: "Behold, in that day that he shall suffer death the sun shall be darkened and refuse to give his light unto you; and also the moon and the stars; and there shall be no light upon the face of this land, even from the time that he shall suffer death . . . to the time that he shall rise again from the dead" (Helaman 14:20).

Samuel describes the "thunderings and lightnings" and earthquakes that will accompany and presumably produce this period of darkness. He concludes with more words of exhortation to righteousness and a prophecy that the Lamanites will be preserved in the long term.

Those who believe Samuel seek out the head of the Nephite church, who is named Nephi, confessing their sins and asking for baptism. Those who do not believe attempt to kill Samuel, shooting arrows and throwing rocks at him as he stands on the wall. When they realize that they are unable to hit him, a few conclude that his protection has come from God, and they seek out Nephi as well. Most of the people do not believe Samuel, however, and demand that the guards seize him. Samuel jumps down from the wall and goes back to his own country.

He is not heard from among the Nephites again.

5 to 3 B.C.E. Samuel's sermon has little effect. There are no significant changes in behavior among the Nephites.

2 B.C.E. Signs and wonders begin to appear in the heavens. Angels are seen by some. A core of believers sees these things as the beginning of the fulfillment of Samuel's prophecies, but most of the Nephites remain skeptical. Calling the expectation of Christ a "wicked tradition" and the place of his birth "a land

151

which is far distant, a land which we know not," they reject Samuel's message. "Satan did get great hold upon the hearts of the people upon all the face of the land" (Helaman 16:20, 23).

1 B.C.E. The prophet named Nephi, who has been holding the church together, turns all the records over to his eldest son, also named Nephi, after which "he departed out of the land, and whither he went, no man knoweth" (3 Nephi 1:3). *From here on, all references to Nephi are to this son. We are at the eve of the birth of Jesus Christ.*

1 C.E. Although "there began to be greater signs and greater miracles wrought among the people," there are some who "say that the time was past" for the prophecies of Samuel the Lamanite to be fulfilled. Those who believe are "very sorrowful" because the skeptics are now sure that nothing is going to happen as predicted. They set a deadline and say that "all those who believed in those traditions should be put to death except the sign should come to pass, which had been given by Samuel the prophet" (3 Nephi 1:4–5, 7, 9).

Nephi *(son of the Nephi who departed from the land of Zarahemla)* goes out to pray. He "bowed himself down upon the earth and cried mightily to his God in behalf of his people, . . . who were about to be destroyed because of their faith. . . . The voice of the Lord came unto him, saying: Lift up your head and be of good cheer; for behold, the time is at hand, and on this night shall the sign be given, and on the morrow come I into the world, to show unto the world that I will fulfill all that which I have caused to be spoken by the mouth of my holy prophets" (3 Nephi 1:11–13).

Accordingly, as the sun goes down, there is no darkness all that night. Many of the people fall down in a swoon, aware of how badly they had sinned in refusing to believe. "A new star did appear, according to the word." While Satan tries to harden the hearts of the people, "the more part of the people did believe" (3 Nephi 1:21–22). Nephi goes among them, preaching and baptizing, and there is peace in the land for a time.

In the following decade, a threat to the peace comes from the Gadianton robbers, living in the mountains, who cannot be destroyed. Old patterns reassert themselves.

"The people began to wax strong in wickedness and abominations; and they did not believe that there should be any more signs or wonders given; and Satan did go about, leading away the hearts of the people" (3 Nephi 2:3).

"The people did still remain in wickedness" (3 Nephi 2:10).

12 and 13 C.E. The Gadianton robbers are so numerous and have killed so many people that both the Nephites and the Lamanites are compelled to go to war with them, with the very survival of the Nephites hanging in the balance. Converted Lamanites unite with the Nephites and are numbered as Nephites. When this happens, "their curse was taken from them, and their skin became white like unto the Nephites; . . . and they were numbered among the Nephites, and were called Nephites" (3 Nephi 2:15–16).

All of the book's sermons make it clear that skin color doesn't matter with God—righteousness is the issue—but this reference suggests that it does, as we saw in Story One. It appears that the book is trying to have things both ways.

Some believers have suggested that the change in skin color mentioned here came from intermarriage between the righteous Lamanites and the Nephites and assign Mormon's description of lighter skin to the resulting children. It seems unlikely, given the tone of the statement in the book, and is more of an excuse than an explanation. This passage is a legitimate forgery issue.

14 through 28 C.E. There are more wars with the robbers, with the tide switching back and forth until the Nephites finally prevail. The Nephites "did forsake all their sins . . . and did serve God with all diligence day and night." As a result, the secret combinations are ended among the Nephites (3 Nephi 5:3, 6). "There [is] great order in the land": Highways are built, old cities are repaired, and new cities are built, as "the people had continual peace" (3 Nephi 6:4, 9).

29 C.E. Once again old habits reemerge. "There began to be some disputings among the people; and some were lifted up unto pride and boastings because of their exceedingly great riches, yea, even unto great persecutions; . . . the people began to be distinguished by ranks, according to their riches and their chances for learning; yea, some were ignorant because of their poverty, and others did receive great learning because of their riches" (3 Nephi 6:10–12).

"And thus Satan did lead away the hearts of the people to do all manner of iniquity; therefore they had enjoyed peace but a few years" (3 Nephi 6:16).

30 C.E. "They were in a state of awful wickedness" (3 Nephi 6:17). Holy prophets are sent among them—*Mormon gives no names or explanation of where they came from*—who testify boldly of the coming of Christ. The prophets are secretly killed by some of the judges, and the conspirators pledge to each other, in secret oaths, to help bring down the existing government and go back to a monarchy. The chief judge is murdered, and this time the judgment seat is not filled; indeed, the whole system of government falls.

"The people were divided one against another; and they did separate one from another into tribes, every man according to his family and his kindred and friends; and thus they did destroy the government of the land" (3 Nephi 7:2).

Thus the century-old system of judges, set up back in King Mosiah's time, is eliminated and replaced by tribal rule. Such a fundamental governmental realignment could not have happened without a great deal of internal decay in the old system, but there has been no warning whatsoever that it was coming. Why not? Did the forger slip up? Or was Mormon preoccupied with other things?

Whatever its cause, I find this a stunning development, because it is remarkably similar to political forces we have seen in our own day in the Balkans, Afghanistan, and the Middle East. When central control broke down in these places and governmental chaos ensued, the result was reversion to ancient tribal allegiances. Whoever wrote a similar outcome into the Book of Mormon had a good understanding of how power shifts take place in the real world of politics—not one of Joseph Smith's obvious strong points.

31 C.E. Although the tribal leaders are not righteous, they enter into agreements with one another that they will not go to war with each other. The peace is thus kept, even though the people are caught up in their wickedness. "Nephi—having been visited by angels and also the voice of the Lord . . . and having had power given unto him that he might know concerning the ministry of Christ . . . went forth among them . . . to testify, boldly, repentance and remission of sins through faith on the Lord Jesus Christ." Mormon says that Nephi "did minister with power and with great authority" (3 Nephi 7:15–17).

32 C.E. Overall, conditions remain the same, but Nephi has some success. "There were many . . . that were baptized unto repentance" (3 Nephi 7:26).

33 C.E. The people remember that Samuel the Lamanite had said "there should be darkness for the space of three days over the face of the land" after thirty-three years. Nothing of the sort happens during this year, and "there began to be great doubtings and disputations among the people" (3 Nephi 8:3–4).

And then it comes. "In the thirty and fourth year, in the first month, on the fourth day of the month, there arose a great storm, such an one as never had been known in all the land. And there was also a great and terrible tempest; and there was terrible thunder, insomuch that it did shake the whole earth as if it was about to divide asunder. And there were exceedingly sharp lightnings, such as never had been known in all the land. And the city of Zarahemla did take fire. And the city of Moroni did sink into the depths of the sea, and the inhabitants thereof were drowned" (3 Nephi 8:5–9).

Mormon goes on, with specific mention of cities and tempests and whirlwinds, for many more paragraphs. When the devastation ceases, after three hours, "behold, there was darkness upon the face of the land" (3 Nephi 8:19). It lasts for three days, during which no light could be seen.

A voice is heard in the darkness, "crying: Wo, wo, wo unto this people; wo unto the inhabitants of the whole earth except they shall repent; for the devil laugheth, and his angels rejoice, because of the slain of the fair sons and daughters of my people; and it is because of their iniquity and abominations that they are fallen!" (3 Nephi 9:1–2). The voice names city after city that has been destroyed and lists the sins that were committed. It tells the survivors, "Behold, I am Jesus Christ the Son of God. I created the heavens and the earth, and all things that in them are. I was with the Father from the beginning. I am in the Father, and the Father in me; and in me hath the Father glorified his name" (3 Nephi 9:15).

He tells them that they are no longer to offer up burnt offerings but to offer a sacrifice of a broken heart and a contrite spirit. "And whoso cometh unto me with a broken heart and a contrite spirit, him will I baptize with fire and with the Holy Ghost, even as the Lamanites, because of their faith in me at the time of their conversion, were baptized with fire and with the Holy Ghost, and they knew it not. Behold, I have come unto the world to bring redemption unto the world, to save the world from sin" (3 Nephi 9:20–21).

The people are so astonished that they stop "howling for the loss of their kindred," and there is silence "for the space of many hours." Then the voice comes again and laments the unfaithfulness of the people who "would not" when they received the call to gather themselves to Christ and thus are now fallen (3 Nephi 10:2, 5).

The darkness clears. The people rejoice at their survival and raise their voices in "praise and thanksgiving unto the Lord Jesus Christ, their Redeemer" (3 Nephi 10:10).

A "great multitude" forms around the temple, in the "land Bountiful" (3 Nephi 11:1). *The book does not give a definite time frame as to how long after the devastation this gathering occurs.* They talk about the tremendous changes that have taken place, as well as discuss Jesus Christ, whose voice they have heard.

As they do this, they again hear a voice and look around to try to find its source. They do not understand what it is saying.

It is "not a harsh voice, neither was it a loud voice; nevertheless . . . it did pierce them that did hear to the center . . . ; yea, it did pierce them to the very soul, and did cause their hearts to burn" (3 Nephi 11:3).

The voice comes again, and they still do not understand. Then, "the third time they did hear the voice," they look toward heaven, from which the voice seems to be coming, and this time they understand (3 Nephi 11:5).

"Behold my Beloved Son," the voice says, "in whom I am well pleased, in whom I have glorified my name—hear ye him" (3 Nephi 11:7). As they look toward heaven, they see a man clothed in a white robe descending towards them. They dare not speak.

Many think the man is an angel, but he says, reaching out his hand, "Behold, I am Jesus Christ, whom the prophets testified shall come into the world. . . . I am the light and the life of the world; and I have drunk out of that bitter cup which the Father hath given me, and have glorified the Father in taking upon me the sins of the world, in the which I have suffered the will of the Father in all things from the beginning" (3 Nephi 11:10–11).

The people fall to the earth, realizing that this is indeed the fulfillment of the prophecies that had been made to them. Jesus says, "Arise and come forth unto me, that ye may thrust your hands into my side, and also that ye may feel the prints of the nails in my hands and in my feet, that ye may know that I am the God of Israel, and the God of the whole earth, and have been slain for the sins of the world" (3 Nephi 11:14).

They do as Jesus directs, "going forth one by one until they had all gone forth, and did see with their eyes and did feel with their hands, and did know of a surety and did bear record, that it was he, of whom it was written by the prophets, that should come. And when they had all gone forth and had witnessed for themselves, they did cry out with one accord, saying: Hosanna! Blessed be the name of the Most High God! And they did fall down at the feet of Jesus, and did worship him" (3 Nephi 11:15–17).

He calls twelve men out of the multitude and declares them to be his representative disciples among the people; he then delivers a sermon that closely approximates chapters 5 through 7 of Matthew in the King James Version of the Bible, the Sermon on the Mount.

But it is not identical. For example, the words "Thy kingdom come" do not appear in the Lord's Prayer in the Book of Mormon, presumably because, among the Nephites and Lamanites, his kingdom had already come by virtue of his appearance among them. Also, some of Jesus' instructions in the Book of Mormon version are given only to the Twelve rather than to the populace as a whole. There are some additions to phrases we know well, such as "blessed are the poor in spirit who come unto me" and "blessed are all they who do hunger and thirst after righteousness, for they shall be filled with the Holy Ghost."

Is this Jesus sharing the key elements of his message with descendants of the house of Israel? Or is this blatant plagiarism on the forger's part? Critics say it is the latter, on the grounds that the forger couldn't think of anything else to have Jesus say.

When the sermon is finished, Jesus perceives that some of the people are wondering what to do with respect to the law of Moses, which has been their guide. He tells them, "The law is fulfilled that was given unto Moses. Behold, I am he that gave the law, and I am he who covenanted with my people Israel; therefore, the law in me is fulfilled, for I have come to fulfil the law; therefore it hath an end." Continuing, he says, "I am the law, and the light. Look unto me, and endure to the end, and ye shall live" (3 Nephi 15:4–5, 9).

Turning to the Twelve, he tells them that they are "a light unto this people, who are a remnant of the house of Joseph. . . . This is the land of your inheritance; and the Father hath given it unto you" (3 Nephi 15:12–13).

He says that he did not tell their "brethren" in Jerusalem about them because he received no direction from the Father to do so. But, he says, he did tell them

> other sheep I have which are not of this fold; them also I must bring, and they shall hear my voice; and there shall be one fold, and one shepherd. [*This is a verbatim quotation from chapter 15 of the Gospel of John.*]
>
> And now, because of stiffneckedness and unbelief they understood not my word; therefore I was commanded to say no more of the Father concerning this thing unto them.
>
> . . . Ye were separated from among them because of their iniquity; therefore it is because of their iniquity that they know not of you. . . .
>
> . . . Ye are they of whom I said: Other sheep I have which are not of this fold; them also I must bring . . . ; and there shall be one fold, and one shepherd.
>
> And they understood me not, for they supposed it had been the Gentiles; for they understood not that the Gentiles should be converted through their preaching.
>
> And they understood me not that I said they shall

hear my voice; and they understood me not that the Gentiles should not at any time hear my voice—that I should not manifest myself unto them save it were by the Holy Ghost.

But behold, ye have both heard my voice, and seen me; and ye are my sheep, and ye are numbered among those whom the Father hath given me. (3 Nephi 15:14, 17–24)

He then says that he has still other sheep to visit and commands them to write everything down after he has gone, so that at some future time all the records of all the personal appearances he makes can be available to everyone who believes in him. He promises to gather "all the people of the house of Israel" in "from the four quarters of the earth" and then prophesies about the future of both Israelites and Gentiles (3 Nephi 16:5).

Turning back to the multitude, he says, "Behold, my time is at hand. I perceive that ye are weak, that ye cannot understand all my words which I am commanded of the Father to speak unto you at this time. Therefore, go ye unto your homes, and ponder upon the things which I have said, and ask of the Father, in my name, that ye may understand, and prepare your minds for the morrow, and I come unto you again" (3 Nephi 17:1–3).

The people are in tears, hoping he will stay longer. Seeing this, he is filled with compassion for them and asks if they have any sick among them, telling them, "Bring them hither." The people "did go forth with their sick and their afflicted, and their lame, and with their blind, and with their dumb, and with all them that were afflicted in any manner; and he did heal them every one as they were brought forth unto him" (3 Nephi 17:7, 9).

He then asks that they bring their little children. When all the children are sitting around him on the ground, he commands that the adults kneel, kneels himself, and begins to pray. Mormon says, "The things which he prayed cannot be written, and the multitude did bear record who heard him. And after this manner do they bear record: The eye hath never seen, neither hath the ear heard, before, so great and marvelous things as we saw and heard Jesus speak unto the Father; . . . no one can conceive of the joy which filled our souls at the time we heard him pray for us unto the Father" (3 Nephi 17:15–17).

Jesus arises and bids the people to arise; then he takes their children and blesses them, one by one. The heavens open and angels descend; they and the children are encircled with fire. "And the multitude did see and hear and bear record; and they know that their record is true for they all of them did see and hear, every man for himself; and they were in number about two thousand and five hundred souls; and they did consist of men, women, and children" (3 Nephi 17:25).

He sends his disciples for bread and wine and instructs the multitude to sit down. When the bread and wine arrive, he blesses each, gives portions to his disciples, and then instructs them to distribute the same to the multitude. He tells his disciples that those who have authority from him should do the same for everyone who is baptized, serving the bread "in remembrance of my body, which I have shown unto you," and the wine "in remembrance of my blood, which I have shed for you, that ye may witness unto the Father that ye do always remember me" (3 Nephi 18:7, 11). He promises that if they do always remember him and keep his commandments, they will have his Spirit to be with them.

He tells the multitude to "always pray unto the Father in my name; and whatsoever ye shall ask the Father in my name, which is right, believing that ye shall receive, behold it shall be given unto you." He also tells them to "meet together oft" and to allow anyone who wishes to join them, holding up Jesus as the light that should shine throughout the world (3 Nephi 18:19–20, 22).

Turning again to his disciples, he gives them other instructions and, after touching each one of them individually, is overshadowed by a cloud. The multitude does not see him ascend back into heaven.

The multitude disperses, but word of the experience goes through the land during the night, along with the expectation that Jesus will return the next day. When morning comes, there is "an exceedingly great number" of people waiting to see him (3 Nephi 19:3). The Twelve—Mormon lists their names—go into the crowd, which is so large that it is divided into twelve groups, with one of the disciples teaching in each. All are instructed to kneel and pray to the Father in the name of Jesus.

The disciples teach the things Jesus taught the previous day, and when the teaching is over, they go to the water's edge. The leader of the Twelve, Nephi, goes into the water and is baptized; he then baptizes the rest of the disciples. The Holy Ghost falls upon them, and they are encircled with fire as angels descend to them (3 Nephi 19:1–14).

Then Jesus appears among them again, and there is a great deal more of the same sort of ministry. Mormon writes, "There cannot be written in this book even a hundredth part of the things which Jesus did truly teach unto the people." He says, "I was about to write them, all which were engraven upon the plates of Nephi, but the Lord forbade it, saying: I will try the faith of my people. Therefore I, Mormon, do write the things which have been commanded me of the Lord" (3 Nephi 26:6, 11–12).

Jesus teaches the people for three days and after that shows himself often among them, including eating with them. He teaches their children, who "speak unto their fathers great and marvelous things" (3 Nephi 26:14). Then he ascends into heaven for the last time.

AFTERMATH

The effect on the society of this experience with Jesus is immense. "In the thirty and sixth year, the people were all converted unto the Lord, upon all the face of the land, both Nephites and Lamanites, and there were no contentions and disputations among them, and every man did deal justly one with another" (4 Nephi 1:2).

Mormon speaks of improved social conditions, of the rebuilding of cities wherever possible, and of the overall unity that prevails. He says that "surely there could not be a happier people among all the people who had been created by the hand of God. There were no robbers, nor murderers, neither were there Lamanites, nor any manner of -ites; but they were in one, the children of Christ, and heirs to the kingdom of God" (4 Nephi 1:16–17).

After that, Mormon moves rapidly through the centuries that follow the coming of Christ. One hundred ten years after the coming of Christ, he says, "there was still peace in the land, save it were a small part of the people who had revolted from the church and taken upon them the name of Lamanites; therefore there began to be Lamanites again in the land" (4 Nephi 1:20).

Note that these Lamanites take the name by choice, not as a result of actual lineage. During the century when there were no Lamanites, "nor any manner of -ites," it is inevitable that intermarriage would have blurred all racial, tribal, and ethnic lines.

Mormon records that the disciple Nephi, who has been keeping the records for eighty-four years, dies, and the records are given to his son Amos. Amos dies in 194 C.E. and gives the record to his son, also named Amos. Then, when "the second generation had all passed away save it were a few" (4 Nephi 1:22), in 201 C.E. there is trouble.

"There began to be among them those who were lifted up in pride, such as the wearing of costly apparel, and all manner of fine pearls, and of the fine things of the world. . . . And they began to be divided into classes; and they began to build up churches unto themselves to get gain, and began to deny the true church of Christ" (4 Nephi 1:24, 26).

By 210 C.E., there are "many churches in the land; yea, there were many churches which professed to know the Christ, and yet they did deny the more parts of his gospel" (4 Nephi 1:27).

Mormon outlines further difficulties and reports that in 231 C.E., "there was a great division among the people. . . . In this year there arose a people who were called the Nephites, and they were true believers in Christ." Other names are used, but, basically, the believers call themselves Nephites, and those who reject the gospel call themselves Lamanites. *Again, this is by their own choice, with no reported ties to actual lineage.* In 244, "the more wicked part of the people did wax strong, and became exceedingly more numerous than were the people of God." By 260, the "secret oaths and combinations of Gadianton" begin to reappear (4 Nephi 1:35–36, 40, 42).

This time, those who call themselves Nephites do not hold out against these trends. By 300 C.E., "both the people of Nephi and the Lamanites had become exceedingly wicked one like unto another" (4 Nephi 1:45). In 305, Amos, the keeper of the record, dies, and Ammaron, his brother, takes over the responsibility. He is the one who tells Mormon about the records, as we described in Chapter 8, and hides them in 320, so that at some future time "they might come again unto the remnant of the house of Jacob, according to the prophecies and the promises of the Lord" (4 Nephi 1:49).

Mormon's life, as we described in Chapter 6, coincides with the destruction of the people who call themselves Nephites, and his death in 385 C.E. marks the end of Story Two.

10

COMMENTARY ON
STORY TWO

How does Story Two as a whole stand up to the tests for forgery? Before turning to that question, two specific issues arising in the last chapter deserve further comment.

The first deals with Samuel the Lamanite. The Nephites didn't record what he said at the time of his appearance. As Jesus examined the Nephite records, he asked why the prophecies of Samuel were not among them, and Mormon simply records that the Nephites "remembered that this thing had not been written." Jesus then "commanded that it should be written; therefore it was written according as he commanded" (3 Nephi 23:12–13).

Samuel the Lamanite is as significant a prophet as is to be found in the book, but his prophecies were initially left out of the written record. Why?

If the book is authentic, it could be precisely because he *was* a Lamanite. It is possible that a trace of racist views about the Lamanites was present in Nephite thinking, even though the prophets that Mormon quotes made it clear that God does not care about race—it is righteousness that matters with him, not skin color. It is possible that their treatment of Samuel was an authentic description of ambivalent Nephite attitudes on the question.

Was God trying to tell the Nephites something about race that they didn't fully get, by sending them a Lamanite prophet? Or was the forger unsure of which position he wanted to take? This is a legitimate issue for a difference of opinion.

The second item I want to call attention to is the reported age of the record keepers. In Story One, I noted the unusual practice of a record keeper taking possession of the plates when he was very young and then holding them into his elderly years, finally giving them to someone else who was very young.

At the end of Story Two, the same thing happened again. Amos kept the plates for eighty-four years, and Ammaron told Mormon about the plates when the boy was only ten, with the understanding that he would take possession of them in his twenties. Odd as that seems, it could be taken as an internal proof, because it is consistent with prior practice. We must ask, under the heading of motive, why a forger would do this. We will consider that in a moment.

Now, to address Story Two as a whole and apply the tests.

INTERNAL ISSUES

Is the work consistent within itself? Is it consistent with its purported origin? Are there any loose ends—items or stories that start off in one direction but end up somewhere else—indicating that the forger, in his invention, lost track of where he was? What does the work tell us about the person who wrote it?

The size and complexity of the work argue strongly for its

authenticity. It gives us a rich amalgam of historical accounts, political movements, personal experiences, correspondences, battle accounts, and relevant sermons, spanning hundreds of years. It ties into Story One perfectly and offers yet another manifestation of the book's capacity to speak in different voices. Everything fits, which is an indication of authentic history and a very hard test for a forger to pass.

Also, Mormon's point of view, as the author, never falters. He speaks in the third person as he tells the story but shifts to the first person when he comments on it. He gives us verbatim renderings of the more important letters and sermons, and the emphasis of the narrative changes when the reported underlying source changes. At the end, when the account becomes autobiographical and Mormon tells his own story, the tenor of the work changes once again. Through it all, he maintains a strong and consistent central theme, preparing his readers for his description of the appearance and sermons of Jesus Christ.

Such a performance over hundreds of pages would seriously tax the talents of any gifted writer, but it is just what one would expect from a deeply religious prophet with a military background who was working from original material written by others.

The internal evidence says that Story Two is genuine.

EXTERNAL ISSUES

Is there evidence external to its claims that either corroborates or contradicts those claims? Do the things that it says fit with facts that have come to light since its publication? Are there any anachronisms that its original readers may have missed but that are now obvious?

We covered most of this ground with the list of competing Proofs and Problems in Chapter 8, but Chapter 9 raises some additional items on the Problem side.

Critics say that the Book of Mormon description of Christ's visits to the assembled Nephites and Lamanites is just a combination of New Testament themes and Old Testament prophecies, cobbled together to resonate with nineteenth-century readers. They say that such a book emphasizing the divinity of Jesus Christ would find a ready audience on the American frontier in 1830, which is why the forger chose that as the climax of the work.

Harking back to the charge that there are no traces of either Jewish or Christian practices in the traditions of pre-Columbian peoples, critics also focus on the events surrounding both the birth and death of Christ. A night with no darkness and three days when there is no light? These are events that ancient peoples would both remember and celebrate in oral histories, but there are no known examples of such tales.

And, while earthquakes are common in Central and South America, even the strongest ones are over in minutes. The Book of Mormon says the devastation went on for three hours. This appears to be a huge exaggeration on the part of an imaginative writer who was not familiar with earthquakes, which were not common in Joseph Smith's neighborhood.

Believing scholars suggest that the problem can be solved by changing the book's vocabulary. Instead of earthquakes, think of volcanoes.

There are many clear examples in world history where

volcanic eruptions have destroyed whole cities in the manner the Book of Mormon describes, eruptions that have indeed lasted for at least three hours. They have been accompanied by vivid lightning and titanic winds strong enough to spread ash over so large an area that the darkness produced by them lasted for days.

Some volcanic events can be documented. If an eruption is truly huge, it puts a gigantic amount of ash and debris into the upper atmosphere, which eventually falls back to earth in places like the Antarctic or Greenland, where traces of it are preserved in the ice. Through analysis of ice core samples, these traces make it possible to date the eruption with some certainty.

A review of such samples suggests that there may well have been a significant volcanic eruption somewhere on the earth in 36 C.E., give or take a few years. The Book of Mormon account says the devastation in and around Zarahemla took place in 34 C.E.[1]

The Book of Mormon story about hours of destruction and days of darkness is not as outlandish as it once seemed.

SUMMARY

Enough unresolved outstanding issues with respect to Story Two leave it open to debate; however, there is one firm conclusion we can draw with respect to it that is beyond a reasonable doubt:

If Mormon didn't write it, the forger who did was very, very good.

STORY THREE

BEHOLD I, MORONI, DO FINISH the record of my father, Mormon. Behold, I have but few things to write, which things I have been commanded by my father" (Mormon 8:1).

With these words, the authorship of the book shifts from Mormon to his son, who is the author of Story Three. There is nothing further in the book with respect to the Nephites, whose story ends with Mormon's death. It is clear, as he begins his "few things," that Moroni expects to die soon himself.

He is alone; all his kinsfolk are dead. He says that the plates Mormon gave him have little room left on them, and he has no ore from which to make new ones. He is beset with enemies everywhere he looks. "The Lamanites are at war one with another; and the whole face of this land is one continual round of murder and bloodshed; and no one knoweth the end of the war" (Mormon 8:8).

Moroni writes a formal farewell, speaking of the spiritual lessons contained in the history of the Nephites and prophesying of the time when the record will be read. It "shall be brought out of the earth, and . . . shine forth out of darkness, and come unto the knowledge of the people" (Mormon 8:16).

He makes this comment about the work: "If there be faults they be the faults of a man. But behold, we know no fault; nevertheless God knoweth all things; therefore, he that condemneth, let him be aware lest he shall be in danger of hell fire" (Mormon 8:17).

The idea that Mormon, Moroni, and their sources were capable of making mistakes would be a smart thing for a forger to say, because that could be used as cover for any mistakes that might be found later on.

Moroni describes in his prophecy what world conditions will be at the time the record comes to light:

> It shall come in a day when the power of God shall be denied, and churches become defiled and be lifted up in the pride of their hearts. . . .
>
> . . . It shall come in a day when there shall be heard of fires, and tempests, and vapors of smoke in foreign lands;
>
> . . . also . . . wars, rumors of wars, and earthquakes in divers places. . . .
>
> . . . There shall be great pollutions upon the face of the earth; there shall be murders, and robbing, and lying, and deceivings, and whoredoms, and all manner of abominations; when there shall be many who will say, Do this, or do that, and it mattereth not. . . .
>
> . . . There shall be churches built up that shall say: Come unto me, and for your money you shall be forgiven of your sins. (Mormon 8:28–32)

Moroni then speaks directly to those who will be living when the record is made available in later centuries, saying,

> Jesus Christ hath shown you unto me, and I know your doing.
>
> And I know that ye do walk in the pride of your hearts; and there are none save a few only who do not lift themselves up in the pride of their hearts, unto the wearing of very fine apparel. . . .
>
> . . . Ye do love money, and your substance, and your fine apparel, and the adorning of your churches, more than ye love the poor and the needy, the sick and the afflicted. (Mormon 8:35–37)

This prophecy and sermon strike believers as accurate descriptions of our time. However, is it really Moroni giving us a prophetic vision of our world? Or is it Joseph Smith giving us a description of the conditions in his?

Moroni concludes by telling us that the reason the record is written in "reformed Egyptian" rather than Hebrew is that the plates were not large enough for them to have used Hebrew (Mormon 9:32).

But Moroni's farewell turns out to be premature. Instead of dying soon after his father, he lives for at least another thirty-six years. Whether he found some ore, or there was more room on the plates than he originally thought, he says, "And now I, Moroni, proceed to give an account of those ancient inhabitants who were destroyed by the hand of the Lord upon the face of this north country. And I take mine account from the twenty and four plates which were found by the people of Limhi, which is called the Book of Ether" (Ether 1:1–2).

This reference to "the people of Limhi" will be puzzling to those who are not familiar with the Book of Mormon because I did not mention Limhi in my discussion of Story Two, where his history appears. I skipped past him because his history was not part of any of the three core samples I discussed, but Moroni's mention of him means that we need to spend a moment understanding who he was.

He was the leader of an offshoot settlement of Nephites who migrated into Lamanite territory during the reign either of the first Mosiah or of Benjamin; the exact time is not recorded. It was some of his followers who came across the plates spoken of, which were given to Mosiah to interpret when the Nephites joined the Mulekites.

We met Coriantumr, the last survivor of the "ancient inhabitants who were destroyed by the hand of the Lord upon the face of this north country" (Ether 1:1) of which Moroni speaks in the Transition Verses at the end of Story One, but there is nothing in either Story One or Story Two that prepares us for what we are about to review—the history of the Jaredites, as outlined on the twenty-four plates in the writings of a prophet named Ether. Get ready for something completely different from the narratives of Stories One and Two.

THE BOOK OF ETHER

This story begins with Jared, who is the leader of a group of families who flee "from the great tower, at the time the Lord confounded the language of the people" (Ether 1:33). *(The Tower of Babel.)* Jared asks his brother, "a large and mighty man, and a man highly favored of the Lord," to ask the Lord not to confound their language nor the language of their friends, so they can stay together. These prayers are answered, and Jared then asks his brother to ask the Lord "whither we shall go" (Ether 1:34, 38). He is in hopes of getting a better land than the one they have and wants the Lord's guidance.

Jared's brother (who is never named) asks the Lord and is told to gather their kinsmen and their flocks, along with their friends and their flocks, and go "down into the valley which is northward. And there will I meet thee, and I will go before thee into a land which is choice above all the lands of the earth" (Ether 1:42).

The Lord promises that they will become a mighty nation. "And thus I will do unto thee because this long time ye have cried unto me" (Ether 1:43).

The people go the valley of Nimrod, where the Lord comes in a cloud and talks to Jared's brother and sends them "forth into the wilderness, yea, into that quarter where there never had man been" (Ether 2:5). They encounter many waters on this journey and build barges to cross them. The Lord promises Jared's brother that he will eventually lead them across the sea to the land of promise.

When they get to "that great sea with divideth the lands" (Ether 2:13), they pitch their tents, name their place of settlement Moriancumer, and stay there for four years.

Then the Lord returns, in a cloud, and speaks to Jared's brother again. He chastises him for failing to pray and tells him to repent. He does, and the Lord gives him instructions. "Go to work and build, after the manner of barges which ye have hitherto built" (Ether 2:16).

They are going to put to sea in these barges. Jared's brother builds eight of them. They are tight "like unto a dish" (Ether 2:17), so the water will not come in, and "light upon the water" (Ether 2:16), so they will skim along the surface. When the barges are finished, the Lord and Jared's brother start a dialog (Ether 2:19–25).

With the barges so tight, Jared's brother asks the Lord, How will we get air during the voyage, and how will we steer?

Cut a hole in the top, the Lord says, for light and air, and then cut another in the bottom, for use when the barge is flipped over by the waves. Stop up both holes when the waves are high, and open one when the sea is calm enough to permit it.

Jared's brother cuts the holes but says of the barges, There is no light in them. Do you want us to cross the sea in darkness?

The Lord says, You can't have windows because they will break. You will be like a whale, diving in and out of the ocean. I'll get you there with the proper winds and currents, but, as for light, what do you suggest?

Jared's brother goes into a nearby mountain, where he "did molten out of a rock sixteen small stones; and they were white and clear, even as transparent glass; and he did carry them in his hands upon the top of the mount." As he renews the dialog, he prays with great humility, recounting the past sins of the people and asking the Lord to "look upon me in pity, and turn away thine anger from this thy people, and suffer not that they shall go forth across this raging deep in darkness" (Ether 3:1, 3).

He then shows the Lord the stones and asks him to touch each one with his finger, so that they will glow. Putting two stones in each barge will provide the light they will need when the hatches are closed. And then something startling happens:

"The Lord stretched forth his hand and touched the stones one by one with his finger. And the veil was taken from off the eyes of the brother of Jared, and he saw the finger of the Lord; and it was as the finger of a man, like unto flesh and blood; and the brother of Jared fell down before the Lord, for he was struck with fear" (Ether 3:6).

The Lord says:

Arise, why hast thou fallen?

And he saith unto the Lord: I saw the finger of the Lord, and I feared lest he should smite me; for I knew not that the Lord had flesh and blood.

And the Lord said unto him: Because of thy faith thou hast seen that I shall take upon me flesh and blood; and never has man come before me with such exceeding faith as thou hast; for were it not so ye could not have seen my finger. Sawest thou more than this?

And he answered: Nay; Lord, show thyself unto me.

And the Lord said unto him: Believest thou the words which I shall speak?

And he answered: Yea, Lord, I know that thou speakest the truth, for thou art a God of truth, and canst not lie. (Ether 3:7–12)

Jared's brother then sees the full figure of the Lord, who tells him:

Behold, I am he who was prepared from the foundation of the world to redeem my people. Behold, I am Jesus Christ. . . .

And never have I showed myself unto man whom I have created, for never has man believed in me as thou hast. Seest thou that ye are created after mine own image? Yea, even all men were created in the beginning after mine own image.

Behold, this body, which ye now behold, is the body of my spirit; . . . even as I appear unto thee to be in the spirit will I appear unto my people in the flesh. (Ether 3:14–16)

Moroni interjects: "I could not make a full account of these things which are written, therefore it sufficeth me to say that Jesus showed himself unto this man in the spirit, even after the manner and in the likeness of the same body even as he showed himself unto the Nephites" (Ether 3:17).

Jesus instructs Jared's brother not to allow knowledge of this experience "to go forth unto the world, until the time cometh that I shall glorify my name in the flesh; wherefore, ye shall treasure up the things which ye have seen and heard, and show it to no man" (Ether 3:21). He is, however, to write it down before he dies.

Jesus gives him two stones that are to be sealed up with his written account: "I will cause in my own due time that these stones shall magnify to the eyes of men these things which ye shall write" (Ether 3:24).

Joseph Smith said that the two stones Jesus gave to Jared's brother were the Urim and Thummim he received from Moroni.

Jesus then showed Jared's brother, presumably in vision, "all the inhabitants of the earth which had been, and also all that would be; and he withheld them not from his sight, even unto the ends of the earth" (Ether 3:25).

The Lord gave final instructions to Jared's brother: "Write

these things and seal them up; and I will show them in mine own due time unto the children of men" (Ether 3:27).

Moroni again steps into the record in first person to say that this is why King Mosiah did not allow his translation of the twenty-four plates to go before the Nephites. "They should not come unto the world until after Christ should show himself unto his people" (Ether 4:1).

With the Nephites gone and the Lamanites looking for him, Moroni says he is commanded to hide the plates again in the earth. Looking ahead to the time when they will come to light, he speaks directly to the person who will eventually receive the plates.

If the work is genuine, he is speaking to Joseph Smith.

Don't even touch them, he says, unless "it shall be wisdom in God. . . . Ye may be privileged that ye may show the plates unto those who shall assist to bring forth this work; and unto three shall they be shown by the power of God; wherefore they shall know of a surety that these things are true" (Ether 5:1–3).

With that, Moroni goes back to his third-person narrative of Jared and his brother.

Jared's brother comes down from the mount with the glowing stones, puts two in each barge, one at each end, and the group prepares to leave. They pack the provisions they need for themselves and the animals they take with them "and set forth into the sea, commending themselves unto the Lord their God" (Ether 6:4). They are driven by wind and wave for 344 days, until "they did land upon the shore of the promised land" (Ether 6:12), where they spread across the land and "wax strong" (Ether 6:18).

When Jared's brother grows old, he says to Jared, "Let us

gather together our people that we may number them, that we may know . . . what they will desire of us before we go down to our graves" (Ether 6:19). The people are brought together, a census is taken, and they ask for a king.

Jared's brother says, "Surely this thing leadeth into captivity. But Jared said unto his brother: Suffer them that they may have a king. And therefore he said unto them: Choose ye out from among our sons a king, even whom ye will" (Ether 6:23–24).

They choose Pagag, the firstborn of Jared's brother. He refuses. The people ask his father to force him to accept, but he won't. They ask each of Pagag's brothers in turn, but all refuse, as do all the sons of Jared except one—Orihah.

And thus we enter the strange world of the Jaredite kings. The narrative from this point forward is densely detailed and the events it describes are quite repetitive, so we shall only dip into it here and there, as we did in Story Two.

Difficult as it is to follow, we need to review enough of it to get a flavor of Jaredite history, because it is different from anything we have seen before. Here is a tiny sample.

Orihah is a good king, who walks humbly before God, and the people prosper and become "exceedingly rich" (Ether 6:28). Orihah lives a very long time; he has thirty-one children, of whom twenty-three are sons. One of them, Kib, born in Orihah's old age—*Jaredite kings do a lot of "begetting" in their old age*—becomes king and begets Corihor.

When Corihor is thirty-two, he rebels against his father and goes to dwell in the land of Nehor, where he fathers many children and draws a large following. He then marches into the land where Kib lives and takes him captive. Kib, in captivity and in his old age, fathers another son, Shule.

Shule "waxed strong, and became mighty as to the strength of a man; and he was also mighty in judgment." He goes to the hill Ephraim where "he did molten out" steel from which he makes swords for his followers; thus armed, his troops descend on the city Nehor, unseat Corihor, and deliver the kingdom back to Kib. Kib responds by making Shule his heir, and Shule becomes the king. However, when Corihor repents "of the many evils which he had done," Shule gives him a degree of power in the kingdom, so for a time there are two leaders instead of one (Ether 7:8, 9, 13).

There is treachery at court when a son of Corihor seeks to kill Shule, but Shule survives and dies a natural death, at which time his son Omer becomes king. Omer has a son, Jared, who rebels against him and draws support until he is strong enough to overthrow Omer and put him in captivity, where he fathers two sons. When they become of age, they themselves raise an army and attack Jared, who saves his life by agreeing to allow Omer to be placed back on the throne.

But he hates not being king. "Jared became exceedingly sorrowful because of the loss of the kingdom, for he had set his heart upon the kingdom and upon the glory of the world" (Ether 8:7). He wants his throne back.

Jared has a daughter who is "exceedingly fair" (Ether 8:9). She tells her father to read the record that was brought across the waters, in which there is "an account concerning them of old, that they by their secret plans did obtain kingdoms and great glory" (Ether 8:9).

She tells her father to send for Akish, one of Omer's close friends. She will dance for Akish and please him, so that he will desire to take her as a wife, but the price for her will be Omer's head. Things play out as she had anticipated, and when Akish asks for her to be his wife, Jared tells him, "I will give her unto you, if ye will bring unto me the head of my father, the king" (Ether 8:12).

Akish gathers all of his kinsmen into Jared's house and administers oaths, by which they swear to follow Akish and tell no one of their pact, under threat of death. "Akish did administer unto them the oaths which were given by them of old who also sought power, which had been handed down even from Cain, who was a murderer from the beginning. . . . It was the daughter of Jared who put it into his heart to search up these things of old; and Jared put it into the heart of Akish; wherefore, Akish administered it unto his kindred and friends" (Ether 8:15, 17). Akish and his friends succeed in overthrowing Omer, and Jared becomes king.

As agreed, Jared gives his daughter to Akish, who repays his new father-in-law by having Jared murdered on his throne and taking the kingdom for himself.

The narrative goes on like this through a rapid and seemingly inexhaustible line of kings and sons, some righteous, others not. Dethroned kings are often kept in captivity for their entire lives, fathering children who then work to overthrow the ruling king. For the first-time reader, it is terribly confusing and endlessly repetitive. I skip ahead to the time of Ether, the prophet who wrote the record, thus passing over centuries, if not millennia, of royal intrigue and treachery similar to that just described.

Moroni says that Ether "did prophesy great and marvelous things unto the people, which they did not believe. . . ." (Ether 12:5). "They esteemed him as naught, and cast him out; and he hid himself in the cavity of a rock by day, and by night he went forth viewing the things which should come upon the people. And as he dwelt in the cavity of a rock he made the remainder of this record, viewing the destructions which came upon the people, by night" (Ether 13:13–14).

The king at this time is Coriantumr, the man we met in the Transition Verses, the one who was discovered by the Mulekites.

The Lord tells Ether to "prophesy unto Coriantumr that, if he would repent, and all his household, the Lord would give unto him his kingdom and spare the people—otherwise they should be destroyed, and all his household save it were himself. And he should only live to see the fulfilling of the prophecies which had been spoken concerning another people receiving the land for their inheritance; and Coriantumr should receive a burial by them; and every soul should be destroyed save it were Coriantumr" (Ether 13:20–21).

Ether delivers the prophecy, but Coriantumr responds by trying to kill him. He escapes and returns to his cave, and the battles continue.

There is a great deal of detail about generals and kings and who wins which battle; the outcome is that Coriantumr defeats all his enemies except for one final opponent, a vicious general named Shiz.

"There went a fear of Shiz throughout all the land; yea, a cry went forth throughout the land—Who can stand before the army of Shiz? Behold, he sweepeth the earth before him!" (Ether 14:18).

The people are forced to choose sides—"a part of them fled to the army of Shiz, and a part of them fled to the army of Coriantumr. And so great and lasting had been the war, and so long had been the scene of bloodshed and carnage, that the whole face of the land was covered with the bodies of the dead. And so swift and speedy was the war that there was none left to bury the dead, but they did march forth from the shedding of blood to the shedding of blood, leaving the bodies of both men, women, and children strewed upon the face of the land, to become a prey to the worms of the flesh" (Ether 14:20–22).

Shiz pursues Coriantumr eastward to the borders of the seashore, where they fight for three days, after which the armies of Shiz flee to the land of Corihor. There they kill everyone who will not join them and pitch their tents. Coriantumr and his army pitch their tents in the valley of Shurr.

Coriantumr sounds the trumpet, daring Shiz to battle, and there is another terrible fight, in which Shiz wounds Coriantumr so badly that he faints for loss of blood and is carried away as if dead. Shiz's armies cannot pursue Coriantumr's as they retreat, however, because their own losses have been too great.

Coriantumr recovers from his wounds and remembers the prophecy Ether had given him. "He saw that there had been slain by the sword already nearly two millions of his people, and he began to sorrow in his heart. . . . He began to repent of the evil which he had done; he began to remember the words which had been spoken by the mouth of all the prophets; . . . and his soul mourned and refused to be comforted" (Ether 15:2–3).

He writes Shiz a letter, saying that he will give up the kingdom if Shiz will spare the lives of his people. Shiz says he will spare the people only if Coriantumr will present himself to be killed by Shiz personally. Coriantumr's troops are angry at this, Shiz's troops are equally angry, and the battle resumes.

I move to the final confrontation, which takes place after both armies have been destroyed. Shiz has only thirty-two survivors with him; Coriantumr has twenty-seven. Even so, wearily, they keep at it.

"They fought for the space of three hours, and they fainted with the loss of blood. . . . When the men of Coriantumr had received sufficient strength that they could walk, they were about to flee for their lives; but behold, Shiz arose, and also his men, and he swore in his wrath that he would slay Coriantumr or he would perish by the sword" (Ether 15:27–28).

Coriantumr and his men leave the field, but Shiz catches up with them the next day. They fight until Shiz and Coriantumr are the only survivors. Shiz faints from loss of blood, and Coriantumr is about to do the same but, having "leaned upon his sword, that he rested a little, he smote off the head of Shiz." Then he falls to the ground and passes out, "as if he had no life" (Ether 15:30, 32).

But he recovers and wanders about in the wilderness, alone, until he is discovered by the Mulekites, as described in Chapter 5. He lives with them for nine months before he dies, fulfilling Ether's prophecy that he would be buried by the people who took over lands that had belonged to the Jaredites. The date is unknown. We have no idea how long the three civilizations had been sharing the continent before Coriantumr and the Mulekites met.

MORONI'S FINAL FAREWELL

After he has finished with the book of Ether, Moroni returns to his own history, surprised that he is still alive. The

Lamanites are still engaged in fierce wars and kill anyone who will not deny the Christ. "I, Moroni, will not deny the Christ; wherefore, I wander whithersoever I can for the safety of mine own life" (Moroni 1:3). He prepares the record for its storage burial, outlining a few items of church administration and adding one of Mormon's sermons and two of his letters.

When Moroni is finished with his quotations from his father, he writes to those who will receive the book when it comes to light, telling them—us—to pray to God for a knowledge of its truthfulness. He bears his witness of the reality of Christ, calls on us to accept Him as the Messiah, and then says good-bye for the final time.

1 2

COMMENTARY ON
STORY THREE

BEFORE TURNING TO THE BOOK OF Ether, I must call attention
to a golden nugget of forgery evidence found in Moroni's final
comments—an anachronism in the form of a word-for-word
quotation from another source. It is in a sermon Moroni attributes to Mormon, where Mormon talks about faith, hope,
and charity, the same theme that Paul addresses in his letter to
the Corinthians. Mormon's words are just different enough
from Paul's to enable believers to say that they are original until
we get to this:

> If a man be meek and lowly in heart, and confesses by the
> power of the Holy Ghost that Jesus is the Christ, he must
> needs have charity; for if he have not charity he is noth-
> ing; wherefore he must needs have charity.
>
> *And charity suffereth long, and is kind, and envieth*
> *not, and is not puffed up, seeketh not her own, is not easily*
> *provoked, thinketh no evil, and rejoiceth not in iniquity but*
> *rejoiceth in the truth, beareth all things, believeth all things,*
> *hopeth all things, endureth all things.*
>
> *Wherefore, my beloved brethren, if ye have not charity,*

ye are nothing, for charity never faileth. Wherefore, cleave unto charity, which is the greatest of all, for all things must fail—

But charity is the pure love of Christ, and it endureth forever; and whoso is found possessed of it at the last day, it shall be well with him. (Moroni 7:44–47; emphasis added)

The words in italics are not exact quotations from Paul, but they are about 90 percent there, and the differences are insignificant.

One of the surest tests for forgery is the discovery of such a passage, a quotation from a source that was available to a forger but not to the purported author. A forger writing in the 1820s had ready access to the King James Version of Paul's letter, but Mormon was said to be living a hemisphere away from Paul and a millennium before King James.

This is different from the appearance of the Isaiah material in Story One; that was supposedly available to Nephi and Jacob from the brass plates of Laban. It is different from the similarity between the two versions of the Sermon on the Mount; both are attributed to Christ himself. This passage—"charity suffereth long, and is kind . . . seeketh not her own . . . never faileth," etc.—is so clearly the language of Paul's epistle, written in the Middle East, not America, that it is impossible for believers to shrug it off.

There are three attempts at explanation that I have heard.

The first one says that God inspired both men to use the same phrases. That is possible—by definition, God can do whatever he wants—but it is reaching.

The second is that Paul and Mormon were quoting from a common source that predated both of them. There is no evidence of any such source.

The third is that Joseph Smith inadvertently slipped into language with which he was familiar when he came to this sermon. This is the most plausible, but it runs contrary to the position held by some believers, including David Whitmer, that Joseph simply gazed into the interpreters and recited exactly whatever words were shown him. Only if we assume that he understood general ideas rather than specific words as he looked into the interpreters can the appearance of Paul's language be defended. If that was indeed the case, however, then one could argue that more of the book should be in Joseph's language than it appears to be.

Claiming that this passage is not what it appears to be—an obvious anachronism—requires yet another leap of faith.

Now, turning to the book of Ether:

If the exploits of Ammon and his brothers sounded like something out of *Arabian Nights,* what can we say about *this* story?

People and animals, cramped together in watertight barges with enough food to sustain them for a year, tossing about on the ocean with only two glowing stones in each barge to give them light when they are underwater?

Kings kept in captivity for decades but still siring children—in great numbers, and often in their *very* old age—who battle their siblings to put the old king back on the throne?

Wars involving millions that sweep across vast distances,

rage for years, and end only when there are no survivors but the kings?

And what's with the woman who dances for a king and asks for the head of her grandfather as a reward? Isn't this just another item lifted right out of the New Testament? And new "secret combinations" springing up—haven't we had enough of that already?

However you look at it, for the Western reader, the book of Ether is mind-numbingly detailed and repetitive, full of very odd stuff, in a historic setting that has virtually nothing to do with anything in Stories One or Two.

So, why is it here?

If the book is genuine:

Finding Coriantumr was a significant event for the Mulekites. Finding the twenty-four gold plates and the bones of the Jaredite nation was a significant event for the people of Limhi. It would be natural for Moroni, alone and with time on his hands, to want to read the entire story, particularly because Mosiah's refusal to release his translation of the plates would have aroused great curiosity about it. Once he knew what the plates said, it would be equally natural for him to want to add that information to his father's record.

Moroni would not have found the story as strange as we do. The Jaredites were destroyed because they disregarded the revelations their fathers had received, just as the Nephites did. Also, before they fell into iniquity, the Jaredites had a full understanding of the mission of Jesus Christ, a point Moroni would want to emphasize. Strange as the story is, putting it into the final record would have been a logical thing for him to have done.

If the book is a forgery:

Reasons for its inclusion are harder to come by. Story Three doesn't add anything to the book that would make it more believable to an 1830s audience; indeed, its tedious recital of kings and plots and battles does just the opposite. Unlike Stories One and Two, it has no visions other than the story of Jared's brother's vision of the premortal Jesus and no named prophets other than Ether, whose only recorded prophecy has to do with the fate of the king.

The visions of Jared's brother do not resemble Lehi's, just as Jaredite military campaigns do not resemble those managed by the first Moroni and his generals. Jaredite kings do not resemble Benjamin or Mosiah or any of the Lamanite kings. Jaredite society is so different from Nephite society that a forger would require a whole new mindset to construct it. It has little religious content in it, and I cannot think of any logical motive for a forger to put it in, particularly when thinking of a nineteenth-century American audience.

But Fawn Brodie can. She was sure she knew why Joseph did it. Speaking almost as if she had been there and interviewed Joseph directly, she says:

> As his history drew near its close and he began seriously to think of publication, Joseph became more and more dissatisfied with the Indian narrative as it stood. He had written a record of a thousand years—600 B.C. to A.D. 400. But apparently he was troubled by rather widespread speculation that the Indians had been in America almost since the days of the Flood. Many thought they had emigrated at the time of the building of the tower of Babel and the great dispersion of tongues, and Joseph

seems to have realized that if this theory were to gain in popularity the claims of his book might be scorned.

Writers argued variously that the emigrants had sailed in boats, or crossed Bering Strait on the ice, or traversed the sunken continent that was said to have joined the Old World with the New. Caleb Atwater, when examining the Ohio ruins in 1820, wrote that the mounds marked "the progress of population in the first ages after the dispersion, rising wherever the posterity of Noah came."

. . . [Joseph] was impressed with the probability of the "dispersionist" thesis, for in the last weeks of writing he dictated a terse little history of a people called the Jaredites, which he appended to the Nephite record.[1]

There is no evidence that Joseph even knew about the "dispersionist" thesis, let alone that he was impressed by it. He certainly never mentioned it in any of his other speeches and writings. If Brodie were still alive, I would ask her two obvious questions:

First, if Joseph wrote the book of Ether to show his readers that he understood that the ancestors of the American Indians came across the Bering Strait, why did he insist, all his life, that they were descendants of Lehi?

Second, since Joseph never wrote anything else, either in or out of the Book of Mormon, that even came close to resembling it, where did he get the capacity to create something this exotic?

Nibley snorted at Brodie's brush-off of the book as nothing more than a "terse little history" dashed off in a matter of weeks. He was fascinated with the book of Ether and is the only scholar—critic or believer—to spend significant time and effort on it, returning to it again and again. Once again, I quote him extensively because his work in the area has never been refuted. Other than Brodie, most critics (and many believers) have dealt with the book of Ether simply by ignoring it.

Nibley draws a number of parallels between the Jaredites and other ancient civilizations, beginning with the origins and meanings of names, the subject on which he is the most expert. He points out that most Jaredite names do not have Hebrew or Egyptian roots, a fine point that would require great diligence on the part of a forger. He says:

> The Jaredites and Nephites spoke entirely different languages, and even a cursory search will show that Jaredite proper names have a peculiar ring of their own. . . .
>
> . . . It is the proper names that concern us here. When out of the short list of Jaredite names preserved to us, a respectable percentage turn up as Nephite names as well, it is high time to ask, is this one case where the author of the Book of Mormon has slipped up, or is there something significant about those Nephites who bear Jaredite names? The answer is a surprise: Virtually all of these men have Mulekite backgrounds and lead subversive movements against the Nephite state and religion! The significance of this will appear at once if we consider that the only case of definite overlapping between the Jaredite and Nephite peoples is provided in the episode of Coriantumr and the Mulekites.
>
> Coriantumr, the last Jaredite chief, spent the last nine months of his life among the Mulekites. . . . "Coriantumr was *discovered by* the people of Zarahemla" (Omni 1:21, emphasis added). Since Coriantumr had been very badly

wounded and with not a soul to help him, he could not have got very far; the fact that he lingered only nine months after his rescue implies as much, though it does not necessarily prove it. But the evidence strongly suggests that the Mulekites "discovered" Coriantumr shortly after the last Jaredite battle. . . . The overlap between the Mulekite and Jaredite cultures was at least nine months long, and may have extended over many years. At any rate we have proof that the Jaredites made a permanent cultural impression on the Nephites *through Mulek,* for centuries after the destruction of the Jaredite nation we find a Nephite bearing the name of Coriantumr, and learn that this man was a descendant of Zarahemla, the illustrious leader of the Mulekites. . . .

. . . We have here a definite overlapping of the two cultures. What clinches the matter is the fact that our Nephites with Jaredite names all have Mulekite background and connections . . . clearly shown in the *behavior* of men with Jaredite names. Five out of the six whose names are definitely Jaredite betray strong anti-Nephite leanings.[2]

"Nephites with Jaredite names all have Mulekite background and connections"—we meet the information given in the Transition Verses again, here in Story Three. There is a bit of irony in that, because the Transition Verses are perhaps the only part of the book more ignored than the book of Ether.

Let's examine the parallel between Ether's account and the ancient game of chess.

Chess is not a game in which each player piles up points, with the one who has the most points winning, as most modern games are. Chess is a representation of a war in which the object is to capture the other side's king. Destroying his army's ability to fight—the object of modern wars—is not enough. The king himself must be captured, and once that has been accomplished, all the rest of his army is rendered impotent, regardless of its remaining size or firepower. Consequently, every other piece on the board is dispensable, nay, *must* be sacrificed, to ensure the safety of the king.

With that in mind, we read Nibley's comment on what wars are like in the book of Ether:

> You will recall the many instances . . . in which kings were kept in prison for many years but not killed. In the code of medieval chivalry, taken over from central Asia, the person of the king is sacred, and all others must perish in his defense. . . . Shiz was willing to spare *all* of Coriantumr's subjects if he could only behead Coriantumr with his own sword. In that case, of course, the subjects would become his own. The circle of warriors, "large and mighty men as to the strength of men" (Ether 15:26) that fought around their kings to the last man, represent that same ancient institution, the sacred "shieldwall," which our own Norse ancestors took over from Asia and which meets us again and again in the wars of the tribes, in which on more than one occasion the king actually *was* the last to perish. So let no one think the final chapter of Ether is at all fanciful or overdrawn. Wars of extermination are a standard institution in the history of Asia.[3]

Wars of extermination are also demonstrated in the game of chess, which has no ties to the Abrahamic tradition that Lehi followed. Joseph Smith was good at wrestling and stick pulling, but no one has ever suggested that he was a chess player.

Aside from Nibley's work, from my own experience I can say that Brodie's throwaway line about Joseph's decision to "dictate a terse little history" as an afterthought does not ring true to me. An author herself, she should have known better.

Hers is a long and serious book. The experience of writing it undoubtedly taught her—as my own writing has taught me—that one does not sit down and write such a book from start to finish in a straight line. There is a great deal of cutting, pasting, revisiting, and revising required; later chapters bring out points that require a writer to go back to earlier ones and make changes; additions beget further corrections. Inventing the Jaredites and giving them an entirely new society, with significantly different governmental and cultural norms than those ascribed to the Nephites, would have required a huge mental shift on Joseph's part. It would have taken a great deal of time and effort to make sure that no shred of Nephite culture crept into the Jaredite account.

He would also have had to go back into his original work and create the contact between the Mulekites and the Jaredites, insert Jaredite names at the right spots, and make sure that the people so named behaved appropriately. Unlike Mrs. Brodie, Joseph had no skilled editor at Knopf and Company to assist him; all of this would have to have been done in a way that would not disclose to Oliver or anyone else that this farm boy, who earned his living hiring out as a day laborer, was a writer capable of making these changes in the course of producing seven hundred pages of manuscript without anyone knowing what he was doing.

Suggesting that Joseph simply whipped up the book of Ether in a few weeks is nonsense.

Until a few years ago, I would probably have left it at that. Now, however, we must stay with Story Three a little longer, because of recent scientific discoveries, interpretations of which have replaced pre-Columbian archaeology as the principal source of attack from critics.

New DNA studies say that the ancestors of the Indians were Asians, not Semites from the Middle East, bolstering the "dispersionist" theory to which Brodie referred and challenging the notion long held by believers that all American Indians are descendants of the Lamanites. Some believers have even renounced their acceptance of the book as a result of these studies, which appear to contradict Book of Mormon genealogy. We need to spend some time examining what the book itself actually says on the subject.

Everyone mentioned in the beginning of the book had identifiable family ties. Except for Zoram, they were all the children, or spouses of the children, of either Lehi or Ishmael. Although there was a split when Lehi died, it was along religious lines, so the ethnic backgrounds of both Lamanites and Nephites were identical for over 450 years. Then the Mulekites appeared, and Nephite society from Mosiah forward was a racial blend with the descendants of Lehi in the minority.

But Lamanite ethnicity didn't change. Or did it? Let's go back to the Transition Verses and look at the coming of the Mulekites again. There is something significant mentioned there that most people pass by without noticing. I'm talking about relative size.

The old Nephite nation, made up of Nephites alone, was

less than half as large as the new one, made up of Nephites and Mulekites combined. The Lamanite population of the time was roughly two times bigger than the new one, which means that there were more than *four times* as many Lamanites as there were ethnic Nephites. This disparity had grown up over a period of four hundred years.

What could account for that?

Just a higher birth rate? Perhaps. But maybe the Lamanite growth spurt came from outside sources, in the same way that the Nephite growth spurt did. Maybe, during the centuries whose history was lost in the 116 pages, the Lamanites had stumbled into settlements of other peoples, just as the Nephites had come in contact with the Mulekites. If that had happened, and the Lamanites had joined with those peoples as the Nephites did with the Mulekites, it would account for their greater numbers, and—in ethnic terms—significantly change their children's DNA. This would be particularly true if the peoples with whom they joined were not descendants of Semites from the Middle East.

It is not just the book's silence on the subject that leaves open the possibility that Lehi's descendants ran into other people; Lehi himself actually suggests it. He says, in one of his prophecies concerning the future of his family, that if they are not righteous, "Yea, he [God] will bring other nations unto them [Lehi's descendants], and he will give unto them [the other nations] power, and he will take away from them [Lehi's descendants] the lands of their possessions, and he will cause them to be scattered and smitten" (2 Nephi 1:11).

Lehi's prophecy about "other nations" joining with his descendants could easily have been fulfilled during the 430 years between Jacob and Mosiah, years whose record was lost with the 116 pages. If it were, Lamanite numbers would have been significantly enhanced by people whose DNA was different from their own. Some of those people could well have been Jaredites of whom Ether did not know and therefore did not mention in his book.

We have no idea whether anything like that happened because the Book of Mormon is exclusively a Nephite record; it does not talk about any other peoples unless they intrude on Nephite society. The Lamanites could have added a significant new ethnic strain to their numbers without the Nephite record keepers even knowing about it.

Now, let us review again Mormon's description of the society that existed after the coming of Christ, when everyone was converted and their descendants all lived in peace. He tells us that Nephites and Lamanites disappeared as identifiable ethnic groups; there were "no manner of -ites" for more than a hundred years.

A hundred-plus years with "no manner of -ites," with everyone living in peace, means that there would have been no barriers to ethnic intermarriages. When the labels Nephite and Lamanite reappeared, in 201 C.E., remember that they did not represent ethnic lineage. The labels were self-applied, as people chose to call themselves one or the other.

That means that the Nephites who were destroyed in Mormon's last battle were not necessarily pure descendants of the original Nephites; indeed, it is probable that few, if any, of them were. Ethnically, those who were killed and those who did the killing were all of the same racial pool—an amalgam of Nephites, Lamanites, Mulekites, very likely Jaredites, and whatever other peoples their ancestors may have met that the authors of the book didn't know about.

I say "very likely Jaredites" because the book of Ether makes it clear that the Jaredites inhabited the continent at the same time the Nephites, Lamanites, and Mulekites did and occasionally in the same places.

Back to Nibley, the only scholar who has examined this issue. Speaking of the Jaredites, he says:

> They were past masters at dodging and hiding. Their history begins with Nimrah and Omer hiding in the wilderness and ends with Shiz and Coriantumr and Ether himself doing the same. Are we to believe of such people that when "part of them fled to the army of Shiz, and a part of them fled to the army of Coriantumr" (Ether 14:20), none of them attempted to flee to the wilderness? Or that no one *tried* to get away when "the cry went throughout the land" that Shiz was approaching, sweeping the earth before him? (Ether 15:18). . . . The picture is that of people doing their best to get out of the way, the classic picture of those who "flee to the mountains" or break for the woods on the approach of the Assyrian king, the Mongol hordes, or the modern Chinese general. . . . Nowhere is there any indication that none made their escape, either during the final war or at an earlier time.[4]

Referring to material covered in the Transition Verses, Nibley notes

> how closely the editors of the Book of Mormon stick to the business at hand, shunning any kind of digression and stubbornly refusing to tell about any people but the

announced subjects of their history. The people of Zarahemla [Mulekites] are only mentioned because they have to be—since they in time become bona fide Nephites. But the brief and grudging nod to their past is a priceless clue for us. It is a reminder that just because Lehi's people had come from Jerusalem by special direction we are not to conclude that other men cannot have had the same experience. And by the same token the fact that the Jaredites were led to the land of promise at the time of the dispersion gives us no right to conclude that no one else was ever so led, either earlier or later than they. It is nowhere said or implied that even the Jaredites were the first to come here.[5]

Nibley then takes direct aim at the American Indian question, even though he was writing several decades before DNA was discovered:

Why all this insistence on the possible survival of a few Jaredite escapees prowling in the woods? Because it would take no great number of such renegades to perpetuate "upon the face of this north country" the ways of the Jaredite nomads and hunters. We have said that when the Asiatics hide in the mountains and the woods their way of life becomes just like that of the Indians. Indeed Professor Grousset can think of no way of life so perfectly like that of the scattered and disorganized tribes of Asia after the destruction of the great nations than that of the North American Indians at the time of their discovery by the whites. And what is more natural than that conditions in the north country, littered with bones and haunted by savage hunters, should present after the passing of the

Jaredite nation just the sort of wreckage and savagery that make the Asiatic scene after the passing of empire? In time descendants of Jaredite hunters and robbers would combine with Lamanite riffraff, as their ancestors did with the Mulekites, and the old Jaredite stock would survive, like the Nephite, as a "mixture" only (1 Nephi 13:30). . . . This complicates the picture considerably, but for that matter the anthropologists themselves now begin to detect just such complications in their own picture. . . .

Now all this is as the book of Ether would have it. That account tells us that at the very dawn of history, many thousands of years ago, a party of nomad hunters and stock raisers from west central Asia crossed the water—very probably the North Pacific—to the New World, where they preserved the ways of their ancestors, including certain savage and degenerate practices, and carried on a free and open type of steppe warfare with true Asiatic cruelty and ferocity; it tells us that these people moved about much in the wilderness, for all they built imposing cities, and that they produced a steady trickle of "outcasts" through the centuries. A careful study of the motions of the Jaredites, Mulekites, Nephites, and Lamanites should correct the absurd oversimplification by which the Book of Mormon as a history is always judged. It will show as plain as day that the Book of Mormon itself suggests the Asiatic origin of some elements at least of the Indian race and culture long before the anthropologists got around to it. The scientists *no longer* hold that one migration and one route can explain everything about the Indians. The Book of Mormon *never did* propound a doctrine so naive. Though it comes to us a digest and an abridgment, stripped and streamlined, it is still as intricate and complex a history as you can find; and in its involved and tragic pages nothing is more challenging than the sinister presence of those fierce and bloody-minded "men out of Asia" known in their day as Jaredites. . . .

. . . I think by now it should be apparent that the Book of Mormon account is not as simple as it seems. Ether alone introduces a formidable list of possibilities, few of which have ever been seriously considered. Foremost among these is the probability, amounting almost to certainty, that numerous Jaredites survived in out-of-the-way places of the North to perpetuate a strong Asiatic element in the culture and blood of the American Indian.[6]

"The Book of Mormon itself suggests the Asiatic origin of some elements at least of the Indian race and culture long before the anthropologists got around to it" and "Jaredites survived . . . to perpetuate a strong Asiatic element in the culture and blood of the American Indian."

Interesting comments from the foremost—if not the sole—expert on the book of Ether, made long before scientists even knew about DNA. Measured against them, recent DNA studies that say the first ancestors of the Indians came from Asia almost sound like evidence of the book's authenticity instead of proof of its fraud. Focus again on the word *mixture,* used in an early prophecy to Nephi about the future of his seed; follow the historical record laid out in the three Stories. At the time of the final battle in 385 C.E., when Mormon died, we are talking about a people whose predecessors—those descendants of the original passengers on Lehi's and Mulek's ships—had been on the continent for a thousand years. During that time some of their forebears had mixed with others whose ancestors had been here for thousands of years before that, and it is possible that there were other contacts with other peoples of whom we have no record.

A thousand more years went by with no record at all, after which Columbus arrived. Any number of other influences could have entered their society during that time, including "other nations"—Lehi's phrase—whose roots were, like those of the Jaredites, not in the Middle East.

Five hundred more years have now passed since Columbus. It is inevitable that the DNA of the members of the family that sailed here on Lehi's boat would be only a "mixture" in the DNA of any American Indian tribe living here twenty-five hundred years later.

Remember the allegory of the olive tree, quoted by Jacob and attributed to the prophet Zenos? It outlines, in excruciating detail, how the branches of the original tree, representing the house of Israel, are pruned and grafted and regrafted onto the branches and roots of other trees to ensure their ability to bring forth good fruit. Zenos did not know about DNA, but his allegory is an amazingly accurate description of the jumbled genealogical scene just described.

So, for the Book of Mormon to survive the attack from the DNA studies, all that is necessary is that Lehi's descendants' DNA be present as a "mixture" in the bloodlines of modern American Indians to qualify them as Lamanites, as Joseph Smith always said they were.

SUMMARY

Moroni's brief entries are what we would expect from one of Mormon's sons. The book of Ether, on the other hand, is totally unexpected, very much unlike anything else anywhere in the Book of Mormon.

It depicts an entirely different age and an entirely different migration to America, describing a society unrelated to anything one would find in either Jerusalem or Egypt.

It further fortifies the "different voices" argument, introducing a narrative style that has no resemblance to anything that has come before.

It provides a possible explanation for the DNA evidence that has come forward with respect to the ancestry of the American Indians, and it was written before DNA was discovered.

And it is so tedious in its telling that many readers simply can't get through it, raising the question, "Why would a forger have put it in?"

The only certain conclusion we can draw, beyond a reasonable doubt, is that Story Three shows that the Book of Mormon is much more complex than its casual readers, believers and critics alike, think it is.

THE THREE STORIES
TOGETHER

HAVING EXAMINED EACH OF ITS separate stories, we now know that the Book of Mormon story has the following attributes:

It claims roots in three different Old World cultures.

The Tower of Babel, Jerusalem, and Egypt.

It is attributed to four different primary authors, with verbatim quotations from a number of others, taken from material written by an even greater number of original record keepers.

Nephi, Jacob, Mormon, and Moroni quote directly from Alma, Abinadi, Amulek, Helaman, Zenos, Samuel the Lamanite, and others, along with Jesus himself.

It was written for an audience living in our times—1830 onward.

It was inscribed on metal plates so the writing would not fade.

It covers a wide variety of topics.

There are descriptions of revelations, visions, dreams, miracles, religious doctrine, Middle Eastern geography, earthquakes and military strategy, along with significant commentary on government, political intrigue, monetary systems and secret societies, all offered with a high degree of specificity regarding ancient names, poetry, and agricultural practices.

It declares that the heavens are still open for angelic visitation in modern times.

Four individuals living in the 1830s claim to have seen and conversed with such an angel.

It comes from a young man in his twenties who had no previous demonstration of either scholarly bent or literary talent, who dictated it out loud to a scribe in a period of sixty-five days.

Joseph Smith never again produced anything even vaguely resembling it.

Through it all, it maintains a consistent and insistent central message, testifying of the divinity of Jesus Christ.

With that summary before us, it is time to apply the forgery tests.

INTERNAL ISSUES

Is the work consistent within itself? Is it consistent with its purported origin? Are there any loose ends—items or stories that start off in one direction but end up somewhere else—indicating that the forger, in his invention, lost track of where he was? What does the work tell us about the person who wrote it?

The preponderance of evidence shows that the Story passes these internal tests in the following ways:

It passes the internal tests with respect to the interrelationship of its structure to its claimed origin and the circumstances of its production.

Moroni's account of his own life fits Joseph Smith's

description of him in Story One. The awkwardness of entering Mormon's ongoing narrative in the middle is consistent with Joseph Smith's claim of having lost the first 116 pages. Stories One and Two contain clues that tie them to Story Three. The entire work is just what it should be if Joseph's claim of its provenance is correct.

It passes the internal tests in its consistency of point of view.

Its narrative is always consistent with its description of who is writing at the time and always stays true to its claim to be exclusively a Nephite record; there is nothing in it regarding Lamanite, Mulekite, or Jaredite activities except where there is a Nephite source for such a discussion. Even when the Lamanites are reportedly more righteous than the Nephites, and thus more favored by God, the Nephite record keepers do not offer any details of the Lamanite leaders, their cultural practices, or their manner of worship.

It passes the internal tests in the way it handles the differences that arise from claimed divergent original sources.

Mormon's narrative changes as he moves from one set of underlying documents to another, consistent with the claim that he is the abridger rather than the originator of the underlying material. The rich store of direct quotations from sermons and letters from others provides multiple examples of the authenticity of the different voices that are heard.

It passes the internal tests in things that are consistent, even when they seem odd.

Its description of record keepers who get the plates as very young boys and then keep them until they are very old, casually made in the Transition Verses, is consistent with later descriptions of the same practice.

It passes the internal tests in the way it handles diversity.

Nephites and Lamanites do things differently from each other, Mulekites add another dimension, and Jaredites are markedly different from any of them.

It passes the internal tests in its size.

The bigger a literary forgery is, the more opportunity there is for internal errors, and here there are none. Throughout all of its more than five hundred printed pages, it never puts a foot wrong internally.

Internal analysis says that the book is authentic.

EXTERNAL ISSUES

Is there evidence external to its claims that either corroborates or contradicts those claims? Do the things that it says fit with facts that have come to light since its publication? Are there any anachronisms that its original readers may have missed but that are now obvious?

External issues are where the arguments start, most of which we have already covered. Here is a quick recap of the main points of support for each side, starting with the arguments of the believers:

It has passed modern computer tests.

The writings attributed to the different authors were, in fact, written by different people, and Joseph Smith was not one of them.

The cited examples of chiasmus did not appear in the book by chance. Although some Americans may have known about chiasmus in 1830, it is clear that Joseph Smith did not, because he never used it in any of his other writings, and he did not call attention to its presence in the Book of Mormon when it would have been to his advantage to do so.

It contains too many items of currently checkable information that no forger could have known in 1830, including the following:

Accurate geographical information about the route and conditions of Lehi's travels in the desert.

Confirmation of the ancient practice of writing on metal plates and burying them in the ground in stone boxes for later people to find.

Egyptian roots for strange names.

Accurate descriptions of Middle Eastern olive farming, poetry, and warfare.

An authentic description of very ancient history in its description of the Jaredites.

There is no logical explanation other than the one Joseph Smith gave about where the book came from.

The critics say the book fails the external tests for the following reasons:

There is no evidence of an ancient Israelite presence in Central or South America.

Modern DNA analysis says that pre-Columbian Indians all came from Asia, not the Middle East.

Although some believers insist that Book of Mormon sites have been found in pre-Columbian America, no nonbelieving archaeologist agrees with them.

There are no signs of Hebrew influence in any of the religious rites of the pre-Columbian tribes.

There are no traces of Old World linguistics in any of the languages of the American aboriginal tribes.

Even with new discoveries, the book still has anachronisms.

It quotes from Deutero-Isaiah and Paul, both of whom lived after Lehi had supposedly left Jerusalem.

Among other things, American Indians didn't have horses before the Spaniards came.

The book is full of topics that were current in Joseph Smith's neighborhood at the time it was written.

These topics include Freemasonry, money digging for treasure, magic stones, Indians as the lost ten tribes, prejudiced racial attitudes, etc.

The stories that it tells are simply too fantastic to credit.

As the arguments flow back and forth over the items on these two lists, believers insist that they have answers to most, if not all, of the critics' complaints:

No record of horses in archaeological digs in pre-Columbian America? It is known that the Huns rode horses when they swept westward across Europe, but no horses' bones have been found in the areas they covered. Does that mean that we must disregard the written accounts of Attila?

No pre-Columbian record that mentions the Lamanites? There are no Egyptian records that mention the Israelites. Does that mean we must disregard the written accounts of Moses?

DNA studies that show the American Indians came from Asia? Nibley was pointing out that the Book of Mormon called for an Asiatic element in the Indians' ancestry decades before DNA was even discovered.

Deutero-Isaiah? A theory only, and one with which some scholars disagree.

No signs of religious or linguistic similarities? Some scholars disagree, and new evidence continues to appear.

The critics do not have an equal number of responses to the claims on the believers' list primarily because they haven't thought that they needed them. They considered the matter closed, with Fawn Brodie delivering the final judgment more than half a century ago. Some of them are beginning to realize that their failure to engage on these issues means that the intellectual high ground that they once held has been slipping away.

Mormon authors are pleased to quote the words of two Protestant scholars, Carl Mosser and Paul Owen, who wrote a paper for their colleagues on the subject of Mormon scholarship and said:

> Currently there are, as far as we are aware, no books from an evangelical perspective that responsibly interact with contemporary LDS scholarly and apologetic writings. In a survey of twenty recent evangelical books criticizing Mormonism reveals that none interact with this growing body of literature. Only a handful demonstrate any awareness of pertinent works. Many of the authors promote criticisms that have long been refuted. . . . A number of these books claim to be "the definitive" book on the matter. That they make no attempt to interact with contemporary LDS scholarship is a stain upon the authors' integrity and causes one to wonder about their credibility. . . .
>
> At the academic level evangelicals are losing the debate with the Mormons. . . . In recent years the sophistication and erudition of LDS apologetics has risen considerably while evangelical responses have not.[1]

That was written in 1996. Things have not changed much since then.

Back to the two lists of competing external claims. Have there been any changes regarding them over the years?

Yes, and the changes have been in favor of the believers. Picture a ledger sheet with the arguments of believers on the right side and of the critics on the left. Label it 1830.

In 1830, all the external evidence was on the left side of the ledger, in favor of the critics. Writing on metal plates? Ridiculous; an obvious invention. Large cities in America, inhabited by the ancestors of the Indians? Nonsense; the Indians are nomadic tribesmen who live in tents. Inspired prophets? Boring prophets is more like it, babbling on about endless wars, with preposterous names that are obvious inventions, and long quotations—containing errors—of various sections of the Bible, particularly the book of Isaiah. All supposed to have been written in "reformed Egyptian"—whatever that is—and given by an angel to an untrustworthy farm boy, known for telling tall tales about seer stones. Ridiculous on its face.

Charles Dickens dismissed the book with a single phrase: "Seeing angels in an age of railways."[2]

Believers had little to say in response in 1830. There were the written statements of the three who claimed to have seen and spoken with Moroni, along with the eight others who said that Joseph showed them the plates. There was also the "untutored farm boy" argument, linked to the sixty-five-day time frame for the book's production. Mainly, however, believers were left with their personal spiritual experiences, which they said they received from God, as the only evidence that the book was "true."

In the decades following Joseph Smith's death, these arguments were easily answered. The witnesses' statements were dismissed as either signs of complicity in the conspiracy or demonstrations of gullibility on the part of the unsophisticated rustics who made up the bulk of the Church, and the Spaulding-Rigdon theory, first propounded in 1834, took care of the "untutored farm boy" question.

The ledger didn't change much for more than a century. B. H. Roberts tried to find additional things to put on the believer's side of it, but he couldn't. He was troubled enough by what he saw—although he remained a believer—that the Church did not publish his paper, fearing, probably correctly, that it would hurt rather than help its case. Although Spaulding-Rigdon had lost its punch, the list of complaints by the critics was still pretty much intact and unchallenged in 1930. Critics believed that careful analysis was not necessary, and they relaxed.

They should not have done so. Think of the same ledger sheet, labeled 2009.

Metal plates with sacred writing on them, hidden in the ground for later generations to find? Joseph was right on that one; move it from the left side of the ledger to the right, as a mark in the book's favor. Big cities among the Indians? Whether they were Nephite cities or not, there were clearly big cities with large populations in Meso-America before Columbus. Writing in Reformed Egyptian? Absolutely—look at all the Egyptian names that show an authentic tie to the Egyptian language.

Add to those items the others we have covered in the previous chapters that have come to light in just the last half century, and it is clear that the passage of time has put a good many new items on the right side of the ledger (in favor of the book) and removed some of the old ones on the left (against it).

Such a trend is significant, because truth *is* the daughter of time. With most forgeries, the farther you get from its date of production, the clumsier it looks. In the case of the Book of Mormon, the farther we get from the date of its production, the better it looks.

So, the internal analysis says it is genuine, but the external analysis is still in some dispute. Can any conclusion about the Story as a whole be drawn without taking a large leap of faith, either way?

Yes. I believe we can conclude beyond a reasonable doubt that Joseph Smith did not produce the Book of Mormon without outside help.

Add it all up:

If it is a forgery based on its author's talent for fictional narrative, it is clear that Joseph showed no such talent in any of his other writings, none of which resemble it.

If it is a forgery based on its author's editing and organizational skills, it is clear that Joseph did not have such skills.

If it is a forgery based on its author's knowledge of the geography, cultures, poetry, language, and military practices of the ancient world, it is clear that Joseph possessed no such knowledge.

If it is a forgery based on its author's motive to deceive the gullible, it is clear that Joseph was unable to produce more of the same kind of writing when he had every motive to do so.

Internal or external, the evidence is overwhelming: Joseph didn't do it by himself.

As noted in Chapter 4, all those who knew Joseph personally, whether friends or foes, came to the same conclusion. They were sure he could not have produced the book without help. They saw the book as an editor of the *Western Banner* did, in May of 1839: "evidently the production of a cultivated mind, yet found in the hands of an exceedingly ignorant illiterate person."[3]

When historical review comes to the same conclusion held by contemporary sources, that is usually a good indication that the conclusion is true.

All right, if Joseph Smith didn't do it by himself, where did his help come from? We are left with just two possibilities—Third Party or God. Since neither one is available for questioning, we have to come up with our own explanations about why either one might have been interested in assisting in the project, which brings us to motive.

MOTIVE

Is there a reason why someone would want to fake this? What would he gain?

Looking for motive is usually a fairly straightforward line of inquiry, but when we are trying to discover the motive of a hidden collaborator who is either divine or dead, things are more complicated. In the case of the Book of Mormon, however, things are a little easier because motive is tied to the final, unique test: relevance.

RELEVANCE

Is there a need, in contemporary times, for its message? Is there unique enlightenment here, for a modern person, that could not have come from some other source? Does this message truly qualify as something that God would want our age to understand?

As far as the Story alone is concerned, the answer to the questions of relevance is "probably not."

That does not mean that the Story is not impressive. On the contrary, as we have seen, it has passed some very tough internal and external tests. If we are going deal honestly with this final test, however, we must admit that the historical narrative, standing by itself, has little modern relevance. No matter how interesting it is to scholars and critics who argue about the topics we've covered, no one really needs to know about the doings of Jaredite kings, or chiasmus, or the details of olive farming, or the location of Nahom, or the source of Egyptian names in order to live a more fulfilling and productive life in the twenty-first century.

When it comes to relevance, the plot, standing alone, is very thin. Other than its affirmation about the divinity of Jesus, it does not have all that much to say to us today.

That means that it's time to listen to the music.

THE DOCTRINE

DOCTRINAL OVERVIEW

DOCTRINAL ANALYSIS DOMINATED early discussion about the Book of Mormon. The critics considered its Story nothing but a silly romance, unworthy of their attention, and concentrated all their fire on the doctrinal side. The book's foremost contemporary religious critic was Alexander Campbell, who had good reason to be upset about it.

Campbell was the son of the founder of Disciples of Christ, then a growing frontier church that turned to the Bible for its doctrine. Campbellite ministers, as its preachers were popularly called, used to stop children in the streets and ask them to hold up five fingers to learn the essential elements of Christ's gospel.[1] They would talk the children through a description of what each finger represented, in the following order:

Faith in Jesus Christ
Repentance
Baptism
Remission of sins
The gift of the Holy Ghost

The children who successfully memorized the list were told to go home, recite it to their parents, and then tell them about the meeting where the ministers would preach.

Anyone familiar with the teachings of Joseph Smith will see similarities with the five-finger recital; indeed, it is almost word for word the same as a statement of the "first principles and ordinances" laid out by Joseph Smith in what have been canonized as the Articles of Faith of The Church of Jesus Christ of Latter-day Saints.

The name of Sidney Rigdon resurfaces here. He was a Campbellite minister with a fairly large following centered near Kirtland, Ohio, a town not far from Cleveland. When Rigdon embraced the Book of Mormon and joined Joseph's church, he took most of his congregation with him, and Kirtland became the Mormons' headquarters. Furious, Campbell considered Joseph not only an imposter but a thief, one who had made off with preacher, converts, and doctrine that were not properly his. (He seems not to have considered that since Joseph read the same Bible he did, he could have discovered the same five points on his own.)

Campbell's primary attack was the standard one regarding a suspected forgery—he said it contained nothing new. He saw it firmly rooted in the religious discussion of Joseph's time and locale. He wrote:

> This prophet Smith, through his stone spectacles, wrote on the plates of Nephi, in his Book of Mormon, every error and almost every truth discussed in New York for the last ten years. He decides all the great controversies:—infant baptism, ordination, the trinity, regeneration,

repentance, justification, the fall of man, the atonement, transubstantiation, fasting, penance, church government, religious experience, the call to the ministry, the general resurrection, eternal punishment, who may baptize, and even the question of free masonry, republican government, and the rights of man. . . . But he is better skilled in the controversies in New York than in the geography or history of Judea. He makes John baptize in the village of Bethabara, and says Jesus was born in Jerusalem.[2]

Campbell's comment about the book's failure to describe Middle Eastern geography accurately is amusing now, given the external evidence we have examined in the previous chapters, and his two specific complaints—Bethabara as the place of Jesus' baptism and Jerusalem as the place of his birth—are easily answered.

Bethabara means "house of the ford," indicating that it was located at a place where people routinely forded, or crossed, the River Jordan. That is a likely spot for baptisms, and there is nothing in the Bible to rule it out.

Regarding Jerusalem as the birthplace of Jesus, Campbell missed a seemingly minor but important point. The Book of Mormon routinely uses place names to designate both cities and lands. Early critics said that the book's mention of the "*land* of Jerusalem" (see, for instance, 1 Nephi 7:2) demonstrated Joseph's ignorance, but the book is consistent in this use of place names. Zarahemla, for example, appears as the name of both a city and a land, as do other Nephite place names.

Nibley cites sources that confirm this particular double usage as standard in Lehi's time. Instead of showing that Joseph knew nothing about Middle Eastern geography and language,

Campbell's comments show that he was the one who was un-informed. Bethlehem is clearly in the "land"—the outer environs—of Jerusalem. Joseph's use of the term is consistent with the language of the time in which the book was suppos-edly written.

Campbell's criticisms of the book's doctrine are not so eas-ily dismissed. No one knew the religious issues under discus-sion in the 1820s better than he. The fact that so many of those issues are in the book is consistent with forgery and therefore a legitimate red flag. By claiming that its message was not signifi-cantly different from other teachings of the time, Campbell cut squarely to the issue of relevance. If the work had nothing new to say, why would God have gone to such lengths to pro-duce it?

At the front of every copy of the Book of Mormon is a statement attributed to Moroni that offers an answer to this question. Titled "An Account Written by the Hand of Mormon," it gives a summary of what the book is and to whom it is addressed—"the Lamanites, who are a remnant of the house of Israel; and also to Jew and Gentile." As I read it, it says that the book was produced for three reasons (brackets added by me; capitals in the original):

> **[One]** to show unto the remnant of the House of Israel what great things the Lord hath done for their fathers; **[Two]** that they may know the covenants of the Lord, that they are not cast off forever—**[Three]** to the convincing of the Jew and Gentile that JESUS is the CHRIST, the ETERNAL GOD, manifesting himself unto all nations.

I separated story and doctrine to make the book easier to follow, but Moroni's summary makes it clear that they are inextricably entwined. The Story has told us "what great things the Lord hath done"; the prophets we have met all testified "that Jesus is the Christ, the Eternal God"; and the doctrine we will review in this section emphasizes "the covenants of the Lord" that were made. They fit together.

Nonetheless, I think Moroni's summary falls a bit short. Considering the book in our time, not Joseph Smith's, I see a message in it that God would want our society to hear but that neither Mormon nor Moroni would have thought of emphasizing. Mentioning it, for them, would have been like recording the daily rising of the sun. Here it is:

God exists and is in charge.

This message suggests that God's motive in aiding Joseph in bringing the book forward was to convince people in "an age of railways" that His existence is not an ancient superstition but a vital contemporary fact.

Alexander Campbell and other critics of his time would have said something like this: It is presumptuous; indeed, it is arrogant for Joseph Smith to pretend to instruct us on such an obvious truth. The Bible has made it clear that God exists and is in charge. Nothing needs to be added to it.

And, in 1830, that was indeed the prevailing public sentiment with regard to the Bible. The Book of Mormon spoke to it directly, in words that critics consider an example of Joseph Smith's blatant cheekiness. Defending God's right to say as many words as he chooses to, Nephi quotes the Lord as saying:

My words shall hiss forth unto the ends of the earth, for a standard unto my people, which are of the house of Israel;

And because my words shall hiss forth—many of the Gentiles shall say: A Bible! A Bible! We have got a Bible, and there cannot be any more Bible. . . .

. . . Know ye not that I, the Lord your God, have created all men . . . ; and that I rule in the heavens above and in the earth beneath; and I bring forth my word unto the children of men, yea, even upon all the nations of the earth?

Wherefore murmur ye, because that ye shall receive more of my word? Know ye not that the testimony of two nations is a witness unto you that I am God, that I remember one nation like unto another? Wherefore, I speak the same words unto one nation like unto another. And when the two nations shall run together the testimony of the two nations shall run together also.

And I do this that I may prove unto many that I am the same yesterday, today, and forever; and that I speak forth my words according to mine own pleasure. And because that I have spoken one word ye need not suppose that I cannot speak another; for my work is not yet finished; neither shall it be until the end of man, neither from that time henceforth and forever.

Wherefore, because that ye have a Bible ye need not suppose that it contains all my words; neither need ye suppose that I have not caused more to be written. (2 Nephi 29:2–10)

Bold words, and Joseph was ridiculed for them. In frontier America in 1830, the Bible was indeed accepted as being everything the world needed.

Today, however, things are different. The validity of the Bible is under attack from many directions. Archaeologists say they cannot validate the Moses story; they find no evidence that the children of Israel were ever in Egypt. Some challenge the historical existence of Jesus and argue about the true authorship of the Gospels. Even many Christian scholars say that the stories of Jesus' miracles and his resurrection are fables and embellishments that grew up after his death; they say he was a great moral teacher, whose ideas were transcendent above all others, but that he had no divine powers.

Garry Wills, in his book *What Jesus Meant,* reports on a team of scholars that calls itself "the Jesus Seminar" and prints a Bible that works from the "assumption that anything odd or dangerous or supernatural is prima facie suspect. That disqualifies the Resurrection from the outset. The Seminar's founder, Robert Funk, agreed with Jefferson that Jesus was 'a secular sage,' and the team trims the gospels even more thoroughly than Jefferson did. . . . Overall the Seminar retains fewer than a fifth of the gospel acts of Jesus and fewer than a fifth of his words."[3]

Wills calls this "the new fundamentalism. It believes in the literal sense of the Bible—it just reduces the Bible to what it can take as literal quotation from Jesus. Though some people have called the Jesus Seminarists radical, they are actually very conservative. They tame the real radical, Jesus, cutting him down to their own size. Robert Funk called Jesus 'the first Jewish stand-up comic'—which is not as far as it might at first glance seem from Jefferson's view of him as the last sit-down Stoic sage."[4]

In short, in many circles in our time, the Bible isn't The Bible any more. In our increasingly skeptical world, if it is true scripture, it could use some defenders.

And Mormon comes to its defense, during his farewell. The relevant passage:

> And now, behold, I would speak somewhat unto the remnant of this people who are spared, if it so be that God may give unto them my words, that they may know of the things of their fathers; yea, I speak unto you, ye remnant of the house of Israel . . .
>
> Know ye that ye must come to the knowledge of your fathers, and repent of all your sins and iniquities, and believe in Jesus Christ, that he is the Son of God. . . .
>
> Therefore repent, and be baptized in the name of Jesus, and lay hold upon the gospel of Christ, which shall be set before you, not only in this record but also in the record which shall come unto the Gentiles from the Jews, which record shall come from the Gentiles unto you.
>
> For behold, this [the Book of Mormon] is written for the intent that ye may believe that [the Bible]; and if ye believe that ye will believe this also; and if ye believe this ye will know concerning your fathers, and also the marvelous works which were wrought by the power of God among them. (Mormon 7:1–9)

So, in Mormon's last message to those who will receive his book in later centuries, he says that it was "written for the intent" that they should accept the Bible as well.

That means the first Nephi accurately predicted how the Book of Mormon would be received as an affront to the Bible in the age of Alexander Campbell, and Mormon accurately predicted how it would furnish support for the Bible in the age of Sigmund Freud. Not bad.

Of course, it is not just the Bible that is under attack; it is the very idea of the existence of God. Since the coming of Darwin and Freud and their successors and the rise of the secular disciplines in academe, the number of influential voices claiming that God is a myth has grown to a loud chorus with many followers.

Go to Europe, throughout the countries that make up what the historians call Christendom. Polls in some of them show that the proportion of the population that believes in God has fallen to single digits. As my wife and I have traveled there, we have seen the many cathedrals that have no religious function because nobody comes to worship in them anymore; they have been turned into concert halls. Karen Armstrong, the author quoted in Chapter 3, told me that in intellectual circles in Europe today, a person who claims to have deep religious faith of any kind is viewed with "disdain."

It is somewhat different in America, where a larger proportion of the general populace still believes in God, but among the intellectual elite here there is also widespread skepticism about his existence. The issue is current and controversial enough that Dr. Armand M. Nicholi Jr., a psychiatrist, has been teaching a class on it at Harvard for the last thirty years. In 2002, he published a book titled *The Question of God.*

In it, as in his classes, he stages a "debate" between Freud, the most celebrated of modern atheists, and C. S. Lewis, the most widely published and best-read modern defender of Christian faith. Although the two never met, their writings address the same issues often enough that the confrontation in print comes across as if they had indeed spent time together on the podium, probing and disagreeing with each other.

Nicholi points out that Freud and Lewis held directly opposite world views, between which there is no middle ground. He notes that both views "have existed since the beginning of recorded history—the spiritual worldview, rooted primarily in ancient Israel, with its emphasis on moral truth and right conduct and its motto of Thus saith the Lord; and the materialist or 'scientific' worldview, rooted in ancient Greece, with its emphasis on reason and acquisition of knowledge and its motto What Says Nature?"[5]

He says: "We will examine several of the basic issues of life in terms of these two conflicting views. We will look at both views as objectively and dispassionately as possible and let the arguments speak for themselves."[6]

Nicholi adds, however: "I am aware that no one—including the author—is neutral on such emotionally charged issues. None of us can tolerate the notion that our worldview may be based on a false premise and, thus, our whole life headed in the wrong direction."[7]

In short, the argument about the existence of God is serious stuff—and the Book of Mormon has serious things to say about it. It is extraordinary that a book published in 1830 would address such a current topic.

I will not follow Alexander Campbell into his list of religious issues and argue about each one, because the items he lists are not externally checkable questions, as is the location of Nahom or the existence of metal plates in the ancient world. I will concede Campbell's point that these topics were current in

Joseph's time, but, once again, that is not the point. Are they current now?

The fact that I think they are is also not the point. Readers will have to determine for themselves whether or not the book's doctrinal statements are relevant to their own lives. In the following chapters I will present what I consider to be the most basic of those statements. Because I cannot analyze every doctrinal comment the book contains—there are far too many of them for that—I will focus on the issues that I think are the most relevant to a twenty-first-century audience.

I expect grumbling from believers who read these chapters because they will complain that I have left out their favorite passages. My only defense is that we are looking for just enough of an understanding of the doctrine in the Book of Mormon to determine, if we can, if it has something to say to us now. I will include some fairly long portions of a few of the more pertinent sermons, so readers who wish to do so can experience their flavor, but those who want to capture its complete doctrinal sweep should turn to the book itself.

At the start, however, there is one particular doctrinal concept I want to highlight. It comes from Moroni. As he was writing the book's final good-bye and speaking directly to those whom he assumed would read his words in later centuries, he made the statement which is the most quoted passage in the book:

> Behold, I would exhort you that when ye shall read
> these things, if it be wisdom in God that ye should read
> them, that ye would remember how merciful the Lord
> hath been unto the children of men, from the creation of

Adam even down until the time that ye shall receive these things, and ponder it in your hearts.

And when ye shall receive these things, I would exhort you that ye would ask God, the Eternal Father, in the name of Christ, if these things are not true; and if ye shall ask with a sincere heart, with real intent, having faith in Christ, he will manifest the truth of it unto you, by the power of the Holy Ghost.

And by the power of the Holy Ghost ye may know the truth of all things. (Moroni 10:3–5)

The promise that God will validate the authenticity of the book to anyone willing to pray about it "with a sincere heart, with real intent, having faith in Christ," is a serious doctrinal statement all by itself. It says that God not only exists but that he will respond to any individual who humbly and prayerfully seeks confirmation of that fact.

Is this an insertion by a clever forger, written to catch the gullible by preying on their credulity?

Or a sincere promise from God, set forth to convince his children that he actually exists?

That is for readers to decide for themselves, as we turn to the doctrinal particulars.

AGENCY AND FAITH

Lᴇᴛ's sᴛᴀʀᴛ ᴏᴜʀ ᴅᴏᴄᴛʀɪɴᴀʟ ʀᴇᴠɪᴇᴡ with one of the most de-
bated of current questions: How responsible for our actions are
we really? What forces control our lives?

In Joseph Smith's day, the Calvinist doctrine of predestination was still strong. It had been taught by the Scottish minister
John Knox, considered the father of Presbyterianism, and
Jonathan Edwards, the early American Puritan preacher who
said that those who were saved were chosen for heaven entirely
as a result of God's whim, regardless of what they did in their
lives.

To illustrate how firmly deterministic that doctrine was, the
story is told that John Knox caught a man stealing one of his
sheep and started to beat him for it.

"Don't beat me, Reverend Knox," the man pleaded, "I was
predestined to steal this sheep!"

"You're right," said Knox, as he continued his blows, "just
as I was predestined to beat you for it."

The doctrine of predestination is not completely dead, even
now. It shows up in various forms. Several decades ago I was on

an airplane reading *Passages,* a popular best-seller written by Gail Sheehy. In it she sets forth the deterministic idea that all of us go through predictable phases in our lives, unavoidable "passages" in which we think we are freely making decisions but where our actions are actually based on where we are in the life cycle.

As a predicate for this proposition, she cites the familiar childhood phase called the "terrible twos," which comes when children first learn to say no. She says there is no reason to assume that the progression—passage—from phase to phase we see in children will stop just because we become adults. For example, after looking around her own circle of acquaintances and noting that most of them were divorced, and then reading a study about how long marriages typically last, she says that the "seven-year itch" of literature, referring to the time it takes for married people to tire of their mates, is an actual phenomenon validated by scientific research. I doubt that her research protocol would stand up under rigorous scientific tests for methodology, but that is beside the point. She embraces a form of "predestination" that says divorce is inevitable, although she certainly does not suggest that the predestination comes from God.

A flight attendant saw me reading *Passages* on the airplane and said she was reading it as well. "I can't wait to find out what is going to happen to me next," she said with some seriousness. She had bought the idea that her life's pattern was not hers to control.

Sigmund Freud did not use determinist language as strong as that employed by John Knox—he was willing to admit that we do make choices—but he too insisted that we are not free agents. He said that our actions and thoughts are the results of involuntary childhood experiences, including the desire to believe in something or someone greater than ourselves. Freud insisted that those who believe in God simply turn their childhood attachments to their fathers into religious faith. He thought they were not very bright.

Freud's theories have been vigorously challenged, but the notion that we are not fully responsible for our actions remains strong. Those who have done studies into the physical structure of the brain and its response to various stimuli offer their own version of determinism. We have seen the emergence of the phrase "It's in your DNA," indicating that what we do is "hardwired" into our genes by countless generations of evolutionary processes.

I do not denigrate the importance of research into brain structure and genetic predispositions. We have discovered much about serious and specific mental conditions, such as bipolar status and genetic sources of learning disabilities, conditions that clearly affect, if not severely limit, the decision-making prowess of those who have them, driving some into depression and sometimes even suicide. But do our genes make robots of us all?

As the Nicholi book points out, C. S. Lewis said no on religious grounds. Lewis wrote:

> "God created things which had free will. That means creatures which can go either wrong or right. Some people think they can imagine a creature which was free but had no possibility of going wrong; I cannot. If a thing is free to be good it is also free to be bad. And free will is what

has made evil possible. The more intelligent and more gifted the person God creates, the greater the capacity to love and to be a positive force in the universe, but also, if that person rebels, the greater capacity to cause evil, to inflict pain and to cause unhappiness. Our remote ancestors rebelled and used their free will to transgress the moral law . . . and to become their own masters . . . to invent some sort of happiness for themselves, apart from God."[1]

"Free will is what has made evil possible." That twentieth-century statement by Lewis is worth discussing, because one of the main modern arguments against the existence of God is the fact that there is evil in the world.

That argument goes like this: If there is a God, and he created the world, that means he created evil, because the world contains evil. So, God cannot be good, which means that he cannot be God, which means that he cannot be, period.

I will deal with the question of evil in the world in the next chapter. For now, let's see what the prophets quoted in the nineteenth-century Book of Mormon had to say on the subject of free will, or as Joseph Smith called it, free agency.[2] I start with Lehi.

LEHI'S VISION OF THE TREE OF LIFE

After his sons returned from Jerusalem with the brass plates of Laban, Lehi told them he had "dreamed a dream; or, in other words, I have seen a vision" (1 Nephi 8:2).

It began with Lehi in "a dark and dreary wilderness," where he was met by a man in a white robe, whom he followed into "a dark and dreary waste." He traveled "for the space of many hours in darkness" and then prayed for mercy, after which he saw "a large and spacious field," in which there was a tree "whose fruit was desirable to make one happy" (1 Nephi 8:4, 7–10).

He ate the fruit. "It was most sweet, above all that I ever before tasted. Yea, and I beheld that the fruit thereof was white, to exceed all the whiteness that I had ever seen. And as I partook of the fruit thereof it filled my soul with exceedingly great joy; wherefore, I began to be desirous that my family should partake of it also" (1 Nephi 8:11–12).

As he looked for his family, he saw a river, running near the tree. At the head of the river he saw his wife, Sariah, with Sam and Nephi, standing as if they were in doubt about which way to go. He beckoned and called to them to join him "and partake of the fruit also" (1 Nephi 8:16), which they did. Then he saw Laman and Lemuel as well, but they refused to come to the tree.

He saw "a rod of iron [which] extended along the bank of the river, and led to the tree by which I stood. . . . A strait and narrow path [ran alongside] the rod of iron," and it led not only to the tree but also to "the head of the fountain, unto a large and spacious field, as if it had been a world" (1 Nephi 8:19–20).

There were "numberless concourses of people, many of whom were pressing forward, that they might obtain the path which led unto the tree." As they got on the path, they were overshadowed by "an exceedingly great mist of darkness, insomuch that they who had commenced in the path did lose their way, that they wandered off and were lost." However, those who pressed forward while holding firmly to the iron rod were able to pass safely through the "mist of darkness" and get to the tree and eat its fruit (1 Nephi 8:21, 23–24).

Some of these people began to "cast their eyes about as if they were ashamed." He saw, on the other side of the river, "a great and spacious building; and it stood as it were in the air, high above the earth. And it was filled with people, both old and young, both male and female; and their manner of dress was exceedingly fine; and they were in the attitude of mocking and pointing their fingers towards those who had come at and were partaking of the fruit" (1 Nephi 8:25–27).

As a result of this taunting, some who "had tasted of the fruit . . . were ashamed . . . ; and they fell away into forbidden paths and were lost" (1 Nephi 8:28).

Lehi saw others come forward to partake of the fruit, holding the rod of iron, while still others were "feeling their way towards that great and spacious building." Many of those in the latter group "were drowned in the depths of the fountain; and many were lost from his view, wandering in strange roads." Those who made it to the "great and spacious building" mocked those who were at the tree, eating the fruit, but Lehi said "we heeded them not" (1 Nephi 8:31–33). Lehi said the dream made him fearful for Laman and Lemuel, because they refused to come to the tree.

Nephi wanted to understand what all these things meant, and "believing that the Lord was able to make them known unto me, as I sat pondering in mine heart I was caught away in the Spirit of the Lord." He found himself on "an exceedingly high mountain" (1 Nephi 11:1).

Asked by the Spirit what he wanted, he replied, "To behold the things which my father saw" (1 Nephi 11:3). He was given his own vision, which corresponded to Lehi's but included a number of other prophetic views.

When Laman and Lemuel questioned Nephi about Lehi's dream, he gave them the interpretations of its elements. The tree was the tree of life, he said, and represented "the love of God, which sheddeth itself abroad in the hearts of the children of men; wherefore, it is the most desirable above all things. . . . Yea, and the most joyous to the soul. . . . The great and spacious building was the pride of the world" (1 Nephi 11:22–23, 36), the "vain imaginations" (1 Nephi 12:18) of those who embrace the ways of the world.

The "rod of iron" was "the word of God; and whoso would hearken unto the word of God, and . . . hold fast unto it . . . would never perish" (1 Nephi 15:23–24). The "mists of darkness" which caused people to let go of the rod and lose their way were "the temptations of the devil, which blindeth the eyes, and hardeneth the hearts of the children of men" (1 Nephi 12:17). The river, into which the people who let go of the rod fell and were lost, was filthiness, "an awful gulf, which separated the wicked from the tree of life, and also from the saints of God. . . . It was a representation of that awful hell, which the angel said unto me was prepared for the wicked" (1 Nephi 15:28–29).

COMMENTARY

Before analyzing the contents of the dream for doctrine, we must take a detour, because Fawn Brodie considers Lehi's dream a clear proof of forgery. She notes that it corresponds closely to a dream that Joseph Smith Sr. had, which Lucy Smith, Joseph's mother, records in her history. Brodie lays out the similarities:

Lehi: . . . me thought I saw a dark and dreary wilderness. . . .

Joseph Sr.: I thought I was thus traveling in an open and desolate field, which appeared very barren. . . .

Lehi: I beheld a tree, whose fruit was desirable, to make one happy . . . most sweet, above all that I ever had before tasted. . . .

Joseph Sr.: . . . a tree, such as I had never seen before. . . . I found it delicious beyond description.

Lehi: I began to be desirous that my family should partake of it also. . . .

Joseph Sr.: As I was eating, I said in my heart, "I cannot eat this alone, I must bring my wife and children." . . .

Lehi: And I beheld a rod of iron; and it extended along the bank of the river, and led to the tree. . . .

Joseph Sr.: I beheld a beautiful stream of water, which ran from the east to the west. . . . I could see a rope running along the bank of it. . . .

Lehi: . . . a great and spacious building . . . filled with people, both old and young, both male and female; and their manner of dress was exceeding fine, and they were in the attitude of mocking and pointing their fingers towards those which had come at, and were partaking of the fruit.

Joseph Sr.: I beheld a spacious building . . . filled with people, who were very finely dressed. When these people observed us in the low valley, under the tree, they pointed the finger of scorn at us.[3]

Brodie drew the obvious conclusion that Lehi's vision of the tree of life is simply a repetition of a dream that Joseph Smith's father had.

The timing is right, for a forgery, because Joseph Smith Sr.'s dream came before the publication of the Book of Mormon. It impressed him enough that he told his family about it. It is entirely logical that Joseph Jr. was so taken by it that he decided to put it in his book.

Also, because Nephi is the one who fully understood its meaning and explained it to his brothers, those who seek to psychoanalyze Joseph insist that they have found another autobiographical touch—the father had the dream, but it was the son who was spiritually capable of telling the world what it meant.

All of which points strongly to forgery. Is there any other logical alternative?

Only if you accept Joseph's claim of divine assistance.

If God really was involved in the book's creation and had a purpose for its emergence, it would suit his purposes to be sure that Joseph had the support of his own family. What better way to ensure that support than to show Lehi's dream to the head of that family, so that he would recognize it as genuine when his son came forward with a scriptural account of it?

Almost two centuries after the events took place, we cannot be sure beyond reasonable doubt why either Joseph—father or son—did anything. Nonetheless, rejecting Brodie's list of similarities requires another leap of faith.

Now, back to the question: What does the dream say, in doctrinal terms?

In his conversation with his brothers, Nephi makes it clear

that the central figure in God's plan is "the Lamb of God . . . the Son of the everlasting God," who "was lifted up upon the cross and slain for the sins of the world" (1 Nephi 11:32–33). Everything comes from faith in him.

The dream says the blessings that flow from the love of God are beyond anything we can imagine and are available to anyone who wants them enough to seek them. But God will not force them on us. We are free to reject them if we choose, which is why Satan does everything he can to blind us with "mists of darkness" so that we will lose our way.

Successful navigation through the wilderness of the contemporary world to God's love—the tree of life—therefore requires daily obedience to "the word of God," be it ancient scripture or contemporary inspiration, so that the "vain imaginations" and "pride of the world" will not be able to make us drift away.

Also, choosing to follow the correct path is not a one-time decision. Lehi's dream would have us reject the notion of "once saved, always saved." Remember the dream's depiction of those who, after coming to the tree of life, responded to the taunts and ridicule of others and left the tree to join the scoffers. As they did so, they were carried away in the torrent and became contaminated by the filth of the river in which they were caught. They were therefore unable to enter the kingdom of God, where no unclean thing is permitted, even though they had gone to the tree at one time in their lives.

The doctrine taught in Lehi's dream also opposes the notion that our power to choose between good and evil is unduly circumscribed by God, our childhoods, or our genes. These forces are present and powerful in our lives, but they are not ultimately determinative. There are those in contemporary society who agree; an avuncular Dumbledore told an anxious Harry Potter, worried about who he was by lineage, that it is the choices you make, not your abilities, that determine what kind of person you are.

Lehi's dream and the doctrine of agency show up again and again in the Book of Mormon. When Alma the Younger was preaching to some poor people who were forbidden to enter the synagogues because they were not considered good enough to mingle with the more fortunate, he incorporated the image of the tree of life in a sermon on the importance of seeking faith. It is one of the longer sermons in the book, so I have shortened it a bit, but I have tried to preserve the full sweep of the doctrinal statement as well as the flavor of Alma's distinctive preaching style. He uses rhetorical questions as a teaching device more often than any other Book of Mormon prophet.

Those interested in the issue of "different voices" will want to compare this sermon with the samples from Joseph Smith, Lehi, and Jacob, which have been put forward in earlier chapters.

ALMA'S SERMON TO THE ZORAMITES

Behold thy brother hath said, What shall we do?—for we are cast out of our synagogues, that we cannot worship our God.

Behold I say unto you, do ye suppose that ye cannot worship God save it be in your synagogues only?

. . . Do ye suppose that ye must not worship God only once in a week?

I say unto you, it is well that ye are cast out of your

synagogues, that ye may be humble, and that ye may learn wisdom; . . . that ye are brought to a lowliness of heart; for ye are necessarily brought to be humble.

And now, because ye are compelled to be humble blessed are ye; for a man sometimes, if he is compelled to be humble, seeketh repentance; and now surely, whoso-ever repenteth shall find mercy; and he that findeth mercy and endureth to the end the same shall be saved.

. . . Do ye not suppose that they are more blessed who truly humble themselves because of the word?

Yea, he that truly humbleth himself, and repenteth of his sins, and endureth to the end, the same shall be blessed—yea, much more blessed than they who are com-pelled to be humble because of their exceeding poverty. . . .

. . . There are many who do say: If thou wilt show unto us a sign from heaven, then we shall know of a surety; then we shall believe.

Now I ask, is this faith? Behold, I say unto you, Nay; for if a man knoweth a thing he hath no cause to believe, for he knoweth it. . . .

. . . Faith is not to have a perfect knowledge of things; therefore, if ye have faith ye hope for things which are not seen, which are true.

. . . I would that ye should remember, that God is merciful unto all who believe on his name; therefore he desireth, in the first place, that ye should believe . . . on his word.

And now, he imparteth his word by angels unto men, yea, not only men but women also. Now this is not all; little children do have words given unto them many times, which confound the wise and the learned. . . .

But behold, if ye will awake and arouse your faculties, even to an experiment upon my words, and exercise a particle of faith, yea, even if ye can no more than desire to believe, let this desire work in you, even until ye believe in a manner that ye can give place for a portion of my words.

Now, we will compare the word unto a seed. Now, if ye give place, that a seed may be planted in your heart, behold, if it be a true seed, or a good seed, if ye do not cast it out by your unbelief, that ye will resist the Spirit of the Lord, behold, it will begin to swell within your breasts; and when you feel these swelling motions, ye will begin to say within yourselves—It must needs be that this is a good seed, or that the word is good, for it beginneth to enlarge my soul; yea, it beginneth to enlighten my understanding, yea, it beginneth to be delicious to me.

Now behold, would not this increase your faith? . . .

. . . Yea, it will strengthen your faith: for ye will say I know that this is a good seed; for behold it sprouteth and beginneth to grow. . . .

. . . As the tree beginneth to grow, ye will say: Let us nourish it with great care, that it may get root, that it may grow up, and bring forth fruit unto us. And now behold, if ye nourish it with much care it will get root, and grow up, and bring forth fruit.

But if ye neglect the tree, and take no thought for its nourishment, behold it will not get any root; and when the heat of the sun cometh and scorcheth it, because it hath no root it withers away, and ye pluck it up and cast it out.

Now, this is not because the seed was not good,

neither is it because the fruit thereof would not be desirable; but it is because your ground is barren, and ye will not nourish the tree, therefore ye cannot have the fruit thereof.

And thus, if ye will not nourish the word, looking forward with an eye of faith to the fruit thereof, ye can never pluck of the fruit of the tree of life.

But if ye will nourish the word, yea, nourish the tree as it beginneth to grow, by your faith with great diligence, and with patience, looking forward to the fruit thereof, it shall take root; and behold it shall be a tree springing up unto everlasting life.

. . . Behold, by and by ye shall pluck the fruit thereof, which is most precious, which is sweet above all that is sweet, and which is white above all that is white, yea, and pure above all that is pure; and ye shall feast upon this fruit even until ye are filled, that ye hunger not, neither shall ye thirst.

Then, my brethren, ye shall reap the rewards of your faith, and your diligence, and patience, and long-suffering, waiting for the tree to bring forth fruit unto you. (Alma 32:9–43)

So, Alma tells us that those who choose to nurture and build their faith in God will be rewarded with a sure knowledge of him, but they must work at it. And, in a message that might have been aimed at today's world, where we demand instant solutions and happy endings before the final commercials run, he also instructs us on the value of patience.

After Alma was finished, another prophet, Amulek, spoke

to the same group. At the end of his sermon he had this to say about the importance of making right choices, now.

AMULEK

For behold, this life is the time for men to prepare to meet God; yea, behold the day of this life is the day for men to perform their labors.

And now, as I said unto you before, as ye have had so many witnesses, therefore, I beseech of you that ye do not procrastinate the day of your repentance until the end; for after this day of life, which is given us to prepare for eternity, behold, if we do not improve our time while in this life, then cometh the night of darkness wherein there can be no labor performed.

Ye cannot say, when ye are brought to that awful crisis, that I will repent, that I will return to my God. Nay, ye cannot say this; for that same spirit which doth possess your bodies at the time that ye go out of this life, that same spirit will have power to possess your body in that eternal world.

For behold, if ye have procrastinated the day of your repentance even until death, behold, ye have become subjected to the spirit of the devil, and he doth seal you his; therefore, the Spirit of the Lord hath withdrawn from you, and hath no place in you, and the devil hath all power over you; and this is the final state of the wicked.

And this I know, because the Lord hath said he dwelleth not in unholy temples, but in the hearts of the righteous doth he dwell; yea, and he has also said that the righteous shall sit down in his kingdom, to go no more out; but their garments should be made white through the blood of the Lamb.

And now, my beloved brethren, I desire that ye should remember these things, and that ye should work out your salvation with fear before God, and that ye should no more deny the coming of Christ;

That ye contend no more against the Holy Ghost, but that ye receive it, and take upon you the name of Christ; that ye humble yourselves even to the dust, and worship God, in whatsoever place ye may be in, in spirit and in truth; and that ye live in thanksgiving daily, for the many mercies and blessings which he doth bestow upon you. (Alma 34:32–38)

SUMMARY

The Book of Mormon strongly teaches the doctrine of agency, the right of every individual to choose to accept or reject God. It also says that those who accept him must work at nourishing and strengthening their faith throughout their lives, but it promises that when they do, their reward will be "sweet above all that is sweet, . . . white above all that is white, . . . and pure above all that is pure" (Alma 32:42).

This is an exhortation to good works and righteous choices, motivated by faith in Christ's atonement for sins and voluntarily embarked upon. We don't know if it is the same as the ideas Joseph Smith would have heard discussed in his neighborhood—I rather doubt it—but we do know it is relevant to our present society today.

16

THE FALL AND THE ATONEMENT

WHENEVER CHRISTIANS TALK ABOUT evil, they talk about the fall of man. It was that fall, they say, that brought death into the world and created the need for a Redeemer. The apostle Paul summarized the connection this way:

"For as in Adam all die, even so in Christ shall all be made alive" (1 Corinthians 15:22).

What does the Book of Mormon have to say on this subject? To open this discussion, we again begin with Lehi. Old Testament patriarchs routinely gave formal blessings to their sons, and Lehi acts in this tradition, just before his death, when he gathers his posterity around him.

LEHI'S BLESSING TO JACOB

Speaking to "my first-born in the days of my tribulation in the wilderness," Lehi says, "I know that thou art redeemed, because of the righteousness of thy Redeemer; for thou hast beheld that in the fulness of time he cometh to bring salvation unto men. . . . And the way is prepared from the fall of man, and salvation is free" (2 Nephi 2:1, 3–4).

He tells Jacob that because of the Fall, the workings of the law with respect to acts of disobedience mean that men are "cut off" and "miserable" (2 Nephi 2:5), but that condition is neither permanent nor inevitable.

Redemption cometh in and through the Holy Messiah; for he is full of grace and truth.

Behold, he offereth himself a sacrifice for sin, to answer the ends of the law, unto all those who have a broken heart and a contrite spirit; and unto none else can the ends of the law be answered. . . .

And because of the intercession for all, all men come unto God; wherefore, they stand in the presence of him, to be judged of him according to the truth and holiness which is in him. . . .

For it must needs be, that there is an opposition in all things. If not so, my first-born in the wilderness, righteousness could not be brought to pass, neither wickedness, neither holiness nor misery, neither good nor bad. . . .

And if ye shall say there is no law, ye shall also say there is no sin. If ye shall say there is no sin, ye shall also say there is no righteousness. And if there be no righteousness there be no happiness. And if there be no righteousness nor happiness there be no punishment nor misery. And if these things are not there is no God. And if there is no God we are not, neither the earth; for there could have been no creation of things, neither to act nor to be acted upon; wherefore, all things must have vanished away. (2 Nephi 2:6–13)

However, he says:

There is a God, and he hath created all things, both the
heavens and the earth, and all things that in them are,
both things to act and things to be acted upon.

And to bring about his eternal purposes in the end of
man, after he had created our first parents, and the beasts
of the field and the fowls of the air, and . . . all things
which are created, it must needs be that there was an opposition; even the forbidden fruit in opposition to the tree
of life; the one being sweet and the other bitter.

Wherefore, the Lord God gave unto man that he
should act for himself. (2 Nephi 2:14–16)

So the doctrine of agency applied right from the beginning,
with Adam and Eve in the Garden of Eden. They had the
power to make choices, but that power would have been mean-
ingless if there were no choices to be made. Temptation was
permitted.

"Man could not act for himself save it should be that he
was enticed by the one or the other" (2 Nephi 2:16).

It was Satan who did the enticing, hoping to get Adam and
Eve to disobey God. When they did, they became subject to
physical death and also were expelled from the garden, which was
a spiritual death—a separation from the presence of God.

Yet their actions in the garden actually furthered rather than
frustrated God's plan, as Lehi explains:

If Adam had not transgressed he would not have fallen,
but he would have remained in the garden of Eden. And
all things which were created must have remained in the

same state in which they were after they were created; and they must have remained forever, and had no end.

And they would have had no children; wherefore they would have remained in a state of innocence, having no joy, for they knew no misery; doing no good, for they knew no sin.

But behold, all things have been done in the wisdom of him who knoweth all things.

Adam fell that men might be; and men are that they might have joy. (2 Nephi 2:22–25)

The Fall led to joy? What is the source of that joy? Again, it is Christ.

The Messiah cometh in the fulness of time, that he may redeem the children of men from the fall. And because that they are redeemed from the fall they have become free forever, knowing good from evil; to act for themselves and not to be acted upon, save it be by the punishment of the law at the great and last day, according to the commandments which God hath given.

Wherefore, men are free according to the flesh; and all things are given them which are expedient unto man. And they are free to choose liberty and eternal life, through the great Mediator of all men, or to choose captivity and death, according to the captivity and power of the devil. (2 Nephi 2:26–27)

This is not a doctrine Joseph Smith would have picked up from listening to the local preachers in his neighborhood. There, the Fall would have been depicted simply as sexual sin— as one old pun puts it, "It wasn't the apple on the tree; it was the pair on the ground." Joseph's contemporaries believed that it was the sex act between Adam and Eve that was the original sin, the act which, by descent, contaminated all their posterity. Biblical comment of the time spoke of Adam's "shameful fall."

But Lehi says that instead of being conceived in sin and born in sin, as the doctrine of original sin would have it, descendants of Adam and Eve are entitled to have joy as a consequence of the saving power of the atonement of Christ. That is one of the reasons why Mormon teaches against infant baptism; the rite is delayed until a child is old enough to make choices.

Lehi is saying that God anticipated that a law would be broken, which would require a punishment, so he provided a way whereby that punishment could be set aside—"redemption . . . in and through the Holy Messiah . . . [who] offereth himself a sacrifice for sin, to answer the ends of the law, unto all those who have a broken heart and a contrite spirit" (2 Nephi 2:6–7).

When shall that redemption take place? Lehi discusses that as well, but the clearest answer comes from Amulek, one of Alma's preaching companions. In an exchange with a hostile lawyer who was seeking to turn people against him, Amulek talks specifically about death:

There is a death which is called a temporal death; and the death of Christ shall loose the bands of this temporal death, that all shall be raised from this temporal death.

The spirit and the body shall be reunited again in its perfect form; both limb and joint shall be restored to its proper frame, even as we now are at this time; and we shall be brought to stand before God, knowing even as we

know now, and have a bright recollection of all our guilt.
(Alma 11:42–43)

This is familiar ground, speaking of what Christians know
as the resurrection. It will be universal:

> Now, this restoration shall come to all, both old and
> young, both bond and free, both male and female, both
> the wicked and the righteous; . . . [all] shall be brought
> and be arraigned before the bar of Christ the Son, and
> God the Father, and the Holy Spirit, which is one Eternal
> God, to be judged according to their works, whether they
> be good or . . . evil.
>
> Now, behold, I have spoken . . . concerning the death
> of the mortal body, and also concerning the resurrection
> of the mortal body. . . . This mortal body is raised to an
> immortal body, that is from death, even from the first
> death unto life, that they can die no more; their spirits
> uniting with their bodies, never to be divided. (Alma
> 11:44–45)

Read again Paul's statement, this time with emphasis:
"For as in Adam *all* die, even so in Christ shall *all* be made
alive."

After Amulek has finished, Alma steps into the discussion
and explains the conditions of the Judgment and the emotions
that will be felt by those who have not repented.

> And now behold, I say unto you then cometh a
> death, even a second death, which is a spiritual death;
> then is a time that whosoever dieth in his sins, as to a tem-
> poral death, shall also die a spiritual death; yea, he shall

die as to things pertaining unto righteousness. (Alma 12:16)

The *mortal* death Amulek speaks about is the separation of one's spirit from his or her body, but the *spiritual* death Alma talks about is the separation of one's spirit from the presence of God, or "all things pertaining unto righteousness."

Adam and Eve suffered both kinds of death as a result of their transgression. Their spirits were separated from God when they left the Garden of Eden, and their spirits were separated from their bodies when they died as mortals. The atonement of Christ delivers all from mortal death, but deliverance from spiritual death comes only to those who use their agency to follow God's paths and keep his commandments.

The doctrine of agency and the doctrine of overcoming spiritual death are linked together.

Alma gave a long and insightful exposition of this subject to a wayward son who was concerned about his sins, one of which was sexual activity with a harlot. Here is a portion of that sermon.

ALMA'S INSTRUCTIONS TO CORIANTON

And now, my son, I perceive there is somewhat more which doth worry your mind, which ye cannot understand . . . concerning the justice of God in the punishment of the sinner; for ye do . . . suppose that it is injustice that the sinner should be consigned to a state of misery.

Now behold, my son, I will explain this thing unto thee. . . . The Lord God sent our first parents forth from the garden of Eden, to till the ground, from whence they were taken. . . .

There was a time granted unto man to repent, yea, a probationary time, a time to repent and serve God.

. . . If Adam had put forth his hand immediately, and partaken of the tree of life, he would have lived forever, . . . having no space for repentance . . . and the great plan of salvation would have been frustrated.

But behold, it was appointed unto man to die. . . .

. . . Ye see by this that our first parents were cut off both temporally and spiritually from the presence of the Lord; and thus we see they became subjects to follow after their own will. . . .

Therefore, as . . . the fall had brought upon all mankind a spiritual death as well as a temporal, that is, they were cut off from the presence of the Lord, it was expedient that mankind should be reclaimed from this spiritual death.

Therefore, as they had become carnal, sensual, and devilish, by nature, this probationary state became a state for them to prepare. . . .

And now remember, my son, if it were not for the plan of redemption, . . . as soon as they were dead their souls were miserable, being cut off from the presence of the Lord.

And now, there was no means to reclaim men from this fallen state, which man had brought upon himself because of his own disobedience. . . .

. . . The plan of mercy could not be brought about except an atonement should be made; therefore God himself atoneth for the sins of the world, to bring about the plan of mercy, to appease the demands of justice, that God might be a perfect, just God, and a merciful God also.

Now, repentance could not come unto men except there were a punishment, which also was eternal as the life of the soul should be, affixed opposite to the plan of happiness, which was as eternal also as the life of the soul.

Now, how could a man repent except he should sin? How could he sin if there was no law? How could there be a law save there was a punishment? . . .

. . . If there was no law given against sin men would not be afraid to sin.

And if there was no law given, if men sinned what could justice do, or mercy either, for they would have no claim upon the creature?

But there is a law given, and a punishment affixed, and a repentance granted; which repentance, mercy claimeth; otherwise, justice claimeth the creature and executeth the law, and the law inflicteth the punishment; if not so, the works of justice would be destroyed, and God would cease to be God.

But God ceaseth not to be God, and mercy claimeth the penitent, and mercy cometh because of the atonement; and the atonement bringeth to pass the resurrection of the dead; and the resurrection of the dead bringeth back men into the presence of God . . . to be judged according to their works, according to the law and justice. . . .

And thus God bringeth about his great and eternal purposes, which were prepared from the foundation of the world. . . .

And now, my son, I desire that ye should let these

things trouble you no more, and only let your sins trouble you, with that trouble which shall bring you down unto repentance.

. . . Deny the justice of God no more. Do not endeavor to excuse yourself in the least point because of your sins, by denying the justice of God; but do you let the justice of God, and his mercy, and his long-suffering have full sway in your heart; and let it bring you down to the dust in humility. (Alma 42:1–30)

Joseph Smith summarized it all in two sentences:

We believe that men will be punished for their own sins, and not for Adam's transgression.

We believe that through the Atonement of Christ, all mankind may be saved, by obedience to the laws and ordinances of the Gospel. (Articles of Faith 1:2–3)

SIN

CALVIN COOLIDGE, SO THE STORY GOES, once attended church without his wife. When he returned home, she asked what the subject of the sermon had been.

"Sin," he replied.

Well, she inquired, what had the minister said about it?

"He was against it."

Every religion is against sin—that's not news. Does the Book of Mormon have anything special to add?

Maybe.

I spoke earlier of the Nephite cycle, a pattern of obedience, prosperity, and happiness, followed by forgetfulness, sin, destruction, and repentance, followed by a new round of obedience, prosperity, and happiness, followed by a new round of forgetfulness, sin, destruction, etc. The Nephites paid dearly, over and over again, for their propensity to forget the "great things the Lord hath done for [them]" (1 Nephi 7:11). What was the one great sin that always took them down the back side of the cycle?

Pride.

In the Book of Mormon, pride is the universal sin that leads the way to every other sin.

Nephi warned of it, right from the beginning. The "great and spacious building" he saw in his vision, where the mockers of the righteous lived, represented "the pride of the world" (1 Nephi 11:36). Nephi talked scathingly of "the wise, and the learned, and the rich, that are puffed up in the pride of their hearts," tying them to "all those who preach false doctrines, and all those who commit whoredoms, and pervert the right way of the Lord." He declared, "They shall be thrust down to hell!" (2 Nephi 28:15).

When they got to the Americas, Jacob worried because the Nephites "began to search much gold and silver" and, as a result, "began to be lifted up somewhat in pride" (Jacob 1:16). Alma the Younger was the first chief judge after the Nephites abandoned the monarchy, but he gave up the judgment seat to devote full time to preaching because "he saw great inequality among the people, some lifting themselves up with their pride, despising others, turning their backs upon the needy and the naked and those who were hungry" (Alma 4:12).

Samuel the Lamanite berated the Nephites for their support of those who said it was acceptable to "walk after the pride of your eyes, and do whatsoever your heart desireth" (Helaman 13:27). Mormon said that the Nephites who lived just before the appearance of Christ were "lifted up unto pride and boastings because of their exceedingly great riches, yea, even unto great persecutions" (3 Nephi 6:10). These were destroyed in the great earthquakes. At the end of his life, Mormon told Moroni that "the pride of this nation . . . hath proven their destruction" (Moroni 8:27).

Can pride really be that serious? Ezra Taft Benson was one of Joseph Smith's successors as president of The Church of Jesus Christ of Latter-day Saints. He spent most of his energy while in that position urging Church members to read and heed the teachings of the Book of Mormon, and he had this to say about pride:

> Pride is a very misunderstood sin, and many are sinning in ignorance. . . .
>
> Most of us think of pride as self-centeredness, conceit, boastfulness, arrogance, or haughtiness. All of these are elements of the sin, but the heart, or core, is still missing. . . .
>
> Pride is essentially competitive in nature. We pit our will against God's. . . .
>
> The proud cannot accept the authority of God giving direction to their lives. (See Hel. 12:6.) They pit their perceptions of truth against God's great knowledge, their abilities versus God's . . . power, their accomplishments against His mighty works.
>
> Our enmity toward God takes on many labels, such as rebellion, hard-heartedness, stiff-neckedness, unrepentant, puffed up, easily offended, and sign seekers. The proud wish God would agree with them. They aren't interested in changing their opinions to agree with God's.
>
> Another significant portion of this very prevalent sin of pride is enmity toward our fellowmen. . . .
>
> . . . It is manifest in so many ways, such as faultfinding, gossiping, backbiting, murmuring, living beyond our means, envying, coveting, withholding gratitude and praise that might lift another, and being unforgiving and jealous. . . .
>
> Selfishness is one of the more common faces of pride. . . .

Another face of pride is contention. Arguments, fights, unrighteous dominion, generation gaps, divorces, spouse abuse, riots, and disturbances all fall into this category of pride. . . .

The antidote for pride is humility—meekness, submissiveness. . . . It is the broken heart and contrite spirit.[1]

The passage in the Book of Mormon that Benson cites, Helaman 12:6, is part of a sermon given just before the birth of Christ. The relevant passages read as follows, with the cited verse in italics:

O how foolish, and how vain, and how evil, and devilish, and how quick to do iniquity, and how slow to do good, are the children of men; yea, how quick to hearken unto the words of the evil one, and to set their hearts upon the vain things of the world!

Yea, how quick to be lifted up in pride; yea, how quick to boast, and do all manner of that which is iniquity; and how slow are they to remember the Lord their God, and to give ear unto his counsels, yea, how slow to walk in wisdom's paths!

Behold, they do not desire that the Lord their God, who hath created them, should rule and reign over them; notwithstanding his great goodness and his mercy towards them, they do set at naught his counsels, and they will not that he should be their guide. (Helaman 12:4–6; italics added)

The sin most often linked to pride by the Nephite prophets was the sin of neglecting the poor. As we have seen, both Jacob and Alma warned that excessive pride would make the Nephites reject their obligations to the less fortunate. The seriousness of those obligations is emphasized by Amulek. We reviewed a portion of his sermon in Chapter 15; here are the verses in which he urges his listeners to seek God through prayer and then serve the less fortunate:

May God grant unto you, my brethren, that ye may begin to exercise your faith unto repentance, that ye begin to call upon his holy name, that he would have mercy upon you;

Yea, cry unto him for mercy; for he is mighty to save.

. . . Humble yourselves, and continue in prayer unto him.

Cry unto him when ye are in your fields, yea, over all your flocks.

Cry unto him in your houses, yea, over all your household, both morning, mid-day, and evening.

. . . Cry unto him against the power of your enemies.

Yea, cry unto him against the devil, who is an enemy to all righteousness.

Cry unto him over the crops of your fields, that ye may prosper in them.

Cry over the flocks of your fields, that they may increase.

But this is not all; ye must pour out your souls in your closets, and your secret places, and in your wilderness.

Yea, and when you do not cry unto the Lord, let your hearts be full, drawn out in prayer unto him continually for your welfare, and also for the welfare of those who are around you.

And now behold, my beloved brethren, I say unto you, do not suppose that this is all; for after ye have done all these things, if ye turn away the needy, and the naked, and visit not the sick and afflicted, and impart of your substance, if ye have, to those who stand in need—I say unto you, if ye do not any of these things, behold, your prayer is vain, and availeth you nothing, and ye are as hypocrites who do deny the faith.

Therefore, if ye do not remember to be charitable, ye are as dross, which the refiners do cast out, (it being of no worth) and is trodden under foot of men. (Alma 34:17–29)

Jesus said, "Inasmuch as ye have done it unto one of the least of these my brethren, ye have done it unto me" (Matthew 25:40). Those infected with the sin of pride, who "turn away the needy, and the naked, and visit not the sick and afflicted, and impart of [their] substance, if [they] have" (Alma 34:28), have, by this standard, turned away Jesus. They are so self-centered that they are in competition with God.

And that's why pride is the universal sin.

Is pride a problem in the world today? The question answers itself. Along with its standard denunciations of what we might call the standard sins—murder, rape, adultery, lying, stealing, etc.—the emphasis in the Book of Mormon on the role of pride as a sin is an insight from which our current society can benefit.

We turn again to Alma and a sermon he gave when he relinquished his political position to concentrate on calling the Nephites to repentance. Here are portions of it:

I ask of you, my brethren of the church, have ye spiritually been born of God? Have ye received his image in your countenances? Have ye experienced this mighty change in your hearts?

Do ye exercise faith in the redemption of him who created you? Do you look forward with an eye of faith . . . to stand before God to be judged according to the deeds which have been done in the mortal body?

. . . Can you imagine to yourselves that ye hear the voice of the Lord, saying unto you, in that day: Come unto me ye blessed, for behold, your works have been the works of righteousness upon the face of the earth?

Or do ye imagine to yourselves that ye can lie unto the Lord in that day, and say—Lord, our works have been righteous works upon the face of the earth—and that he will save you? . . .

I say unto you, ye will know at that day that ye cannot be saved; for there can no man be saved except his garments are washed white; yea, his garments must be purified until they are cleansed from all stain, through the blood of him of whom it has been spoken by our fathers, who should come to redeem his people from their sins. . . .

Behold, are ye stripped of pride? I say unto you, if ye are not ye are not prepared to meet God. Behold ye must prepare quickly; for the kingdom of heaven is soon at hand, and such an one hath not eternal life.

. . . Is there one among you who is not stripped of envy? I say unto you that such an one is not prepared; and I would that he should prepare quickly, for the hour is close at hand, and he knoweth not when the time shall come; for such an one is not found guiltless.

. . . Is there one among you that doth make a mock of his brother, or that heapeth upon him persecutions?

Wo unto such an one, for he is not prepared, and the time is at hand that he must repent or he cannot be saved!

Yea, even wo unto all ye workers of iniquity; repent, repent, for the Lord God hath spoken it!

Behold, he sendeth an invitation unto all men, for the arms of mercy are extended towards them, and he saith: Repent, and I will receive you.

Yea, he saith: Come unto me and ye shall partake of the fruit of the tree of life; yea, ye shall eat and drink of the bread and the waters of life freely;

Yea, come unto me and bring forth works of righteousness, and ye shall not be hewn down and cast into the fire. . . .

I speak by way of command unto you that belong to the church; and unto those who do not belong to the church I speak by way of invitation, saying: Come and be baptized unto repentance, that ye also may be partakers of the fruit of the tree of life. (Alma 5:14–62)

"By way of command" to those who belong to the church and "by way of invitation" to those who do not—a call to repentance for the former and a statement of promise for the latter. At the root of it all is the idea that all sin is a determination to follow our own wills in a way that is competitive with God's will.

If we would be forgiven of our sins—including pride—we must be humble and turn to Christ, who atoned for them all.

JESUS IS THE CHRIST

ON THE TITLE PAGE OF EVERY copy of the Book of Mormon is this statement regarding the book's purpose:

> to the convincing of the Jew and Gentile that JESUS is the CHRIST

Some are confused by that construction—"Jesus is the Christ." They say his full name is simply "Jesus Christ," and that saying "Jesus is the Christ" is like saying "George is the Washington" or "Abraham is the Lincoln."

In modern usage, we do refer to him as if Christ were his last name, but when he lived in Palestine, he had only one name. In his own language it was Yeshua, or Joshua, one of the most common of names at the time. It means *God is help*. However, as the story of his ministry was written down and circulated beyond the borders of Palestine, first in the letters of Paul and then in the four Gospels, it was recorded in Greek, the most widely used language of the time.

Thus, in our Bibles, the Hebrew name *Yeshua* is rendered as the Greek name Jesus and the Hebrew word *Messiah* as the

Greek word *Christ.* To say "Jesus is the Christ" is to say that Yeshua from Nazareth is the promised Messiah of ancient Hebrew prophecy and scripture.

The claim that Jesus is the Christ is the key doctrine of the Book of Mormon. That's why, in recent years, Church leaders have added a subtitle to the book. Its cover and title page now read: "The Book of Mormon—Another Testament of Jesus Christ."

Alexander Campbell undoubtedly thought there was no need for "another testament," that such a thing would be superfluous if not blasphemous. But in today's world of biblical commentary, that is not the case. Today, some scholars challenge the idea that Jesus even existed; others, the idea that he had any special relationship with God. One historian whose work I have read speculates that he was the illegitimate child of a Roman soldier. He reasons that Mary, embarrassed at her condition, told Joseph she was carrying the promised Messiah, and he was either gullible enough or sympathetic enough to go along with her story. Other alternative explanations regarding Jesus' origins and history abound.

The Gospels do not allow such alternatives, which is why such doubters as Thomas Jefferson and the modern Jesus Seminarians insist that the Gospels cannot be taken as gospel. If these critics are right and Jesus never existed—or, if he did exist, had no special relationship with God—then the Book of Mormon must be a forgery, regardless of all the historical items it gets right. If they are wrong, however—if Jesus really did live and really *is* the Christ—then the necessity of contradicting their modern skepticism provides a logical motive for God to assist Joseph Smith in bringing forward a record that supports the biblical accounts of Jesus' mortal birth and literal resurrection.

The importance of such accounts cannot be overemphasized. Reading them was an important turning point in C. S. Lewis's conversion. Armand Nicholi Jr. describes it:

> Lewis had spent his life reading ancient manuscripts. As an atheist, he, like Freud, considered the New Testament story simply another of the great myths. He knew well the ancient myths and legends—especially Norse mythology—and they moved him deeply. . . . Many of these myths . . . contained stories similar to the one in the Bible—of a god coming to earth, dying to save his people, and rising again from the dead. Lewis had always considered the New Testament story simply another one of these myths.
>
> But the Gospels, Lewis noted, did not contain the rich, imaginative writings of these talented, ancient writers. They appeared to be simple eyewitness accounts of historical events, primarily by Jews who were clearly unfamiliar with the great myths of the pagan world around them. Lewis writes: "I was by now too experienced in literary criticism to regard the Gospels as myths. They had not the mythical taste." He observes that they were different from anything else in literature. "If ever myth had become fact, had been incarnated, it would be just like this." . . . "The story of Christ is simply a true myth: a myth working on us in the same way as the others, but with this tremendous difference that it really happened. . . ."
>
> . . . "As a literary historian, I am perfectly convinced that whatever else the Gospels are they are not legends. I have read a great deal of legend (myth) and I am quite

clear that they are not the same sort of thing. They are not artistic enough to be legends. From an imaginative point of view they are clumsy, they don't work. . . . Most of the life of Jesus is totally unknown to us . . . and no people building up a legend would allow that to be so.[1]

Believing readers of the Book of Mormon respond to it the same way Lewis responded to the New Testament, accepting it as an eyewitness account of something that really happened. And every eyewitness quoted in the book speaks of Jesus as the Messiah, the early ones as prospective, that is, coming in the future, and those who lived at the time of his appearance as present, ministering to them in his resurrected condition.

A few examples.

Jacob tells his people:

Rejoice, and lift up your heads forever, because of the blessings which the Lord God shall bestow upon your children.

For I know that ye have searched much, many of you, to know of things to come; wherefore I know that ye know that our flesh must waste away and die; nevertheless, in our bodies we shall see God.

Yea, I know that ye know that in the body he shall show himself unto those at Jerusalem, from whence we came; for it is expedient that it should be among them; for it behooveth the great Creator that he suffereth himself to become subject unto man in the flesh, and die for all men, that all men might become subject to him. (2 Nephi 9:3–5)

Jacob, speaking to those who would come after him, says:

For this intent have we written these things, that they may know that we knew of Christ, and we had hope of his glory many hundred years before his coming; and not only we ourselves had a hope of his glory, but also all the holy prophets which were before us.

Behold, they believed in Christ and worshiped the Father in his name, and also we worship the Father in his name. And for this intent we keep the law of Moses, it pointing our souls to him. . . .

Wherefore, brethren, seek not to counsel the Lord, but to take counsel from his hand. For behold, ye yourselves know that he counseleth in wisdom, and in justice, and in great mercy, over all his works.

Wherefore, beloved brethren, be reconciled unto him through the atonement of Christ, his Only Begotten Son, and ye may obtain a resurrection, according to the power of the resurrection which is in Christ, and be presented as the first-fruits of Christ unto God, having faith, and obtained a good hope of glory in him before he manifesteth himself in the flesh. (Jacob 4:4–11).

King Benjamin told his people:

And moreover, I say unto you, that there shall be no other name given nor any other way nor means whereby salvation can come unto the children of men, only in and through the name of Christ, the Lord Omnipotent.

. . . Men drink damnation to their own souls except they humble themselves and become as little children, and believe that salvation was, and is, and is to come, in and through the atoning blood of Christ. . . .

For the natural man is an enemy to God, and has

been from the fall of Adam, and will be, forever and ever, unless he yields to the enticings of the Holy Spirit, and putteth off the natural man and becometh a saint through the atonement of Christ the Lord. (Mosiah 3:17–19)

Abinadi told the priests of a wicked king:

Ye have said that salvation cometh by the law of Moses. I say unto you that it is expedient that ye should keep the law of Moses as yet; but I say unto you, that the time shall come when it shall no more be expedient to keep the law of Moses.

. . . Salvation doth not come by the law alone; and were it not for the atonement, which God himself shall make for the sins and iniquities of his people, that they must unavoidably perish, notwithstanding the law of Moses. (Mosiah 13:27–28)

And now if Christ had not come into the world, speaking of things to come as though they had already come, there could have been no redemption.

And if Christ had not risen from the dead, or have broken the bands of death that the grave should have no victory, and that death should have no sting, there could have been no resurrection.

But there is a resurrection, therefore the grave hath no victory, and the sting of death is swallowed up in Christ.

He is the light and the life of the world; yea, a light that is endless, that can never be darkened; yea, and also a life which is endless, that there can be no more death. (Mosiah 16:6–9)

Similar passages can be found in the sermons of the two Almas, Samuel the Lamanite, and the two men named Nephi who lived just before the coming of Christ. At the time of his appearance among them, after his resurrection, the voice of the Father proclaimed him, saying, "Behold my Beloved Son, in whom I am well pleased, in whom I have glorified my name—hear ye him" (3 Nephi 11:7).

So what's new? Isn't this simply a regurgitation of what every Christian believes?

Maybe not. The idea that prophets in the ancient world, thousands of years before Christ was born, knew of him by name and taught that he was the Savior and sole creator of the world is not accepted Christian doctrine. The fact that the Book of Mormon teaches that a full knowledge of Christ's mission was available at such an early stage in religious history puts it in a class by itself.

Follow me into a side story that explains why I say that.

In my final quarter at the University of Utah, in 1957, I took a class in the English department titled "The Bible as Literature," taught by Dr. Louis Zucker. Dr. Zucker was Jewish, and he told us at the beginning of the course that we had a "short quarter" that year, so we wouldn't have time to get into the New Testament.

I couldn't see that the number of class meetings was any different from any other quarter, but I didn't mind. I reveled in the idea of having a Jewish scholar of his stature open up the Old Testament to me. I was not disappointed. We saw the Old Testament through the eyes of one who was not only a superb teacher but also a lifelong student and practitioner of the

Hebraic traditions. I still have my notes from that class, more than fifty years later.

When we got to Amos, Dr. Zucker made this comment: "Amos was the first monotheist, the first to teach that there is only one God."

What? Because of my Book of Mormon perspective, I had always read the Hebrew scriptures as monotheistic from the very first, and I raised my hand. How about Moses? What about the First Commandment, the "no other gods before me" bit? Wasn't that a monotheistic statement on its very face?

No, Dr. Zucker said, it was henotheistic. I had to learn the meaning of a new word.

Henotheism is defined as the belief in multiple gods, unconnected with each other but nonetheless possessed of divine attributes and powers. Dr. Zucker explained that henotheists would hold that Jehovah could be a true god for the Israelites but that some other god could be a true god for some other group. He pointed out that the statement "I am the Lord thy God, which have brought thee out of the land of Egypt, out of the house of bondage. Thou shalt have no other gods before me" is subject to a henotheistic interpretation, depending on where you put the emphasis.

"I am the Lord *thy* God" could mean that he was exclusive to the Hebrews; "*Thou* shalt have no other gods before me" could mean that it was only they who should not worship other gods. There was no requirement that the Egyptians should follow this commandment.

No, Dr. Zucker repeated, the Ten Commandments are not monotheistic. Human understanding of God—for all humans, including the Hebrews in Egypt—has evolved over time. The ancient prophets did not become monotheistic until Amos started to tell the Israelites that *their* God was *the* God, the only God.

That seems to fit their history. Their failure to understand that their God was *the* God seems to have been the cause of much of their difficulty up to that point. When things weren't going the way they liked, didn't they want to go back to the gods of Egypt? After they got to Canaan, didn't they spend time in the hedonistic groves of the gods of the Philistines? And why not? If you are henotheistic and you think your god isn't doing the job for you, it makes sense to go shopping for another one. If things don't work out with the new deity, the old one is still around; you can go back, if you like. That's the sort of thinking Dr. Zucker said Amos and his successors in the Old Testament preached against—there is only one God, folks, and you had better start acting accordingly.

Not long after this discussion, Dr. Zucker took a few days off to attend an out-of-town seminar of some kind, and we had a substitute for a few classes. She began by telling us somewhat pointedly that she was *not* Jewish, so we should expect that her perspective of the Bible would be different from the one we had been getting from him.

Nonetheless, she affirmed, in the strongest of terms, from what she called a mainstream Protestant point of view, the idea that human understanding of the nature of God has evolved and changed over the centuries. She emphasized even more strongly than Dr. Zucker had that early biblical peoples believed one thing and later ones another, that it was not until relatively late in the game that people came to believe in a single Creator—and, for Christians, a single Savior—of the world.

The Book of Mormon says that isn't true.

The Book of Mormon says that Christ told ancient prophets of his position as the Creator and Messiah at the dawn of recorded history. Remember, when he showed himself to the brother of Jared in spirit form thousands of years before he was born in the flesh, he declared:

> Behold, I am he who was prepared from the foundation of the world to redeem my people. Behold, I am Jesus Christ. I am the Father and the Son. In me shall all mankind have life, and that eternally, even they who believe on my name; and they shall become my sons and my daughters.
>
> . . . This body, which ye now behold, is the body of my spirit; and man have I created after the body of my spirit; and even as I appear unto thee to be in the spirit will I appear unto my people in the flesh. (Ether 3:14, 16)

Moroni's comment on this vision was, "It sufficeth me to say that Jesus showed himself unto this man in the spirit, even after the manner and in the likeness of the same body even as he showed himself unto the Nephites" (Ether 3:17).

There is no room here for an "evolving" or "maturing" understanding of Jesus' role. He makes it clear long before either Moses or Amos that He is the Creator. His place at the beginning of history is affirmed by all the Book of Mormon prophets, from the brother of Jared through the first Nephi, in 600 B.C.E.; from Alma to Samuel the Lamanite, in 6 B.C.E.; from Mormon to Moroni, in 421 C.E.; from Joseph Smith, in 1830.

Moroni's final words to his readers focus again on Christ, telling them—us—that

> if ye by the grace of God are perfect in Christ, and deny not his power, then are ye sanctified in Christ by the grace of God, through the shedding of the blood of Christ, which is in the covenant of the Father unto the remission of your sins, that ye become holy, without spot. (Moroni 10:33)

So, why do some insist that Mormons are not Christians?

Perhaps it is because Mormons do not accept some of the nonbiblical statements that have become part of the Christian tradition. Joseph Loconte, an evangelical who is a senior fellow at the Ethics and Public Policy Center, in Washington, D.C., says, "If you can't sign on to the Nicene Creed—Catholics and Protestants do, but Mormons don't—then you're outside the boundaries of traditional Christianity."[2]

Let's consider that.

The Nicene Creed was first propounded in 325 C.E. The council that produced it was convened by Constantine, the Roman pagan who converted to Christianity around that time. He wanted the Christian scholars and clerics to stop arguing among themselves about the nature of God and settle on a single definition. The creed that was adopted in response to his pressure was not revealed by an angel nor taken from biblical statements; rather, it was the product of debate, compromise, and vote, with several drafts offered before the final version was settled in 381 C.E.

I am a practicing politician; I understand fully how such a process works and how the statements that emerge from it are arrived at. To accept the Nicene Creed as the authentic, definitive, and final word on what one must believe in order to be a Christian, one must make the leap of faith to believe that the members of the fourth-century councils that fashioned the first draft, as well as the others that influenced the changes that were made in it, were inspired—nay, controlled—by God, even though they were neither apostles nor prophets and made no such claim. That is as big a leap as believing in angels in an age of railways.

Instead of debating the matter, when I am asked if Mormons are Christians, I simply say, "Some are, some aren't." I'm not ducking the issue. I'm admitting that I am not competent to make such a decision.

There is only one who is.

Jesus said at the conclusion of the Sermon on the Mount:

> Not every one that saith unto me, Lord, Lord, shall enter into the kingdom of heaven; but he that doeth the will of my Father which is in heaven.
>
> Many will say to me in that day, Lord, Lord, have we not prophesied in thy name? and in thy name have cast out devils? and in thy name done many wonderful works?
>
> And then will I profess unto them, I never knew you: depart from me, ye that work iniquity. (Matthew 7:21–23)

The decision of who is a Christian and who is not will be made by Jesus Christ himself on the basis of who is willing to "[do] the will of my Father which is in heaven." It is not for me, or anyone else currently on Earth, to decide.

The Book of Mormon makes the same point. Jacob says:

> O then, my beloved brethren, come unto the Lord, the Holy One. Remember that his paths are righteous. Behold,

the way for man is narrow, but it lieth in a straight course before him, and the keeper of the gate is the Holy One of Israel; and he employeth no servant there; and there is none other way save it be by the gate; for he cannot be deceived, for the Lord God is his name. (2 Nephi 9:41)

I take great comfort in that statement: "The keeper of the gate is the Holy One of Israel." I accept the proposition that "he cannot be deceived." It means that I don't have to worry about the opinions of anyone but Jesus.

If Jesus judges me—or anyone else—a Christian, then it doesn't matter what the rest of the world may say. Conversely, if he decides that I am not, all the testimonies from all my friends, from the boards of trustees of all the churches that use Christ's name, or even from the leaders of the Church I have chosen, will not help me. "He employeth no servant there."

Like the Bible, the Book of Mormon teaches that simply claiming Christian status is not enough, for a Mormon or anybody else. Such status will finally come solely from Christ himself, and it will only be bestowed, as he said in the Sermon on the Mount, on those who "[do] the will of my Father which is in heaven."

SUMMARY

The primary doctrinal message of the Book of Mormon is that Jesus is the Christ, the resurrected Messiah, that his sacrifice atoned for all human sins, and that He will be the final and sole judge of each one of us. It also teaches that ancient prophets back to the beginning of recorded time knew that.

In today's skeptical world, where even some of the teachers

and scholars well within the historic Christian tradition doubt the reality of Christ's resurrection, this is a message of tremendous import—if true. It is significant enough to provide a motive for God to have been involved in bringing the Book of Mormon forward in our time.

Assuming, of course, that God exists. If you are going to believe in the book, you first have to believe in God, which is the most important leap of faith of all.

The Final Question

WHO WROTE THE BOOK OF MORMON?

WE HAVE COME TO THE END OF our examination. We have examined the Plot and listened to the Music. It is time to make some final judgments.

I believe that all honest observers will agree that the Book of Mormon is a large and complex work, containing much more than a simple "good guys, bad guys" story with some pedestrian nineteenth-century sermons thrown in. It goes far beyond anything suggested by *View of the Hebrews* or any other nineteenth-century book; it has all of the complexities and nuances of an authentic history.

I separated Story from Doctrine to make the book easier to follow, but the original author(s) did not, and, given the book's stated purpose, we now see that the two fully intertwine. We could not understand Lehi's instructions to his family and the promises he gives them if we did not know the details of his journey. We could not fully understand the sermons calling the Nephites to repentance if we hadn't been told the specifics of their disobedience. We could not understand the effects of pride in Nephite society if we didn't know about the incursions of the Gandianton band into their government or the effect on their society of war with the Lamanites. The story is essential to making the doctrine relevant.

That is the norm when dealing with ancient sacred writings, and not just the Bible. Think of the Dead Sea Scrolls, discovered by a shepherd boy who happened upon them in some caves in the 1940s. They contain passages from almost every book of the Old Testament, with heavy emphasis on Isaiah, but the first thing the scholars wanted to know, as they tried to decipher them, was who the people were who had placed them in the caves in the first place. Things that are written down are far more understandable if we can place them in the proper context of the community that produced them.

The Dead Sea Scrolls are relevant to our discussion of the Book of Mormon because their discovery touched off a hunger for more documents, more enlightenment about the ancient world, more records that might be authentic windows into the religious teachings of the past. No one had such a hunger in 1829. No one in Christendom then ever considered that religious groups like the Qumran Community, which produced the Dead Sea Scrolls, even existed, or that they wrote sacred things on metal plates.

But the author of the Book of Mormon did. Listen again to the words Nephi attributes to the Lord, and consider them in this age of discovery of additional ancient religious writings:

> Know ye not that there are more nations than one?
> Know ye not that I, the Lord your God, have created all
> men, . . . and that I rule in the heavens above and in the
> earth beneath; and that I bring forth my word unto the

children of men, yea, even upon all the nations of the earth? . . .

. . . And because that I have spoken one word ye need not suppose that I cannot speak another; for my work is not yet finished; neither shall it be until the end of man, neither from that time henceforth and forever.

Wherefore, because that ye have a Bible ye need not suppose that it contains all my words; neither need ye suppose that I have not caused more to be written. (2 Nephi 29:7–10)

By claiming that God has spoken to "more nations than one," the Book of Mormon is much more in tune with twentieth-century scholarship than it was with nineteenth.

But that still doesn't tell us who wrote it, or, more properly, who assisted Joseph Smith in producing it. If we reject the book's own claims, there is no clear indication of who that was, but this much is clear—whoever did it had a broad background in ancient cultures and languages, Middle Eastern geography, military strategy, and biblical scholarship, and went to a great deal of painstaking effort. Such a person does not easily come to mind, and coming up with a clear explanation of how a forgery this large and this complex might have been done is very difficult.

But that doesn't mean we cannot try.

When confronting a body of evidence like the one we have assembled, lawyers will construct a "theory of the case" that makes sense out of the facts they have before them. Because we are faced with two possibilities for the source of Joseph's assistance, we need to construct two such theories, one for each

alternative—God, working through centuries of inspired record keepers, or Third Party, living and writing in the early
1800s.

The theory of the case for God as Joseph's source of help
rests on the idea that he did it to inform a doubting modern
world that the ancient scriptural record is true, that belief in
him and obedience to him is still a matter of eternal importance
in our lives. If God exists, that makes it logical for us to accept
him as Joseph's collaborator.

But if God does not exist, or if he does but didn't help
Joseph, that means Third Party existed. What theory of the case
can be built for him (or her) that would be logical enough for
us to accept?

Let's begin with what we know.

The Book of Mormon is primarily a religious book with a
heavy and consistent emphasis on the mission of Jesus Christ
as Messiah and Savior; it is also long, complex, and well constructed.

Those two facts suggest a biblical scholar with very good
writing skills—not an unusual combination. That's where we
will start.

As we visualize such a man, in order to give him maximum
resources on which to draw, let's put him at a college somewhere, with a large library and learned colleagues at his dis-
posal. In the early 1800s, he would also need to have some time
on his hands.

What's his motive?

Consider this one:

The author of the book is a strong believer in Christ. Our
man could well have become involved in arguments with a few

of his fellow professors who considered themselves part of the intellectual elite. Along with Thomas Jefferson, who was still alive at the time, they would have been skeptical about Jesus' resurrection. Third Party felt duty bound to show them the light.

They do not accept the Bible as authoritative; I need some proof of the literal divinity of Jesus from outside the Bible.

Also, he resented their ridicule on this issue. His motive could have been a combination of a sense of religious duty and a desire for a little revenge. If he could provide proof of the reality of Christ's resurrection, he could convince his associates of the error of their sectarian views and, at the same time, bring them down a peg in retaliation for their having belittled his intellectual abilities.

He began to think about what sort of proof that would be.

The Bible contains references to missing books, prophetic writings that did not survive to be included in it. What would be in such a book? Who might have written it?

As a "lark"—Clifford Irving's word—he drew up an outline of what such a book might be like. He conceived an ancient Israelite family that left Jerusalem just before the Babylonian invasion, taking scriptures with them.

If they kept a record of their wanderings and maintained their belief in the Messiah, that might make their descendants eligible for a visit from him, after his resurrection. But their new location would need to be far enough away from Jerusalem that they couldn't have heard of his birth or death otherwise.

He tried to imagine where they might go.

They would have to go south, into the desert, away from the Babylonians. That would take them towards Egypt, but that's too *close. I know—suppose they built a ship and sailed off to America. There's a new book out—*View of the Hebrews—*that says the ancestors of the American Indians are the lost tribes of Israel. This is consistent with that idea.*

He started to write all this down, and, as the work progressed, it took hold of him. As in the Pygmalion story of the mythical sculptor who created a statue of the perfect woman and then fell in love with it, he fell in love with his own creation. He began to believe that these people might have actually existed.

Meticulous in his search for authenticating details, he turned to a colleague at the college who knew Egyptian, from whom he got enough information to give some of his characters authentic Egyptian names. He knew other scholars who knew about ancient forms of battle, and, after several quiet dinners and some long conversations, with a pile of notes made afterward, he sat down and outlined several decades of detailed battle tactics. Captain Moroni was born.

He found a mathematician who could devise a coinage system based on eights instead of tens, which he put in just to show how advanced these people were.

Then something incredibly fortunate happened. One of the school's professors who had been to the Middle East brought back an Arab for an extended visit. Amazingly, the Arab had learned enough English to be part of that professor's lecture series. Third Party and the Arab talked for days, and the Arab gave him a description of desert geography and poetry that was unlike anything available in any American library. It was exotic to him—wonderfully different—and he decided to use it in his opening narrative. But he needed some human interest angle.

Along with the desert stuff, I'll need some drama, right at the first, to grab my readers. A little derring-do, perhaps, on the part of my narrator. And a family quarrel—that's the way to do it. People will relate to that.

Nephi emerged triumphant from his clash with Laban.

Putting his fictional Nephites and Lamanites in the Western Hemisphere nearly six hundred years before Christ meant he had to create a very long story in order to keep things going until Jesus could come to them.

Too much work; I can't do it. I'll say that some of the record was lost, to cut down the amount of ground I have to cover. Also, as a filler, I'll put in some quotes from Isaiah. Actually, lots of quotes from Isaiah, since this book is about the coming of the Messiah, and Isaiah is the best Old Testament source for messianic prophecies.

He concocted a series of missionary experiences, side narratives, flashbacks, and sermons to fill the abbreviated time frame, letting his creative juices flow. Alma and his son appeared and accomplished wonderful things.

Third Party was one of the few people in America who knew about chiasmus. He put it into the mouths of some of his prophets for two reasons. First, he knew that chiasmus was a form considered sacred by the ancient Jews, and he wanted his creations to be as scholarly as he was. Second, he saw it as a way to have the book authenticated.

The average reader will not notice. But then, when the book comes out, people will seek some sort of validation for it, and they'll bring it to me, because of my reputation as an expert on these matters. I'll study it carefully and, to everyone's amazement, "discover" the chiasmus—clear proof of its ancient origins. Everyone will be convinced, and my reputation will be enhanced.

He realized that the sermons were a problem, because if he wrote them all, they would all sound alike. So, choosing the different themes he wanted to cover, he approached his colleagues in the Divinity School.

I've been thinking about the importance of serving one's fellowmen. Do you think you could write me a sermon on service? And, please, make it Christ-centered. I'd be so grateful.

What do you think an ancient prophet might say about the relationship between the law of Moses and Christ? Could you put a few thoughts on paper for me, on that? Thank you so much.

I've been rereading the Sermon on the Mount. Presumptuous, I know, but what editing changes do you think Christ might make in it if he were to review it as presented in the King James Version? Could you give it some thought and get back to me with your ideas? That would be so much appreciated.

You are familiar with the practice of the patriarchs giving blessings to their sons—have a little fun with me. Write out some blessings that you think a prophet-father might give to his sons, some who are righteous and some who not. It will be a good stretch for you to try it!

He himself became Alma, the most prolific sermonizer, but King Benjamin, Abinadi, Amulek, Samuel the Lamanite, and others joined him, as the book filled up with sermons that sounded different from one another because they *were* different. Third Party missed the fact that one of his unwitting collaborators had used the language of Paul when discussing charity.

Then he came across the issue of Freemasonry with its founding myths.

Wonderful stuff! Secret societies, ancient oaths, metal plates with inscriptions on them—say, why not have the entire book in-scribed on metal plates? That way they won't fade. And by con-demning the wickedness of secret societies in the strongest terms, I will win the heart of every anti-Masonic editor in the country.

Gadianton and his followers thus came to life.

It took him years, but when he had it all done, he had the Nephites become unrighteous one last time so God could use the Lamanites to wipe them out. With a nod towards *View of the Hebrews,* he left open the suggestion that the victors would become the ancestors of the dark-skinned people who greeted Columbus, thus tying the whole thing to the idea of the Indians being the lost ten tribes.

Then he ran into Professor X from another college. X had theories about ancient civilizations that were unconnected with the Israelites or Jerusalem. The people X concentrated on were rooted in Asia, and he reported some *very* strange cultural prac-tices among them. X maintained that it was these Asians who were the ancestors of the Indians, and he had a following in some academic circles. Our man got worried.

I should ignore this stuff—it is really far-fetched—but there is a possibility that some critics of the book will ask X to take a look at it, instead of me. I'd better include some of his theories and cultural descriptions in it, just in case.

Jared and his brother appeared.

To put them properly into context, however, our man had to spend enough time with X to understand his theories and become acquainted with the world he was describing. He wrote and rewrote his summary of those theories several times, trying his best to duplicate X's tedious recitation of kings and sons and cousins killing each other in a perpetual struggle for the throne, because he knew he had to make it sound different from his previous work. When that was finished, he had to do a lot of additional editing and rewriting of his first text; inventing the Jaredites was hard enough, but making them fit was even harder.

I'll go back to the part where I had the break in the original story. There is enough ambiguity about what went on during the time covered by the "lost" pages that I can fit something in there. But I don't think I can have them meet directly. I need some sort of bridge between the two societies.

And so the Mulekites were born. But they didn't last.

This is dangerous ground—too much opportunity to get things all confused. I'll have them absorbed by the Nephites right away, so I won't have to deal with them any more. Still, just to make sure there is some cohesion, I'd better sprinkle a few Jaredite names among their descendants.

This took still more time, but he persisted because the book had become his obsession, his masterpiece, and he was now fully committed to the idea of bringing it forward.

He started looking around for the necessary "someone else" who would discover it, someone unconnected to him in any way. One of his students told him of a farm boy named Smith in New York State who pretended to have visions. He made some discreet inquiries and found that the boy was said to have a "seer stone" that enabled him to find buried treasure.

Perfect—this Smith fellow is young enough to be pliable and yet well enough known as a mystic to be credible, at least among his gullible neighbors. He's also poor enough that he should be willing to help out for a piece of the profits, as the book sells. And he is obviously not educated enough for anyone to believe that he did it himself. That supports the whole idea of divine intervention.

Here was the plan: Joseph would announce to the world that he had met Moroni and received some plates from him. Reading from the manuscript Third Party would provide, Joseph would dictate the "translation" of the plates to a gullible scribe and then, after the book was published and controversial, insist that Professor Third Party—an outside expert with impeccable credentials—be called in to examine the work.

Third Party would examine it carefully and discuss it with his colleagues, pointing out all the authentic items he had planted in it, not just the chiasmus but also the geography he had learned from the Arab and the Egyptian names he had picked up at his school. If they accepted it, that would convince them of the reality of Jesus' resurrection and greatly enhance his own reputation.

If it really catches on, I could even start a prosperous lecture tour discussing it, with Joseph as a prop. If it doesn't, I can shrug it off as the delusional production of an ignorant lad.

And so, with nothing to lose and lots to gain—the motive of money having joined that of duty and revenge—he contacted Joseph Smith in a clandestine way and made his offer.

The young man eagerly agreed.

So, what happened?

Any number of things could have happened. A heart attack? A cholera epidemic? An accident? Take your pick; there were plenty of ways a man could die suddenly in the 1820s. Let's say that after the work was finished and the manuscript delivered to Joseph, Third Party's horse shied at a sudden movement in the brush. He was thrown from his saddle onto a rock and died of the injuries. None of his colleagues or family members had any idea what he had been up to, and Joseph was left with the manuscript and no need to share its glory with anyone.

He had con artist abilities of his own. He realized that the fact that he couldn't write very well was a significant plus for him because it gave credibility to his claim of divine assistance. He went forward with the story as planned, lined up some willing witnesses and collaborators to support it, had the book published, and waited for its sales to make him rich.

When they didn't, he changed course. Surrounded by people who believed him, he started himself a church.

This theory of the case is filled with many highly dubious and unprovable assumptions, including the English-speaking Arab who rivals with Moroni for the title of the unlikeliest player in the drama. But it is the best one I can think of whereby someone in the 1820s could have produced the book we have. It is far more credible than the idea that Joseph did it by himself, even if he had read *View of the Hebrews*.

While this theory takes a very big leap of faith to accept, so does the leap required of believers, as illustrated by an incident related to me by Dr. Wilfred Griggs, a professor who specializes in ancient languages and archaeological digs, primarily in the Middle East.

Wilfred, who is a believer, gave a copy of the Book of Mormon to one of his professional colleagues. "Look this over," he said, "and tell me what you think." The colleague agreed to do it.

When next they met, the colleague said, "It is an ancient book, but there is a problem. You've got to get rid of the angel."

That is the nub of the matter. One cannot believe the book to be authentic and "get rid of the angel." It is the angel—Moroni—that holds the whole thing together.

He is the one who buries the plates in the first place. He is the one who shows Joseph where they are and delivers them to him. He is the one who appears to the three witnesses to confirm that Joseph is telling the truth and then takes the plates back when the translation is finished.

He does not appear in Story One, but he is the sole survivor of Story Two and the author of Story Three, where his summary of the book of Ether introduces the book's most exotic tale. Believers are stuck with him.

SUMMARY

Aside from the obvious conclusion that Joseph Smith could not have written it by himself, no final answer can be drawn about the authorship of the Book of Mormon on the basis of analysis alone. No matter which way one chooses to go, a leap of faith is required.

Accepting the idea that Joseph Smith got his outside help from Third Party requires a leap that jumps over a huge pile of evidence that says the book is genuine; it leaves one pondering the identity of one of the greatest unknown forgers of all history.

Accepting the idea that Joseph Smith got his outside help from God requires a leap that jumps over the problems that still remain unresolved; it leaves one pondering the implications of miracles and angels in our time.

Readers get to decide for themselves which leap to take.

Epilogue

I SAID IN THE INTRODUCTION that I am a believer and made my decision to accept the Book of Mormon on the basis of faith rather than scholarship. Allow me, if you will, to expand on that position here at the end.

I have already quoted Moroni's instructions to those who receive the book, telling them to "ask God, the Eternal Father, in the name of Christ, if these things are not true." He promises them that if they will "ask with a sincere heart, with real intent, having faith in Christ, he will manifest the truth of it unto you, by the power of the Holy Ghost" (Moroni 10:4).

Before I went to Scotland as a missionary, I had not put Moroni's promise to the test. I was very familiar with the book, of course, but I had never read it all the way through and then, in the way Moroni urges, prayed for a personal witness of its authenticity. I realized I needed to do that if I was to avoid being a hypocrite, because that is what I was urging the Scots to do.

So, in the first weeks of my mission, I read the book in every spare moment, riding on buses, waiting for streetcars, or trying to settle into bed. When I was finished, I knelt down in prayer and did my best to "ask with a sincere heart, with real intent, having faith in Christ" for God to tell me if it was, in fact, what it claimed to be.

Moroni's promise was fulfilled. I received a strong personal, spiritual confirmation that the book was the word of God.

Or not.

A case can be made that what happened to me was simply an internal reaffirmation of indoctrination that had been implanted in my brain for years. Certainly that's what Freud would have said. I was raised in a home where both of my parents and all of my brothers and sisters were believers, I was taught that the book was "true" from the day I was old enough to attend Church classes and services, and I grew up and went to school in a city where most of my playmates and classmates were believers. Freud would have insisted that I was preconditioned to be open to the affirmative answer that I received.

That's why I began this book with Bill and Marion Proctor's story, not mine. My experience is fully credible to me, but I think theirs is more credible to outside observers.

Whatever the differences in our backgrounds, however, the lasting effect of our acceptance of the book in our respective lives has been the same. Though Bill is dead now, he was as committed a member of the Church as I have been. During our adult lives, both of us held a number of time-consuming and demanding positions, including that of bishop, a twenty-hour-a-week calling with no remuneration. Bill's later assignments were even more significant than mine. For him and for me and for millions more, a strong personal, spiritual witness that Jesus is the Christ, as the Book of Mormon testifies, has been a powerful sustaining force, one based on more than analysis alone.

Moroni's final plea, offered in the last verses of the book, is for its readers to "come unto Christ, and be perfected in him, and deny yourselves of all ungodliness." He promises that "by his grace" those who do "may be perfect in Christ" (Moroni 10:32).

That is the message of the Book of Mormon.

I believe it.

I have made the leap of faith.

NOTES

CHAPTER 1: INTRODUCTION

1. Book of Mormon, Introduction.
2. Bushman, *Joseph Smith,* 87.

CHAPTER 3: DISCOVERY

1. Book of Mormon, Testimony of Eight Witnesses.
2. Book of Mormon, Testimony of Joseph Smith.
3. Armstrong, *Islam,* 4.
4. Ibid., 4–5.
5. Dickinson, *New Light on Mormonism,* 3.
6. Ibid., 3.
7. Ibid., 4.
8. Ibid., 16; italics in original.
9. Ibid., 16–17.
10. Brodie, *No Man Knows My History,* 68.
11. Roberts, *Studies of the Book of Mormon,* 250.
12. John M. Allegro, *The Treasure of the Copper Scroll* (New York: Doubleday, 1960), 61–62, as quoted in Nibley, *Since Cumorah,* 221.
13. Ostling and Ostling, *Mormon America,* 276.

CHAPTER 4: STORY ONE

1. Book of Mormon, A Brief Explanation about the Book of Mormon.

CHAPTER 5: COMMENTARY ON STORY ONE

1. Madsen, "Valley of Lemuel," in *Journey of Faith* [DVD].
2. Madsen, "Nahom," in ibid.
3. Widtsoe, "Is Book of Mormon Geography Known?" *Improvement Era*, June 1950, 547; or *Evidences and Reconciliations*, 3:93.
4. Thomas, *Arabia Felix*, 48–49.
5. Nibley, *Approach to the Book of Mormon*, 274–75.
6. Ibid., xii.
7. Nibley, *Lehi in the Desert*, 102–4.

CHAPTER 6: INTRODUCTION TO STORY TWO

1. Brodie, *No Man Knows My History*, 62.

CHAPTER 7: THE HISTORY OF STORY TWO

1. Brodie, *No Man Knows My History*, 62–63.
2. Ibid., 63–64.
3. Ibid., 65.
4. Ibid., 66n.
5. Ibid.
6. Ibid.

CHAPTER 8: COMMENTARY ON THE HISTORY OF STORY TWO

1. Nibley, *Lehi in the Desert*, 25–28.
2. Ibid., 28, 30.
3. Edwards and Edwards, "Does Chiasmus Appear in the Book of Mormon by Chance?" 110–11.
4. Ibid., 111.
5. See Hilton, "On Verifying Wordprint Studies," 89–108.
6. Nibley, *Prophetic Book of Mormon*, 245–46.

Chapter 10: Commentary on Story Two

1. Jordan, "Volcanic Destruction in the Book of Mormon," 78–87.

Chapter 12: Commentary on Story Three

1. Brodie, *No Man Knows My History,* 70–71; format altered.
2. Nibley, *World of the Jaredites,* 242–43, 245.
3. Ibid., 235.
4. Ibid., 247.
5. Ibid., 249.
6. Ibid., 252–56.

Chapter 13: The Three Stories Together

1. Mosser and Owen, "Mormon Apologetic Scholarship and Evangelical Neglect," 179–205.
2. Dickens, "In the Name of the Prophet—Smith!" 385.
3. Bushman, *Joseph Smith,* 90.

Chapter 14: Doctrinal Overview

1. McGavin, *Historical Background,* 109–10.
2. Campbell, "Delusions," 85–96.
3. Wills, *What Jesus Meant,* xxv.
4. Ibid., xxv-xxvi.
5. Nicholi, *Question of God,* 7.
6. Ibid., 5–6.
7. Ibid., 6.

Chapter 15: Agency and Faith

1. Nicholi, *Question of God,* 104.
2. See Smith, *Teachings,* 49.
3. Brodie, *No Man Knows My History,* 58–59.

Chapter 17: Sin

1. Benson, "Beware of Pride," 4–6.

CHAPTER 18: JESUS IS THE CHRIST

1. Nicholi, *Question of God,* 86–87.
2. Quoted in Miller, "Evangelicals for Romney?"

SOURCES

Armstrong, Karen. *Islam: A Short History.* New York: Modern Library, 2000.

Benson, Ezra Taft. "Beware of Pride," *Ensign,* May 1989, 4–6.

Brodie, Fawn M. *No Man Knows My History: The Life of Joseph Smith.* 2d ed. New York: Alfred A. Knopf, 1971.

Bushman, Richard Lyman. *Joseph Smith: Rough Stone Rolling.* New York: Alfred A. Knopf, 2005.

Campbell, Alexander. "Delusions." *Millennial Harbinger* 2, no. 2 (February 1831): 85–96.

Dickens, Charles. "In the Name of the Prophet—Smith!" *Household Words* (19 July 1851): 385.

Dickinson, Ellen E. *New Light on Mormonism.* New York: Funk & Wagnalls, 1885.

Edwards, Boyd F., and W. Farrell Edwards. "Does Chiasmus Appear in the Book of Mormon by Chance?" *BYU Studies* 43, no. 2 (2004): 110–11.

Hilton, John L. "On Verifying Wordprint Studies: Book of Mormon Authorship." *Brigham Young University Studies,* 30, no. 3 (Summer 1990): 89–108.

Irving, Clifford. *What Really Happened: His Untold Story of the Hughes Affair.* With Richard Suskind. New York: Grove Press, 1972.

Jordan, Benjamin R. "Volcanic Destruction in the Book of Mormon: Possible Evidence from Ice Cores." *Journal of Book of Mormon Studies* 12, no. 1 (2003): 78–87.

Madsen, Truman G. In *Journey of Faith: From Jerusalem to the Promised Land* [DVD]. Copyright Neal A. Maxwell Institute for Religious Scholarship at Brigham Young University. Orem, Utah: Timpanogos Entertainment, 2006.

McGavin, E. Cecil. *The Historical Background of the Doctrine and Covenants.* Salt Lake City: Paragon Printing, 1949.

Miller, John J. "Evangelicals for Romney?" *National Review,* December 18, 2006. See http://nrd.nationalreview.com/article/?q=YWNjMzE2MGMzZGFlZmNjZGZiNDA3YjYyMmFjOWY1NTc; accessed 10 July 2009.

Mosser, Carl, and Paul Owen, "Mormon Apologetic Scholarship and Evangelical Neglect: Losing the Battle and Not Knowing It?" *Trinity Journal* (Fall 1998): 179–205.

Naifeh, Steven, and Gregory White Smith. *The Mormon Murders: A True Story of Greed, Forgery, Deceit, and Death.* New York: St. Martin's Press, 1988.

Nibley, Hugh. *An Approach to the Book of Mormon.* Salt Lake City: Deseret Book, 1988.

———. *The Prophetic Book of Mormon.* Salt Lake City: Deseret Book; Provo: Foundation for Ancient Research and Mormon Studies (FARMS), 1989.

———. *Since Cumorah.* 2d ed. Salt Lake City: Deseret Book, 1973.

———. *Lehi in the Desert and The World of the Jaredites.* Salt Lake City: Bookcraft, 1952. Reprinted, with the addition of *Then There Were Jaredites,* as *Lehi in the Desert; The World of the Jaredites; There Were Jaredites.* Salt Lake City: Deseret Book; Provo: Foundation for Ancient Research and Mormon Studies (FARMS), 1988. Page references are to the 1988 edition.

Nicholi, Armand M., Jr. *The Question of God: C. S. Lewis and Sigmund Freud Debate God, Love, Sex, and the Meaning of Life.* New York: Free Press, 2002.

Ostling, Richard N., and Joan K. Ostling. *Mormon America: The Power and the Promise.* San Francisco: Harper, 1999.

Roberts, B. H. *Studies of the Book of Mormon.* Urbana: University of Illinois Press, 1985.

Smith, Joseph. *Teachings of the Prophet Joseph Smith.* Selected by Joseph Fielding Smith. Salt Lake City: Deseret Book, 1976.

Thomas, Bertram. *Arabia Felix: Across the "Empty Quarter" of Arabia.* New York: Charles Scribner's Sons, 1932.

Wills, Garry. *What Jesus Meant.* New York: Viking, 2006.

Widtsoe, John A. "Is Book of Mormon Geography Known?" *Improvement Era,* July 1950, 547. Also in *Evidences and Reconciliations: Aids to Faith in a Modern Day.* 3 vols. Salt Lake City: Bookcraft, 1951.

INDEX